NATIVE AMERICAN VOICES

A History and Anthology

NATIVE AMERICAN VOICES

A History and Anthology

Edited with an Introduction by
STEVEN MINTZ

BRANDYWINE PRESS • St. James, New York

ISBN: 1-881-089-25-8

1st Printing 1995

Telephone Orders: 1-800-345-1776

Printed in the United States of America

For Susan Kellogg

PREFACE

Most of the history that we acquire comes not from history textbooks or classroom lectures but from images that we receive from movies, television, childhood stories, and folklore. All together, these images exert a powerful influence upon the way we think about the past. Some of these images are true; others false. But much of what we think we know about the past consists of unexamined mythic images.

No part of our past has been more thoroughly shaped by popular mythology than the history of Native Americans. Quite unconsciously, Americans have picked up a complex set of mythic images about the "Indians." For example, many assume that pre-Columbian North America was a sparsely populated virgin land; in fact, the area north of Mexico probably had seven to twelve million inhabitants. Or when many Americans think of early Indians, they conceive of hunters on horseback. In fact, many Native Americans were farmers, and horses had been extinct in the New World for 10,000 years before Europeans arrived.

One of history's most important tasks is to identify myths and misconceptions and correct them. Nowhere is this more important than in the study of the Indian peoples of North America. Until remarkably recently, the history of Native Americans largely reflected the perspective, perceptions, and prejudices of European Americans. Even today, however, many of the distortions of an earlier Eurocentric history persist. Some textbooks still begin their treatment of American history with the European "discovery" of the New World, de-emphasizing the first Americans, who crossed into the New World from Asia and established rich and diverse cultures centuries before Columbus's arrival. Although few textbooks today use the word "primitive" to describe pre-contact Native Americans, many still convey the impression that North American Indians consisted simply of small migratory bands that subsisted through hunting, fishing, and gathering wild plants. In reality, Native American societies were rich, diverse, and sophisticated.

The most dangerous misconception about Native American history is the easiest to slip into. It is to think of Indians as a vanishing people fated for extinction, the passive victims of an acquisitive, land-hungry white population. The view of Native Americans as passive victims is a distortion of history. Far from being passive, Native Americans were active agents who responded to threats to their culture through physical resistance and cultural adaptation. And far from disappearing, today they are a growing population that retains strong cultural traditions.

Throughout their history, Native Americans have been dynamic agents of change. Food they discovered and domesticated would transform the diet of Europe and Asia. They also made many important—though often neglected—contributions to modern medicine, art, architecture, and ecology. During the thousands of years preceding European contact, Native American people developed inventive and creative cultures. They cultivated plants for food, dyes, medicines, and textiles; domesticated animals; established extensive patterns of trade; built cities; produced monumental architecture; developed intricate systems of religious beliefs; and constructed a wide variety of systems of social and political organization ranging from kin-based bands and tribes to city-states and confederations. Native Americans not only adapted to diverse and demanding environments, but also reshaped the natural environments to meet their needs. And after the arrival of Europeans in the New World, they struggled intently to preserve the essentials of their diverse cultures while adapting to radically changing conditions.

During the past quarter century, the history of Native Americans has been totally rewritten, profoundly reshaping our understanding of our collective past. In order to recapture the perspective of American Indians, scholars, many of Indian ancestry, have tapped new sources of evidence, including oral traditions, material remains, and legal records; they have drawn upon the methods and insights of anthropology, archaeology, ethnohistory, and linguistics; and in the process, they have reinvigorated the discipline of history by incorporating previously neglected perspectives and points of view. This book's introduction summarizes the findings of this impressive body of scholarship, which has dramatically altered earlier ways of thinking about the Indian peoples of North America.

In the first half of the twentieth century, the history of Native Americans largely took the form of tragedy. Indian history, from this viewpoint, was the story of declining population, lost homelands, cultural dislocation, and persistent poverty and inequality. There is, however, a much more positive side to Native American history. This is a story of cultural persistence and survival. The key themes of Native American history are continuity, resistance, resilience, and adaptability in the face of extraordinary challenges and dislocations. This book tells that remarkable story through the voices of Native Americans themselves.

TABLE OF CONTENTS

CHRONOLOGY

70,000–25,000 B.C.	Ancestors of the Indians enter the Americas
15,000 B.C.	Glaciers begin to recede and many large animal species become extinct
10,000 B.C.	Sophisticated forms of toolmaking known as Clovis technology appear
9000 B.C.	Plant cultivation begins in central Mexico
8000 B.C.	Immigrants reach the southernmost tip of South America
7000–4000 B.C.	Athabascans settle in the Pacific Northwest
5000 B.C.	Inuits and Aleuts cross the Bering Straits by boat
3000 B.C.	Cultivation of corn begins in the Southwest
1000 B.C.	Beginning of Hohokam and Mogollon cultures
700 B.C.	Adena culture begins
300 B.C.–500 A.D.	Hopewell culture flourishes
700	Mississippian culture develops
1000	Athabascans begin to arrive in the Southwest
1451	Iroquois Confederacy founded
1492	Columbus first arrives in the Caribbean
1622	Opechancanough leads assault against English settlers in Virginia, 12 years of warfare follow
1634	English settlers defeat Opechancanough after renewed warfare erupts in Virginia

1675	King Philip's War begins; colonists defeat southern New England Indians in 1676 and the northern New England Indians in 1678
1680	Indians of New Mexico rise up against the Spanish in the Pueblo Revolt; Spain reconquers the territory in 1692
1700s	Plains Indians adopt the horse
1758	New Jersey establishes an Indian reservation for the Delawares
1763	Britain defeats France in the French and Indian War; Proclamation of 1763 forbids white settlement west of the Allegheny Mountains; Pontiac's War
1794	At Battle of Fallen Timbers near Toledo, Ohio, Anthony Wayne's army defeats Little Turtle's Indian alliance
1811	At Battle of Tippecanoe, William Henry Harrison defeats an Indian alliance led by the Shawnee Prophet Tenskwatawa
1813	Tecumseh dies in Battle of the Thames during the War of 1812
1814	Andrew Jackson's forces defeat Creeks at the Battle of Horseshoe Bend
1816	Land cessions by the Chickasaws, Choctaws, and Creeks
1816–18	First Seminole War in Florida forces Spain to cede the territory
1819	Land cessions by the Cherokees
1820s	Further land cessions by the Choctaws, Creeks, and Seminoles
1830	Congress passes Indian Removal Act
1832	Sauk and Fox Indians unsuccessfully seek to recover territory in Illinois during the Black Hawk War
1835	Second Seminole War begins, lasting for seven years
1838	Cherokee removed along the "Trail of Tears"
1846–64	Navajo warfare
1851	Plains Indians agree to confine hunting to specified regions
1854–90	Sioux wars
1861–1900	Apache warfare
1864	Sand Creek, Colorado, massacre
1867–68	U.S. demands that Plains Indians move to reservations

1872–73	Modoc War begins when Modoc Indians of northern California and southern Oregon seek to return to their homelands
1876	Custer's Last Stand
1877	Nez Percé War begins when Nez Percé refuse to move from their homeland in Oregon's Wallowa Valley
1881	Helen Hunt Jackson's *A Century of Dishonor*
1887	Dawes Severalty Act
1890	Sioux Ghost Dance; Massacre of Lakota Sioux at Wounded Knee
1934	Indian Reorganization Act
1968	American Indian Movement founded
1972	FBI seizes Indian occupants of Wounded Knee, South Dakota
1990	Native American Grave Protection and Repatriation Act requires the return of human remains and sacred funerary objects to the tribes to which they belong
1993	Religious Freedom Restoration Act prohibits states from interfering with the practice of traditional Native American religions

INTRODUCTION

In the spring of 1926, an African-American cowboy named George McJunkin made a discovery that profoundly altered our understanding of the first Americans in North America. While hunting for lost cattle along the edge of a gully near Folsom, New Mexico, he spotted some bleached bones. Those bones, it turned out, were the ribs of a species of bison that had been extinct for 10,000 years. Mixed in with the bones were human-made stone spearheads. The spearheads offered the first unambiguous proof that ancestors of today's Indians lived in the New World thousands of years earlier than most early twentieth-century authorities believed—before the end of the last ice age.

Although the first Europeans to arrive in the Americas in the late fifteenth century called it the "New World," it was a land that had been inhabited for more than 20,000 years. An enormous diversity of societies flourished, each with its own distinctive language, cultural patterns, and history. No written records record these histories. To reconstruct this story, it is necessary to turn to fragile archaeological artifacts that record past human behavior. From snippets of baskets, fragments of pottery, food remains, discarded tools, and oral traditions, anthropologists, archeologists, and historians have pieced together information about these peoples' social organization, technology, and diet, including how these have changed over time. This is a remarkable story, which underscores the ability of the first Americans to adapt to—and reshape—extraordinarily diverse environments, create their own rich and sophisticated cultures independent of outside influences, and establish elaborate trading networks and sophisticated religious systems.

When and how the ancestors of today's Indians arrived in the New World remains one of the most controversial issues in archaeology. Many sixteenth-century Europeans believed that the Indians were descendants of the Biblical "Lost Tribes of Israel" or the mythical lost continent of Atlantis. In 1590, a Spanish Jesuit missionary, José de Acosta, came closer to the truth when he suggested that small groups of "hunters driven from their homelands by starvation or some other hardships" had traveled to America from Asia.

1

Most scholars believe that America's first pioneers crossed into North America in the general area of the Bering Strait—which now separates Siberia and Alaska. Although the dates when the ancestors of today's Native Americans migrated remain disputed, existing evidence suggests that the first migrants arrived between 25,000 and 70,000 years ago. The earth's climate at that time was very different from today's. The earliest Americans entered the New World during one of the earth's periodic ice ages, when vast amounts of water froze into glaciers. As a result, the depth of the oceans dropped, exposing a "land bridge" between Siberia and Alaska. Twice, such a land bridge appeared—between 28,000 and about 26,000 years ago, and between 20,000 and 10,000 to 12,000 years ago. In fact, the term "land bridge" is a misnomer; a vast expanse of marsh-filled land, a thousand miles wide, stretched between Siberia and Alaska. This land mass, now known as Beringia, allowed hunters from northeastern Asia to follow the migratory paths of animals that were their source of food into the more southerly parts of Alaska.

Supporting the notion that the first Americans came from Northeast Asia is the evidence of physical anthropology. Native Americans and northeast Asian people share certain common physical traits: straight black hair; dark brown eyes; wide cheekbones; and "shovel incisors" (concave inner surfaces of the upper front teeth).

Physical and linguistic evidence suggests that the migration into the Americas did not take place all at once. Many scholars believe that it took place in three distinct waves, with the Inuit (Eskimos) and the natives of the Aleutian Islands arriving more recently than the people who would inhabit the Pacific Northwest Coast or other portions of North and South America.

The original settlers of North America were a remarkably adaptable people, capable of surviving in subfreezing temperatures in the tundra. In a climate much harsher than today's, they were able to build fires, construct heavily insulated housing, and make warm clothes out of hides and furs.

Despite a lack of wheeled vehicles and riding animals, the first Americans spread quickly across North and South America. This momentous movement of people was propelled by population pressure, since hunters and gatherers required a great deal of territory to support themselves. Archaeological findings suggest that these people moved along three routes: eastward, across Canada's northern coast; southward, along the Pacific Coast; as well as across the eastern Rocky Mountains, with some groups peeling off toward the eastern seaboard, the Ohio Valley, and the Mississippi Valley.

Prehistoric Patterns of Change

Near Kit Carson, Colorado, archaeologists made an astonishing discovery. There, they found stone spearheads alongside the bones of extinct long-horned bison—evidence of a huge bison hunt around 8200 B.C. During this hunt, Native Americans drove some 200 bison into a gully before killing the animals. To butcher and carry away the 60,000 pounds of meat must have required at least 150 Indians working closely together.

At Bat Cave in southwestern New Mexico archaeologists made another important find: evidence that around 3000 B.C. Indians had learned to domesticate corn, the first grown north of Mexico. It was a primitive form of corn, with stalks barely an inch long and no husk to protect the kernels. Still, it was a sign that these people were no longer wholly dependent on wild food sources; they were now able to supplement their diet by cultivating crops.

It is from discoveries like these that archaeologists reconstruct the prehistory of North America's Indians. The earliest New World pioneers hunted large mammals—bison, caribou, oxen, and mammoths—with stone tipped spears and spear and dart throwers, known as atlatls. Between 6000 and 12,000 years ago, however, many large animal species became extinct. Archaeologists do not agree why these animals died out. Some argue that it was the result of overkilling; others attribute it to climatic changes: rising temperatures, the drying up of many lakes, and the loss of many early forms of vegetation. In any event, the ancestors of today's Indians had to alter dramatically their way of life.

As the larger mammals died out and the Indian population grew, many Indian peoples turned to foraging, gathering plant foods, fishing, and hunting smaller animals. To hunt small game, these people developed new kinds of weapons, including spears with barbed points, the bow and arrow, and nets and hooks for fishing. This era, known as the Archaic period, offers many examples of these peoples' increasing technological sophistication, evident in the proliferation of such objects as awls, axes, boats, cloth, darts, millstones, and woven baskets.

Following the Archaic period comes the Formative period, when some foragers began to domesticate wild seeds. By 3000 B.C., some groups of Southwestern Indians had already begun to grow corn. The rise of agriculture allowed these people to form permanent settlements.

The Cultures of Prehistoric America

Across from present-day St. Louis stands an earthen mound one hundred feet high and covering fifteen acres, bigger at its base than the Great Pyramid of Egypt. This mysterious mound is one of literally thousands that early Native Americans built in the Mississippi and Ohio river valleys, the Great Lakes region, and along the Gulf Coast. Before the 1890s, many authorities refused to believe that Indians could have created these mounds since they lacked horses, oxen, or wheeled vehicles; they thought that the Vikings or the Lost Tribes of Israel or some long vanished civilization constructed

An aerial view of the "Great Serpent Mound" in Adams County, Ohio. *(Courtesy, Smithsonian Institution)*

them. We now know that they were built by Native Americans to serve as burial places and as platforms for temples and the residences of chiefs and priests.

Many of these New World monuments are truly immense. One Ohio mound resembles a huge snake and measures a quarter of a mile long. A Georgia mound has a figure of an eagle across its top. The mounds provide clues to the rich and diverse cultures that Native Americans created during the more than 20,000 years before Europeans reached the New World.

Earthen mounds are not the only magnificent monuments that the Indians produced. On the face of a sandstone cliff in present-day Mesa Verde, Colorado, is a spectacular stone and adobe structure that once housed over four hundred people in two hundred rooms. Located a hundred feet above a nearby plateau, the structure is accessible only by climbing wooden ladders and using toeholds cut in the sandstone. In southern Colorado and

Utah, northwestern New Mexico, and northern Arizona, hundreds of similar communal dwellings are located in shallow caves or under cliff overhangs.

The first Europeans to arrive in the Americas in the late fifteenth and sixteenth centuries were often arrogant, ethnocentric people who drew a sharp contrast between their societies' technological accomplishments and those of the New World Indians. And while it is true that the Indian peoples had no steel or iron tools, wheeled vehicles, large sailing vessels, keystone arches or domes, digital numbers, coined money, alphabet system of writing, or gunpowder, this does not at all mean that they did not create thriving and inventive societies. For one thing, the Indians were the first people to cultivate some of the world's most important agricultural crops: chocolate, corn, long-staple cotton, peanuts, pineapples, potatoes, rubber, quinine, tobacco, and vanilla. In addition, the New World Indians built cities as big as any in Europe, established forms of government as varied as Europe's, and created some of the world's great art and architecture—including temples, pyramids, statues, and canals.

While many Americans are aware of the impressive cultures that thrived in Mexico, Peru, and Guatemala before Columbus's arrival—the Toltec, the Maya, the Aztec, and the Inca—far fewer are familiar with the magnificent ancient cultures to be found north of Mexico. In fact, from the Alaska tundra to the dense evergreen forests of the Pacific Northwest, from the arid deserts of the Southwest to the rich river valleys of the Southeast and the eastern woodlands, prehistoric Native Americans established complex cultures, ingeniously adapted to diverse conditions.

The first Americans had to adapt their ways of life to vastly different environments. Before 2000 B.C., the ancestors of the Inuit and the Aleuts arrived on the coast and frozen tundra of western Alaska, where they adapted ingeniously to arctic conditions. Since few plants grew in the harsh arctic climate, the Inuit relied on hunting and fishing. They drew much of their food from the sea, hunting seals, whales, and other marine mammals. The game they hunted not only provided food, but also protection from the extreme cold. The Inuit wore layers of caribou-skinned clothing and constructed heavily insulated pit houses, dug into the ground and covered with furs and animal skins. The Inuit built sleds for transportation and spread out across the coast. These people were organized in a large number of small bands, which shared certain common cultural patterns while remaining largely autonomous.

Along the Northwest Pacific Coast—an area of dense forests, teeming with caribou, deer, elk, and moose, and rivers rich with sea life—the ancestors of the Haidas, Kwakiutls, and Tlingits developed a distinctive culture oriented toward the water. The mild climate and the abundant marine life—salmon, sturgeon, halibut, herring, shellfish, and sea mammals—meant that these peoples could produce food with very little work. Such

Life in a village along the Pacific Northwest Coast in the 1880s. *(Courtesy, American Museum of Natural History)*

abundance freed these people to create some of the world's most impressive art forms as well as an elaborate ceremonial life. The people of the Northwest Pacific Coast constructed large, gabled-roof plank houses; carved family and clan emblems on totem poles; made elaborately carved wooden masks, grave markers, and utensils; and constructed great seagoing canoes, some more than sixty feet long. The region's abundant resources also produced a highly stratified society, where a few wealthy families controlled each village. Individuals announced their high social status at a feast called a potlatch. During this ritual, which could last for several days, a host demonstrated his wealth by distributing food and gifts to his guests.

It was in the arid Southwest that some of the earliest farming societies developed. The predecessors of the Pueblo and Navajo Indians were able to flourish in a desert environment by developing complex irrigation systems for farming and by developing structures suitable for vast temperature changes.

Shifts in climate appear to have played an important role in encouraging the development of agriculture in the Southwest. Between three and five thousand years ago, the amount of rainfall in this region increased, encour-

A Kwakiutl chief delivers a speech at a potlatch in 1895 in the Pacific Northwest. *(Courtesy, Smithsonian Institution)*

aging many people to migrate to the area, including some from Mexico already familiar with raising corn, squash, and beans. These people raised crops casually, supplementing a diet that depended largely on hunting and foraging. Around 3000 years ago, however, the climate grew drier, killing off many of the region's wild game and vegetation. A people known as the Mogollon, who lived in permanent villages along the rivers of eastern Arizona and western New Mexico, responded to this change by devoting increased energy to farming, raising beans, squash, and corn. The versatility of the Mogollon is also apparent in the housing they constructed. To cope with the desert extremes of heat and cold, they built pit houses—structures burrowed two or three feet into the ground and covered with woven reeds and plaster made out of mud.

In central Arizona, the Hohokam, a group that had migrated from Mexico, constructed elaborate irrigation systems in order to transform the desert into farm land. They dug wells, built ponds and dams to collect rainwater, and created hundreds of miles of canals and ditches to channel water to their crops. The Hohokam combined farming with trade, which involved luxury goods such as precious stones, ornamental seashells, and copper bells.

The Anasazi also used dams and irrigation canals to water their crops. Between A.D. 1000 and 1300, the Anasazi culture spread across much of northern Arizona, northern New Mexico, southern Colorado, and southern Utah, establishing more than twenty-five thousand separate communities spread over sixty thousand square miles connected by a remarkable system

The ruins of the Cliff Palace, a cliff dwelling in Mesa Verde National Park, Colorado. *(Courtesy, American Museum of Natural History)*

of roads. The Anasazi are best known today for their magnificent cliff dwellings—multi-roomed dwellings built atop mesas or along steep cliffs. By 1300, however, the Anasazi abandoned these cliff dwellings and moved to the south and east, apparently in response to incursions from hostile Indians and a severe drought that threatened their food supply. The Anasazi are the ancestors of the modern day Pueblo Indians.

The arrival of a new people into the Southwest, the Athabascans, created an important challenge to the Anasazi way of life. About A.D. 1000, bands of Athabascans, the ancestors of the Navajos and the Apaches, began to migrate to the Southwest from what is now Alaska and Canada. Formidable hunters and raiders, the Athabascans possessed the bow and arrow, and during the fourteenth and fifteenth centuries, raided Anasazi farming communities, and by 1500 had taken over the western desert. They lived in settlements consisting of "forked stick" homes, made by piling logs against three poles joined together at their tops, then covering the outside with mud. Later they fashioned hogans, earthen domes with log frames.

Along the lakes and rivers of the Midwest and the Southeast, prehistoric Americans established complex communities based on flourishing trade and agriculture. One of the earliest farming and trading towns arose approximately 1400 B.C., on the banks of the lower Mississippi River near present-day Vicksburg, Mississippi. Known as Poverty Point, the town showed many signs of Mexican influence, including a cone-shaped burial mound and two large bird-shaped mounds, and other huge earthworks. Networks of trade apparently connected Poverty Point with settlements along the Mississippi, Ohio, Missouri, and Arkansas rivers. Thus, thousands of years before the arrival of Europeans, Native Americans were already engaged in extensive trade of flint, copper, and other goods.

Around 700 B.C., other groups of people, known as the Adena, began to build large mounds and earthworks in southern Ohio. The Adena lived in small villages and supported themselves by hunting, fishing, gathering wild plants, modest farming, and some trading. The Adena built mounds as burial places. The bodies of village leaders and other high ranking people were placed in log tombs before being covered with earth.

From about 100 B.C., a new mound-building culture flourished in the Midwest, known as the Hopewell. These people developed thousands of villages extending across what is now Ohio, Indiana, Michigan, Illinois, Wisconsin, Iowa, and Missouri. The Hopewell supported themselves by hunting, fishing, and gathering, and also cultivated a variety of crops, including corn. The Hopewell developed an extensive trading network, obtaining shells and shark teeth from Florida, pipestone from Minnesota, volcanic glass from Wyoming, and silver from Ontario.

The Hopewell created stratified societies, and buried their leaders in earthen mounds, filled with art works made of materials imported from areas more than a thousand miles away. The Hopewell built many more mounds than the Adena. A colder climate appears to have contributed to the decline of the Hopewell beginning around A.D. 450.

After A.D. 750 another mound-building culture, known as the Mississippians, emerged in the Mississippi Valley and the Gulf Coast. By cultivating an improved variety of corn, and using flint hoes instead of digging sticks, these people greatly increased agricultural productivity, permitting them to build some of the largest cities in prehistoric North America. The largest that we know about was Cahokia, across from present-day St. Louis, which probably had a population of 20,000. To protect the population from raids from neighboring peoples, many of these cities were protected by stockades. Like the Indians of Mexico, the Mississippians built flat-topped mounds in the center of their cities, where chiefs lived and the bones of deceased chiefs were kept.

The largest of the Mississippian settlements may have become city-states, exercising control over surrounding farm country. Within their towns, the Mississippians created a complex, stratified society, with a distinct leadership class, specialized artisans, an extensive system of trade, and priests. The Mississippians practiced a religion known as the Southern Ceremonial Complex. Somewhat similar to Mexican Indian religions, the

"Southern cult," as it is known, provided a set of symbols and motifs of rank and status that recur in Mississippian art, notably a flying human figure with winglike tatoos around the eyes.

The Mississippian cultures grew until the 1500s, when diseases introduced by European explorers resulted in a sharp decline in population. However, one group of Mississippians, the Natchez, survived into the 1700s, long enough to be described by Europeans.

The Eve of Contact

When Columbus arrived in the Caribbean in 1492, the New World was far from an empty wilderness. It was home to as many people as lived in Europe—perhaps sixty or seventy million. Between seven and twelve million lived in what are now the United States and Canada. Not a single, homogeneous population, the people north of Mexico lived in more than 350 distinct groups, which spoke more than 250 different languages and had their own political structure, kinship systems, and economies. These divisions would have fateful consequences for the future, permitting the European colonizers to adopt divide-and-conquer policies that played off one group against others.

In each geographical and cultural area were deeply rooted historic conflicts and vulnerabilities that European colonizers would exploit. In the Southwest, many conflicts arose over control of the arid region's scarce resources, as groups like the Yaquis and Pimas struggled over access to water and fertile land. In the northern portion of the Southwest, village dwellers, such as the Hopi and Zuni, coexisted uneasily with migratory hunters and raiders like the Apache. In the southern Southwest, patterns of land use would make the inhabitants especially vulnerable to Spanish encroachment. The dominant groups, the Pimas and the Papagos, lived in isolated communities known as *rancherias*, spread across a thousand miles along streams and other sources of irrigation. The Spaniards would adopt a policy that sought to "reduce" the dispersed Indian population into supervised towns.

In the Southeast—where the Creeks, the Choctaws, the Cherokees, the Seminoles, and other peoples lived—extensive European colonization was delayed until the seventeenth century because the area lacked precious minerals. Here, Mississippian cultural patterns persisted: towns, with several hundred to a few thousand residents; farming, fishing, and hunting; varying degrees of social stratification; and a pronounced tendency toward matrilineality (tracing descent through the mother's family) and matrilocality (newly married couples residing with and working for the mother's family). Forms of political organization ranged from autonomous towns to sets of villages that paid tribute to a dominant town. A history of intertribal warfare in the Southeast led many tribes to band together for protection in confederations.

Stretching from the Atlantic Coast west to the Great Lakes and southward from Maine to North Carolina lay the eastern woodlands. The eastern woodland's major groups were the Algonquians, the Iroquois, and the Muskogeans.

The Algonquians lived in small bands of from one to three hundred members, combining hunting, fishing, and gathering with some agriculture. A semi-nomadic people, who might move several times a year, the Algonquians would plant crops, then break into small bands to hunt caribou and deer, and return to their fields at harvest time. These people lived in wigwams, dome-shaped structures containing one or more families. A wigwam, made of bent saplings covered with birchbark, typically housed a husband and wife, their children, and their married sons and their wives and children.

During the 1600s, the Algonquians and their allies the Hurons fought a bitter war against the Iroquois. Around 1640, the Algonquians were defeated and driven from their territory. This war and epidemics of measles and smallpox reduced the Algonquian population sharply.

The Iroquois were several related groups of people who still live in what is now central New York State. Scholars disagree about whether the Iroquois had long occupied this area or whether they migrated from the Southeast around 1300. What does seem clear is that beginning in the fourteenth century, bitter feuds broke out among the Iroquois, which grew particularly intense during the sixteenth century. According to Iroquois oral tradition, two reformers, Dekanawidah, a Huron religious leader, and his disciple Hiawatha, a Mohawk chief, responded to mounting conflict by proposing a political alliance of the Iroquois tribes. During the sixteenth century, five Iroquois tribes—the Cayugas, the Mohawks, the Oneidas, the Onondagas, and the Senecas—joined together to form a confederation known as the Iroquois league. A sixth tribe, the Tuscarora, joined the league in the eighteenth century.

Governing the league was a council, consisting of the chiefs of each tribe and fifty specially chosen leaders called sachems. Some scholars argue that the Iroquois League, which combined a central authority with tribal autonomy, provided a model for the federal system of government later adopted by the United States.

Women played a very important role in Iroquois society—which shocked Europeans. Women headed the longhouses that were the basic units of social and economic organization among the Iroquois and were also the leaders of clans, which were comprised of several longhouses. Although women did not sit on the league councils that made decisions involving war and diplomacy, the women who headed the clans did have the power to appoint or remove the men who served on these councils.

Kinship and Religion

Despite differences in language and culture, Native American societies did share certain characteristics in common. Many were organized around principles of kinship. Kinship ties—based on bloodlines or marriage—formed the basis of the political, economic, and religious system. Succession to political office and religious positions, ownership and inheritance of property, and even whom one could or could not marry were determined on the basis of membership in a kin group.

Indian kinship systems included an intricate number of forms, with regulations governing marriages, relations with in-laws, and residence after marriage. In patrilineal societies, like the Cheyenne of the Great Plains, land use rights and membership in the political system flowed through the father. In matrilineal societies, like the Pueblo of the Southwest, membership in the group was determined by the mother's family identity. In the Algonquian-speaking tribes of eastern North America, group membership was based on ties among siblings and cousins.

Many Indian peoples placed less emphasis on the nuclear family—the unit consisting of husband, wife, and their children—than upon the extended family or the lineage. On the Northwest Pacific Coast, the household consisted of a man, his wife or wives, and their children or the man's sister's sons. Among the western Pueblo, the nucleus of social and economic organization was the extended household consisting of a group of female relations and their husbands, sons-in-law, and maternal grandchildren. Among the Iroquoian speakers of the eastern woodlands, the basic social unit was the longhouse, a large rectangular structure that contained about ten families. One sign of the relative unimportance of the nuclear family as opposed to larger kinship ties is that many Indian societies provided for relatively easy access to divorce.

Apart from a common emphasis on kinship, Native American societies also shared certain religious beliefs and practices. Many European colonists regarded Indian religions as a form of superstition. One Catholic priest, Father François du Perron, described Iroquoian beliefs in very negative, but not unusual, terms: "All their actions are dictated to them directly by the devil . . . They consider the dream as the master of their lives; it is the God of the country."

Far from being "primitive" forms of religion, Indian religions possessed great subtlety and sophistication, manifest in a rich ceremonial life, an intricate mythology, and profound speculations about the creation of the world, the origins of life, and the nature of the afterlife. Unlike Islam, Christianity, or Judaism, Native American religions were not "written" religions with specific founders; also, they might be termed mystical religions, since they allowed people to have direct contact with the supernatural through "visions" and "dreams."

The eagle dance of the Senecas. *(Courtesy, Smithsonian Institution)*

Despite rich variations in ritual practices and customs, Native American religions shared certain common characteristics, notably an outlook that might be described as "animistic." This is a belief that there is a close bond between people, animals, and the natural environment, and that all must live together in harmony.

Scholars have identified two dominant forms of Indian religious expression: hunting and horticultural religions. The hunting tradition was distinguished by its emphasis on the human relationship with animals, establishing special rituals and taboos surrounding the treatment of wild animals so as not to offend their spiritual masters. Hunting societies often had a *shaman* (or medicine man or woman), able to contact supernatural beings on behalf of the community.

The agrarian tradition emphasized fertility, celebrated in a yearly round of special ceremonies designed to encourage rainfall and crop productivity. In contrast to the hunting tradition, which tended to emphasize a single male diety, the agrarian tradition had a larger number of gods and goddesses. Also, unlike the less complexly organized hunting societies, agricultural ones tended to have an organized priesthood and permanent temples or shrines.

The centrality of kinship and religion in Indian societies was evident in a series of social rites of passage that demarcated the transition from one life stage to the next. Children were usually born in a special birth hut, located some distance from the family home. Newborn children were dipped in cold water or rubbed with animal oil. Several months later, newborns underwent a special initiation ceremony. In the presence of relatives, a child was given a name from a wealth of family names. Among some peoples, children also underwent a rite involving the piercing of the nose or earlobes.

Girls underwent a puberty ceremony, consisting of isolation at the time of first menstruation. During her isolation, which might last from several weeks to a year, an older woman would care for her and instruct her in her role as an adult. After her return, she began to wear adult dress. Boys also underwent rites of initiation. A number of firsts, including the first tooth, first steps, and the first big game killed by a boy, were recognized in public ceremonies. Among many Indian peoples, when a boy approached adolescence, he went alone to a mountaintop or into a forest to fast and seek a vision from a guardian spirit. On his return he assumed adult status.

The Columbian Exchange

The collision of cultures that occurred when Europeans arrived in the New World had vast consequences for both Europeans and Native Americans. Eating habits were revolutionized, as the potato, corn, and chocolate were introduced to the Old World, and sugar, cattle, chickens, pigs, and sheep were introduced to the New World. Patterns of world trade were also overturned, as New World crops—like tobacco and cotton and vastly expanded production of sugar—ignited growing consumer markets.

Even the natural environment was transformed. Native Americans had not only adapted to the physical environment—they also shaped it to meet their needs. By building irrigation systems and using fire to clear out brush, the Indian people provided themselves with agricultural land and encouraged the growth of wild game. But Europeans had a much more devastating impact on the environment, clearing huge tracts of forested lands and inadvertently introducing a vast variety of Old World weeds. The introduction of cattle, goats, horses, sheep, and swine also transformed the ecology, as grazing animals ate up many native plants.

The horse, extinct in the Americas for 10,000 years, produced a cultural revolution. It radically reshaped the lives of the Plains Indians, transforming hunting, transportation, and warfare. Initially, Indians did not know what to make of these huge animals, which one group described as elk dogs. The introduction of the horse encouraged groups like the Cheyenne, who had been farmers, to become hunters. Horses made hunters much more adept at killing wild game.

Death and disease—these too were consequences of contact. Diseases against which the Indian peoples had no natural immunities caused the greatest mass deaths in history. Within a century of contact, the germs that Europeans carried had killed 50 to 80 percent of the Indian population. Disease radically reduced the resistance that Native Americans were able to offer to the European intruders.

For thousands of years, Indians had lived in biological isolation. Unlike Europeans, who were exposed to a large variety of pathogens from birth, the people of the Americas were immunologically defenseless. They had crossed into the New World in small bands, too small to keep epidemic diseases alive. The extremely cold climate of present-day Alaska and Canada kept many diseases from penetrating southward into the Americas. Furthermore, the Indians had no herds of cattle, horses, pigs, and sheep to keep pathogens active. And in America north of Mexico there were few cities with the thousands of inhabitants necessary to spread diseases. As a result, the peoples of the New World proved extraordinarily vulnerable to cholera, gonorrhea, measles, mumps, smallpox, whooping cough, and yellow fever.

Adult men were particularly susceptible to the ravages of disease. Although sometimes called the "stronger" sex, men between the ages of fifteen and forty were particularly likely to die in epidemics. The spread of disease also strained religious belief systems, persuading many that their ancestral gods had forsaken them and leading some Indians to embrace Christianity. While the ravages of disease caused some people to adopt a more nomadic existence, other Indians responded by establishing new tribes out of the surviving remnants of earlier societies.

With the Indian population decimated by disease, Europeans would introduce a new labor force into the New World: enslaved Africans, who would be put to work in mines and on sugar and tobacco plantations in astonishing numbers. Between 1502 and 1870, when the slave trade was finally suppressed, ten million Africans were shipped to the Americas.

Yet it is important to realize that despite the death, disease, and destruction wrought by contact, the people of North America were not transformed into helpless pawns. They retained vibrant cultures that struggled mightily to adapt to a radically changing environment.

European Perceptions

In 1646, a Christian convert asked the Massachusetts missionary John Eliot: "Why do you call us Indians?" The answer is readily apparent even to young schoolchildren. Because Columbus mistakenly believed he had arrived in the East Indies, near Japan and China, he called the islanders *indios*. Even though Europeans realized within a quarter century that Columbus had not reached the East Indies, the name Indian continued to be used.

The term Indian was a European-imposed concept. There was not a single monolithic Indian culture, nor did the diverse indigenous inhabitants of North America think of themselves as a single people. They were acutely conscious of the diversity of beliefs, customs, and cultures. European colonists, however, were unable to appreciate or comprehend the rich diversity of the Native Americans and tended to conflate the Indian people into a single, undifferentiated group. They classified this vast indigenous population as "Indian," described their color as "red," and considered their religions pagan, their languages incomprehensible, their politics disorganized, and their agriculture and land use patterns primitive. The French philosopher Montaigne reflected a pervasive ignorance about Indians when he pronounced that the Indians had "no knowledge of letters, no intelligence of numbers, no name of magistrate, nor of politics . . . no occupation but idle, no apparel but natural. . . ."

Europeans were shocked by the contrasts between the cultures, particularly in gender roles and childrearing practices. They invariably commented on the essential economic roles performed by Indian women, as farmers, house-builders, traders, and sometimes as *sachems*. And they were also shocked to discover that Indians did not physically punish their children. The Indian young were encouraged to behave properly largely through praise and public rewards for achievement, and were seldom spanked. Convinced that corporal punishment made children timid and dependent, parents praised children when they were good and publicly shamed them when they misbehaved.

Indians offered a screen on which Europeans projected Old World fears and fantasies. Many Europeans regarded the Indians as "natural man," free of all of civilization's restraints. According to this stereotype, the Indians embodied innocence and freedom, lacking sexual restraints, law, and private property, yet possessing health and eternal youth. Arthur Barlowe, who visited Roanoke Island, off the coast of North Carolina, in 1584, described the Native Americans as nature's nobility:

> We found the people most gentle, loving and faithful, void of all guile and treasure, and such as live after the manner of the golden age.

Another favorite stereotype was the somber, wise Indian, divorced from his tribe, who assists whites in their plans to civilize the wilderness. This early stereotype would persist into the nineteenth century in James Fenimore Cooper's literary creation of Chingachgook, the friend of the white frontiersman Natty Bumppo, and into the twentieth century in Tonto, the Lone Ranger's sidekick.

But if some Europeans regarded Indians with fascination, many others looked at them with hatred and fear. A contrasting stereotype, often invoked to legitimate white aggression, was the "bloodthirsty savage" who stood in the way of progress and civilization. Colonists repeatedly referred to Indians in the most pejorative terms, as "inhumanly cruel," "brutish beasts" of "most wilde and savage nature." If the "noble savage" deserved to be "civilized" and "Christianized" in the white man's image, then the "bloodthirsty savage" had to be eliminated. Such self-serving stereotypes long prevented Europeans from seeing Native Americans in their true diversity and individuality.

From an early date, the English colonists were convinced that "civilization" could not coexist with "savagery." Either Indians would have to be reformed in the image of whites or else they had to be removed. This view did not bode well for future relations between the English settlers and their descendants and North America's Indian people.

The Clash of Cultures

Relations between Indians and Europeans during the sixteenth and seventeenth centuries ran the spectrum from cooperation and accommodation to bitter conflict. Where the number of colonists was fewest, relationships were based on trade, and the Indians viewed the Europeans as potential allies, relations were friendliest. Where European numbers were greatest and their primary objective was Indian land or labor, relations were least friendly. By the early eighteenth century, however, it was already clear that friendly relations and cooperation would be the exception, since in areas as diverse as New Mexico, New England, Pennsylvania, and the Chesapeake Bay region of Virginia and Maryland, European colonizers were encroaching on Indian lands and radically disrupting the Indian ways of life.

In Mexico and Central and South America, the Spanish, unlike the English or the French, viewed Indians as a usable labor force—to be put to work raising crops, tending animals, and extracting valuable minerals from mines. In the early 1500s Spanish policy forced many Indians to work on Spanish estates. Under the *encomienda* system, colonists were granted the right to demand tribute from Indians living on a given piece of land. Often the colonists forced the Indians to farm or work in mines as payment. Gradually, the Indians became bound to the land because they had no other way to pay tribute.

North of Mexico, Spain's perspective changed. Relatively few Spaniards migrated to New Spain's northernmost frontiers, because the area lacked mineral riches. Here, Indians were viewed essentially as buffers to protect Spain's New World empire and as objects of religious conversion. Beginning in the 1560s, Jesuit and Franciscan priests established missions in what are now Florida and Georgia and then, starting in the early 1600s, in present-day Arizona, California, New Mexico, and Texas. In Florida and much later in California, missions were enclosed, self-sufficient communities combining farming with the manufacture of pottery, woven blankets, and other goods. In New Mexico, in contrast, where a large Pueblo population inhabited settled villages, Franciscan missionaries established churches on the edge of towns.

During the sixteenth century, cultural conflicts between Spanish missionaries and Indians periodically erupted into violence. The most dramatic uprising took place in New Mexico in 1680, after Franciscan missionaries sought to suppress traditional Pueblo religious practices by desecrating a Pueblo *kiva*—a special room where religious activities took place—flogging Pueblo priests, and destroying sacred Indian artifacts. A Pueblo holy man named Popé led a revolt which killed over 400 Spanish colonists and destroyed every church in New Mexico. Six years later, Spain restored its authority. But in order to maintain peace, Spain reached an accommodation with the Pueblo. In return for a pledge of loyalty to the Spanish crown and attendance at Catholic religious services, Spain promised to protect Pueblo lands from exploitation, abandon forced Indian labor, and tolerate the secret practice of traditional Pueblo religion.

The French and the Indians they encountered reached a different kind of accommodation. France's New World empire was based largely on trade. In 1504, French fishermen sailed into the Gulf of St. Lawrence, looking for cod. Gradually, the French realized that they could increase their profits by trading with the Indians for furs. In exchange for pelts, the French *coureurs de bois* (traders) supplied Indians with textiles, muskets, and other European goods. By the end of the sixteenth century, a thousand ships a year were engaged in the fur trade along the St. Lawrence River and the interior, where the French constructed forts, missions, and trading posts.

Relations between the French and Indians were less violent than in Spanish or English colonies. In part, this reflected the small size of France's New World population. The French government had little interest in encouraging immigration and the number of settlers in New France remained small, totalling just 3,000 in 1663. Virtually all these settlers were men—mostly traders or Jesuit priests—and many took Indian wives or concubines, helping to promote relations of mutual dependency. Common trading interests also encouraged accommodation between the French and the Indians. Missionary activities, too, proved somewhat less divisive in New France than in New Mexico or New England, since France's Jesuit priests did not require them to immediately abandon their tribal ties or their traditional way of life.

English Encounters

Popular mythology recounts many instances of cooperation between English colonists and Native Americans. Grade schoolers learn about Pocahontas, the daughter of Powhatan, an Indian chief in Virginia, who is said to have rescued Captain John Smith when her father was about to kill him. They encounter Squanto, a member of the Pawtuxet tribe of eastern Massachusetts, who taught the Pilgrims how to grow corn. They also hear about William Penn, the Quaker founder of Pennsylvania, who maintained friendly relations with the Indians. But there was another side to this story, missing from popular mythology: settlers poisoning Indians at peace parleys, offering them clothing infected with smallpox, and burning their villages and cornfields.

In fact, encounters between the English and the Indian peoples were more problematic—and violent—than historical mythology suggests. Some English settlers dreamed of discovering gold or silver; others envisioned a lucrative trade in furs. But gradually the primary goal of the English was to acquire land. Unlike the French and Spanish, the English created self-sustaining settler colonies, populated with English, Scot, and Scots-Irish immigrants. And this meant displacing the indigenous inhabitants and expropriating their land.

In English eyes, the Indians held only an ambiguous title to the land. They may have had some vague rights due to discovery and prior occupancy, but they lacked true title since they failed to make improvements. As early as 1609, an Englishman insisted on the right of English colonists to "plant ourselves in their places." "The greater part" of the land, wrote Robert Gray, "possessed and wrongfully usurped by wild beasts, and unreasoning creatures, or by brutish savages, which by reason of their godles[s] ignorance, and blasphemous Idolatrie, are worse than . . . beasts."

The initial English–Indian encounters took place in the Southeast, where the Indian population was better prepared than elsewhere to resist English encroachments. On the eve of contact an estimated one million Indians lived in the region; and even though disease and warfare would soon reduce the indigenous population to just 75,000, these people revealed a remarkable capacity for resistance. In the Southeast, the Mississippian tradition of an urbanized population with centralized political authorities persisted. These people lived in villages, which were often quite sizable, with populations of a thousand or more, protected by wooden fences. In this region, the basic political unit was the chiefdom, consisting of a village or a group of villages ruled by a chief who gained his position through merit, and, in turn, distributed presents and other goods to the people he controlled. When the English entered their land, tribal chiefs in the Southeast were better able than elsewhere to mobilize their people against the outside threat.

The first English settlement in North America was established in 1585 at Roanoke Island, off the coast of what is today North Carolina. A year earlier, Sir Walter Raleigh had sent an expedition to explore the region, and brought two Algonquian Indians back to England: Manteo, who converted to Christianity; and Wanchese, who later led opposition to English colonization.

The English planned to explore Roanoke and the mainland for gold and silver, trade for furs, and raise bananas and sugar and other crops on plantations. Even though the colonists relied on the Indians for food, they treated them in a brutal manner, kidnapping women, burning cornfields, and ultimately beheading the local chief, Wingina. Then, the expedition returned to England.

In 1587, another expedition returned to Roanoke. Unlike the first, which consisted of soldiers and adventurers, this one was made up of families. Clashes erupted between the colonists and local Indians. Later that year, the colonists' leader, John White, returned to England for supplies. He did not return until 1590, when he discovered a shocking sight: buildings in ruin, food and armor scattered on the ground, and the word "CROATOAN" carved on the door post of the colony's crumbling fort. There was no sign of a cross, which White and the settlers had designated as a distress sign. The colony's 84 men, 17 women, and 11 children had vanished.

What happened to the "Lost Colony"? Some scholars believe that Manteo had led the colonists to Croatoan village, fifty miles south of Roanoke Island, where they intermarried with the Indians. Others speculate that the colonists later moved northward toward Chesapeake Bay, where the powerful Chief Powhatan executed the intruders. To this day, no one knows the answer to this historical mystery.

The first permanent English settlement, Jamestown, was built in 1607 in a swampy area, along Virginia's James River. Approximately 30,000 Algonquian Indians lived in the Chesapeake region, divided into some forty tribes. Thirty tribes belonged to a confederacy led by Powhatan. Relations between the colonists and the Indians rapidly deteriorated. Food was the initial source of conflict. More interested in finding precious metals than in farming, Jamestown's residents got part of their food from the Indians, which they exchanged for English goods. When the English began to simply seize Indian food stocks, Powhatan cut off supplies, forcing the colonists for a time to subsist on frogs, snakes, and even decaying corpses.

Relations worsened after the colonists began to clear the land and plant tobacco. Since tobacco production rapidly exhausted the soil of nutrients, the English began to acquire new lands along the James River, encroaching on Indian hunting grounds. In 1622, the growing hostility erupted into violence. Powhatan's successor, Opechancanough, attempted to wipe out the English in a surprise attack. Two Indian converts to Christianity warned the English; still, 347 settlers, or about one third of the English colonists died in the attack. Warfare persisted for ten years, followed by an uneasy peace. In 1644, Opechancanough launched a last, desperate attack. After two years of warfare, in which some 500 colonists were killed, Opechancanough was captured and shot and the survivors of Powhatan's confederacy, now numbering just 2,000, agreed to submit to English rule.

Farther south, English settlers manipulated tribal rivalries to open land to white settlement. In South Carolina, the English effectively pitted groups like the Tuscaroras, the Cherokees, the Creeks, and the Yamasees against one another. The Tuscaroras had taken many Algonquians captive and sold them into slavery. Between 1711 and 1713, the English took advantage of

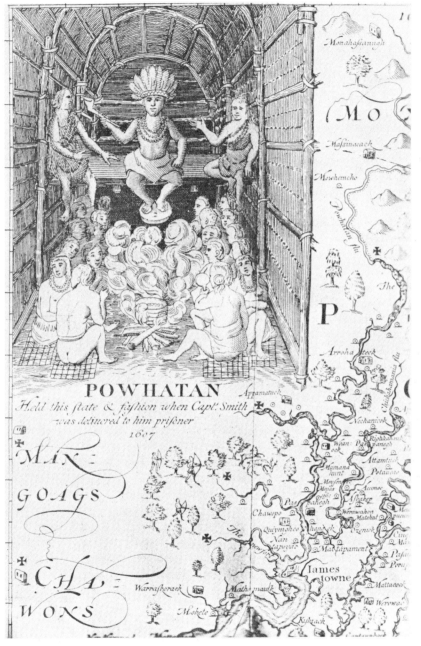

A map of Virginia in 1612, showing Powhatan. *(Courtesy, Smithsonian Institution)*

intertribal hostility by convincing the Algonquians to join them in a war against the Tuscaroras. When the conflict was over, over 1,000 Tuscaroras (a fifth of the tribe) were sold into slavery. Half the remaining Tuscaroras then migrated to New York, where they became the sixth nation of the Iroquois League. Then, in 1715, the European settlers succeeded in mobilizing the Cherokees against the Creeks and the Yamasees, forcing the Creeks to move westward and the surviving Yamasees southward into territory controlled by Spain, clearing valuable rice land of Indians in the process.

In the Northeast, Indians found it difficult to resist the English invaders unless they were able to ally themselves with a European power. Compared to the Southeast, the Northeast was much less densely populated. The 140,000 who inhabited the area in 1600 fell to just 10,000 by 1675. The tribes in this area were also more fragmented politically; except for the Iroquois, they were not organized into political confederacies. Politically, this was a region of autonomous villages that made decisions by consensus. It was also a region with a long history of tribal rivalries.

The migration of Puritan colonists into western Massachusetts and Connecticut during the 1630s provoked bitter warfare. Part of this land was claimed by the Pequots, the region's most powerful people. In 1636, English settlers accused a Pequot of murdering a colonist; in revenge, they burned a Pequot settlement on what is now Block Island, Rhode Island. In 1637, the Pequots struck at Wethersfield in Connecticut, killing several colonists. A force of Puritans and Narragansett Indians retaliated a month later by surrounding and setting fire to the main Pequot village on the Mystic River. Between six and seven hundred Pequot men, women, and children were burned alive. The force's commander declared that God had "laughed at his enemies . . . making them as a fiery oven."

The defeat of the Pequots allowed white settlers to move into the New England interior, where they intruded on Indian homelands. In 1675, the chief of the Pokanokets, Metacomet (whom the English called King Philip), forged a military alliance of two thirds of the region's Indians. In 1675, he led an attack on Swansea, Massachusetts. Over the next year, both sides raided villages and killed hundreds of victims. Twelve out of ninety New England towns were destroyed. Relative to the size of the population, King Philip's War (1675–76) was the bloodiest in American history. Five percent of New England's population was killed—a higher proportion than Germany or Russia lost during World War II. Indian casualties were far higher; perhaps 40 percent of New England's Indian population was killed or fled the region.

The colonists captured Philip's wife and son, and sold them into slavery. Metacomet was killed in 1676, ending war in southern New England. Fighting in the north continued until 1678. When the war was over, the power of New England's Indians was broken. The region's remaining Indians would live in small, scattered communities, serving as the colonists' servants and tenants.

Even in Pennsylvania, whose Quaker founder William Penn envisioned a "peaceable kingdom" where people of diverse backgrounds and religious beliefs could live together harmoniously, Indians were displaced from their lands. Before leaving England, he wrote to the Delawares, the dominant tribe in the region, expressing his hope that "we may always live together as neighbors and friends." True to his word, Penn met with the Delawares and told them that he would not take land from them unless sanctioned by tribal chieftains. Committed to treating Native Americans fairly in negotiating land rights, Penn purchased Delaware lands before reselling them to settlers and prohibited the sale of alcohol. Penn's policies were so unusual that they encouraged the Miamis, the Shawnees, and other peoples to move to Pennsylvania. However, after his death, Penn's own sons and agents reversed his policies, and Pennsylvania's colonists pushed the Delaware and other peoples off their land without compensation.

Native Americans and European Contests for Empire

Along the eastern coast, England, France, the Netherlands, and Spain all competed over trade with the Indians. In the Northeast, England, France, and the Netherlands struggled to control the immensely valuable fur trade. In the Southeast, it was not furs that drew the English, the Spanish, and later the French, but deerskin (used to make clothes, gloves, and book bindings) and Indian slaves. During the early eighteenth century, Indian slaves (many of whom had been converted to Catholicism at Spanish missions before capture) made up a sizable proportion of the slaves in South Carolina and other southeastern colonies.

Competition over furs, skins, and slaves had many destructive effects on Native Americans. It made Indians increasingly dependent on European manufactured goods and firearms. The trade also killed off animals that provided a major part of the hunting and gathering economy. And traders spread disease and alcohol. The fur trade also conflicted with traditional Indian religious beliefs, which charged hunters with never killing more animals than they needed.

Above all, competition over trade encouraged intertribal warfare and thus undermined the Indians' ability to resist white incursions. In what is now New York, for example, the Dutch and the English pitted their allies, the Iroquois, against the Huron, who served as middlemen between French traders and other tribes. In the ensuing warfare, the Hurons were driven westward.

During the late seventeenth and eighteenth centuries, Indians frequently became embroiled in European wars to control North America. Four times between 1689 and 1763, France, England, and their Indian allies waged wars over land between the Allegheny Mountains and the Mississippi River, fishing grounds off Nova Scotia and Newfoundland, and control of the fur trade. The last and most important conflict, the French and Indian War (1754–1763), began partly because the Iroquois started to allow British settlement in the Ohio River valley. The French, afraid that they would be cut out of the fur trade, retaliated by building a chain of forts along Pennsylvania's Allegheny River. France's defeat permitted English colonists to move into newly acquired lands in the interior.

No longer able to play the French off against the British, Indians found it increasingly difficult to slow the rapid advance of white settlers into western parts of South and North Carolina, Virginia and Pennsylvania, New York's Mohawk Valley, and the lower Mississippi River. To stop encroachments on their lands in the Southeast, the Cherokees attacked frontier settlements in the Carolinas and Virginia in 1760. Defeated the next year by British regulars and colonial militia, the Cherokees had to allow the English to build forts on their territory.

Indians in western New York and Ohio suffered a serious defeat in Pontiac's War (1763). With the French threat removed, the British reduced the price paid for furs, allowed settlers to take Indian land without payment, and built forts in violation of treaties with local tribes. In the spring of 1763 an Ottawa chief named Pontiac led an alliance of Delaware, Seneca, Shawnee, and other western Indians in rebellion. Pontiac's alliance attacked forts in Indiana, Michigan, Pennsylvania, and Wisconsin that Britain had taken over from the French, destroying all but three. Pontiac's forces then moved eastward, attacking settlements in western Pennsylvania, Maryland, and Virginia, killing more than 2,000 colonists. Without assistance from the French, however, Pontiac's rebellion petered out by the year's end.

To restore western peace, royal officials issued the Proclamation of 1763, which prohibited colonists from purchasing Indian lands and closed the trans-Mississippi West to white settlement. This scheme failed when land-hungry frontiersmen and speculators repeatedly petitioned the British government to negotiate treaties allowing them to purchase millions of acres of Indian land in the Ohio River valley. To end this pressure, Parliament passed the Quebec Act of 1774, transferring control of Indian trade in the area between the Ohio and Mississippi rivers to the French-speaking province of Quebec. But this act provoked outrage among American colonists, convinced that British government was seeking to transform the West into a preserve for "papists" and "savages." The prohibition on English settlement in the West was a major cause of the American Revolution.

In the 1770s, such tribes as the Delaware, the Wyandot, the Shawnee, and the Cayuga, staged raids into what is now Kentucky and West Virginia in response to an influx of white traders and farmers into the area south of the Ohio River. Whites accused the Indians of transforming Kentucky into a "dark and bloody ground," and struck back. In Lord Dunmore's War (1774), 3,000 British soldiers defeated 1,000 Indians, forcing the Indians to abandon their hunting grounds south of the Ohio River.

During the American Revolution itself, both the British and the American patriots sought to keep Indians neutral. In 1775, the Second Continental Congress asked Indians "not to join on either side," since "you Indians are not concerned in it." Two peoples tried to use the revolution as an opportunity to halt white settlement on their territory, the Shawnee in Kentucky and the Cherokee in frontier Carolina and Virginia. But in each case, these people suffered defeats at the hands of the colonial militias, forcing them to give up land in Kentucky, the western Carolinas, and eastern Georgia to the Americans. The Revolution also had fateful consequences for another group of Indians, the Iroquois Confederacy, who divided over whether to support the British or the Americans. Those Iroquois tribes that aligned with the British—the Cayugas, Mohawks, and Senecas—were defeated in battle in 1779, and left New York State and western Pennsylvania to resettle in British Canada.

Even after the revolution, the eastern Indians still represented a formidable barrier to white expansion. In 1790, there were approximately 150,000 Native Americans east of the Mississippi River—a population greater than the number of European colonists in 1700. The Senecas inhabited the western portions of New York; the Kickapoos, Miamis, Wyandots, and other tribes populated the areas that would become Indiana, Illinois, Michigan, and Wisconsin, while the Cherokees, Chickasaws, Choctaws, and Creeks considered the future states of Alabama, Mississippi, and western Georgia their territory. But pressure on these areas was mounting.

The end of the revolution unleashed a mad rush of pioneers to Kentucky and Tennessee. Between 1784 and 1790, clashes with the Cherokees, Chickasaws, and Shawnees left more than 1,500 whites dead or captured.

Pressure to open up other areas was increasing. In 1790, the United States paid a large bribe to a Creek leader, Alexander McGillivray, to sign a peace treaty allowing whites to occupy lands in central Georgia. Under pressure from Spain, the Creeks renounced the treaty in 1792.

President George Washington also wanted to open the country north of the Ohio River. The British, eager to maintain the lucrative fur trade, had refused to relinquish their military posts from this area and provided aid to the region's Delawares, Iroquois, Miamis, and Shawnees. During the 1790s, George Washington dispatched three armies to clear the Ohio country of Indians. Twice, a confederacy of eight tribes led by Little Turtle, chief of the Miamis, defeated American forces. In the first campaign, the United States suffered 200 casualties and in the second, Indians killed 900 soldiers. But in 1794, a third army defeated the Indians. A 3,000-man force under Anthony Wayne destroyed Indian villages in northwestern Ohio and then overwhelmed a thousand Indians at the Battle of Fallen Timbers. Under the

Treaty of Greenville (1795), Native Americans ceded much of the present state of Ohio, in return for cash and a promise that the federal government would treat the Indian nations fairly in land dealings.

Cultural Survival Strategies

As the eighteenth century drew to a close, the Indians east of the Mississippi faced a fundamental challenge: how to preserve their cultures and heritage in the face of declining populations and a loss of land. As the historian Gary Nash has shown, these people met this challenge by adopting two basic survival strategies. One strategy, physical resistance, was pursued by the Shawnees and other tribes in Indiana and the Creeks in northwestern Georgia and Alabama. The other strategy, cultural adaptation and renewal, was embraced by the Iroquois and the Cherokees.

Few people better illustrate the process of cultural adaptation than the Iroquois. Displaced from their traditional lands and suffering the psychological and cultural disintegration brought on by epidemic disease, rampant alcoholism, and dwindling land resources, the Iroquois reconstituted and revitalized their culture under the leadership of a prophet named Handsome Lake. The prophet endorsed the demand of Quaker missionaries that the traditional Iroquois sexual division of labor emphasizing male hunting and female horticulture be replaced. He argued that men should farm and women rear children and care for the home. He also called for modification of the Iroquois system of matrilineal descent, in which the tie between mothers and daughters had been strong and the bond between spouses had been fragile. Handsome Lake emphasized the sanctity of the marriage bond, and said that marriage should take precedence over all other kinship ties.

As a result of Handsome Lake's religious movement, the Iroquois abandoned their matrilineal longhouses and began to dwell in male-headed households in individual log cabins. They modified their system of matrilineal descent to allow fathers to pass land to their sons. And Iroquois men took up farming, even though this was traditionally viewed as women's work. By adopting those aspects of the encroaching white culture that were relevant to their lives and fitting them into traditional cultural patterns, the Iroquois were largely able to maintain their culture, values, and rituals.

The Cherokees also demonstrated the ability of Native Americans to adapt to changing conditions while maintaining their tribal heritage. During the early nineteenth century, these people developed a written alphabet, opened schools, established churches, built roads, operated printing presses, and even adopted a constitution.

The alternative to cultural revitalization was armed resistance. Between 1803 and 1809, William Henry Harrison, Indiana's territorial governor, acquired thirty-three million acres in cessions from Indians in the Old Northwest. Two Shawnee brothers Tecumseh and Tenskwatawa ("the Shawnee Prophet"), to resist further encroachments, created a pan-Indian

In 1808 Northwest Indians, here dancing and singing, pledged support to Tecumseh. *(Courtesy, Library of Congress)*

alliance, consisting of the Kickapoos, Menominis, Ottawas, Potawatomis, Shawnees, Winnebagos, and Wyandots. In 1811, when Tecumseh was in the South attempting to rally support, Harrison forced a confrontation with the Shawnee Prophet at the battle of Tippecanoe. The Indian stronghold, Prophetstown, was burned, and Indian supplies were destroyed. During the War of 1812, Tecumseh fought in support of the British. But he was killed at the battle of the Thames in 1813, ending effective Indian resistance in the Old Northwest.

The military power of the Creek Indians was also broken during the War of 1812. During his trip to the South, Tecumseh encouraged the Creeks to defend their land from encroaching whites. In retaliation for a Creek attack on an American fort, in which some 500 whites were killed, Andrew Jackson and a force of 4,000 surrounded the chief Creek village at Horseshoe Bend in Alabama. In the ensuing battle, more than 800 Creeks were killed, against 49 white deaths.

The War of 1812 marked a crucial dividing line in the history of the eastern Indians. No longer would they have European allies capable of supplying guns or slowing the advance of white settlers. In the Old Northwest, Britain agreed to abandon its forts on American soil. In the South, Spain ceded part of Florida in 1810 and the rest in 1819, leaving the southeastern Indians, like the Seminoles, without a secure refuge. Abandoned by their British and Spanish allies, the eastern Indians would have to confront a new policy: removing all eastern Indians to lands west of the Mississippi River.

Clearing the Land of Indians

In 1829, at the time Andrew Jackson became president, 125,000 Native Americans still lived east of the Mississippi River. Cherokee, Choctaw,

A sketch of a battle from the Creek War of 1813 and 1814. *(Courtesy, Public Archives of Canada)*

Chickasaw, and Creek Indians—60,000 strong—held millions of acres in what would become the southern Cotton Kingdom stretching across Georgia, Alabama, and Mississippi. The political question was whether these Indian tribes would be permitted to block white expansion. By 1840, Jackson and his successor, Martin Van Buren, had answered this question. All Indians east of the Mississippi had been uprooted from their homelands and moved westward, with the exception of rebellious Seminoles in Florida and small numbers of Indians living on isolated reservations in Michigan, North Carolina, and New York.

Since Jefferson's presidency, two conflicting Indian policies, assimilation and removal, had governed the treatment of Native Americans. Assimilation encouraged Indians to adopt white American customs and economic practices. The government provided financial assistance to missionaries in order to Christianize and educate Native Americans and convince them to adopt single family farms. Proponents defended the assimilation policy as the only way Indians would be able to survive in a white-dominated society. According to the American Board of Commissioners for Foreign Missions, "There is no place on earth to which they can migrate, and live in the savage and hunter state. The Indian tribes must, therefore, be progressively civilized, or successively perish."

The other policy—removal—was first suggested by Thomas Jefferson as the only way to ensure the survival of Indian cultures. The goal of this policy was to encourage the voluntary migration of Indians westward to tracts of land where they could live free from white harrassment. As early as 1817, James Monroe declared that the nation's security depended upon rapid settlement along the southern coast and that it was in the best interests of Native Americans to move westward. In 1825 he set before Congress a plan to resettle all eastern Indians upon tracts in the West where whites would not be allowed to live. Initially, Jackson followed the dual policy of assimilation and removal, promising remuneration to tribes that would move westward, while offering small plots of land to individual Indians who would operate family farms. After 1830, however, Jackson favored only removal.

The shift in federal Indian policy came partly as a result of a controversy between the Cherokee nation and the state of Georgia. The Cherokee people had adopted a constitution asserting sovereignty over their land, and the state of Georgia responded by abolishing tribal rule and claiming that the Cherokee fell under its jurisdiction. The discovery of gold on Cherokee land triggered a land rush, and the Cherokee nation sued to keep white settlers from encroaching upon their territory. In two important cases, *Cherokee Nation v. Georgia* in 1831 and *Worcester v. Georgia* in 1832, the Supreme Court ruled that states could not pass laws conflicting with federal Indian treaties and that the federal government had an obligation to exclude white intruders from Indian lands. Angered, Jackson is said to have exclaimed: "John Marshall has made his decision; now let him enforce it."

The primary thrust of Jackson's removal policy was to encourage Indian tribes to sell all tribal lands in exchange for new lands in Oklahoma and Arkansas. Such a policy, the President maintained, would open new farmland to whites while offering Indians a haven where they would be free to develop at their own pace. "There," he wrote, "your white brothers will not trouble you, they will have no claims to the land, and you can live upon it, you and all your children, as long as the grass grows and the water runs, in peace and plenty."

Pushmataha, a Choctaw chieftain, called on his people to reject Jackson's offer. Far from being a "country of tall trees, many water courses, rich lands and high grass abounding in games of all kinds," the promised preserve in the West was simply a barren desert. Jackson responded by warning that if the Choctaw refused to move west, he would destroy their nation.

During the winter of 1831, the Choctaw became the first tribe to walk the "Trail of Tears" westward. Promised government assistance failed to arrive and malnutrition, exposure, and an epidemic of cholera killed many members of the nation. In 1836, the Creek suffered the hardships of removal. About 3,500 of the tribes 15,000 members died along the westward trek. Those who resisted removal were bound in chains and marched in double file.

The Cherokee, emboldened by the Supreme Court decisions that declared that Georgia law had no force on Indian territory, resisted removal. Fifteen thousand Cherokee joined in a protest against Jackson's policy: "Little did [we] anticipate, that when taught to think and feel as the American citizen . . . [we] were to be despoiled by [our] guardian, to become strangers and wanderers in the land of [our] fathers, forced to return to the savage life, and to seek a new home in the wilds of the far west, and that without [our] consent." The federal government bribed a faction of the tribe to leave the land in exchange for transportation costs and $5 million, but the majority of the people held out until 1838, when the army evicted them from their land. All totaled, 4,000 of the 15,000 Cherokee died along the trail to Oklahoma.

A number of tribes organized resistance against removal. In the Old Northwest, the Sauk and Fox Indians fought the Black Hawk War to recover ceded tribal lands in Illinois and Wisconsin. At the time that they had signed a treaty transferring title to their land, these people had not understood the implications of their action. "I touched the goose quill to the treaty," said Chief Black Hawk, "not knowing, however, that by that act I consented to give away my village." The United States army and the Illinois state militia ended resistance by wantonly killing nearly 500 Sauk and Fox men, women, and children who were trying to retreat across the Mississippi River. In Florida, the military spent seven years putting down Seminole resistance at a cost of $20 million and 1,500 troops, and even then only after the treacherous act of seizing the Seminole leader Osceola during peace talks.

By twentieth-century standards, Jackson's Indian policy was both callous and inhumane. Despite the semblance of legality—ninety-four treaties were signed with Indians during Jackson's presidency—Indian migrations to the West usually occurred under the threat of government coercion. Even before Jackson's death in 1845, it was obvious that tribal lands in the West were no more secure than Indian lands had been in the East. In 1851 Congress passed the Indian Appropriations Act, which sought to concentrate the western Native American population upon reservations.

Why were such morally indefensible policies adopted? The answer is that many white Americans regarded Indian control of land and other natural resources as a serious obstacle to their desire for expansion and as a potential threat to the nation's security. Even had the federal government wanted to, it probably lacked the resources or military means to protect eastern Indians from the encroaching white farmers, squatters, traders, and speculators. By the 1830s, a growing number of missionaries and humanitarians agreed with Jackson that Indians needed to be resettled westward for their own protection. But the removal program was doomed from the start. Given the nation's commitment to limited government and its lack of experience with social welfare programs, removal was destined for disaster. Contracts for food, clothing, and transportation were let to the lowest bidders, many of whom failed to fulfill their contractual responsibilities. Indians were resettled on arid lands, unsuited for intensive farming. The tragic outcome was readily foreseeable.

The problem of preserving native cultures in the face of an expanding nation was not confined to the United States. Jackson's removal policy can only be properly understood when it is seen as part of a broader process: the political and economic incorporation of frontier regions into expanding nation-states. During the early decades of the nineteenth century, European nations were penetrating into many frontier areas, from the steppes of Russia to the plains of Argentina, the veldt of South Africa, the outback of Australia, and the American West. In each of these regions, national expansion was justified on the grounds of strategic interest (to preempt settlement by other powers) or in the name of opening valuable land to settlement and development. And in each case, expansion was accompanied by the removal or wholesale killing of native peoples.

The "Five Civilized Tribes" and the Civil War

There is a tragic postscript to the story of the Trail of Tears. In 1861, many Cherokees, Chickasaws, Choctaws, Creeks, and Seminoles decided to join the Confederacy, in part because some of the tribes' members owned slaves. In return, the Confederate states agreed to pay all annuities that the U.S. government had provided and let these tribes send delegates to the Confederate Congress. A Cherokee chief, Stand Watie, served as a brigadier general for the Confederacy and did not formally surrender until a month after the war was over. Some of these people supported the Union, however, including a Cherokee faction led by Chief John Ross.

After the war, the tribes were severely punished for supporting the Confederacy. The Seminoles were required to sell their reservation at 15 cents an acre and buy new land from the Creeks at 50 cents an acre. The other tribes were required to give up half their territory in Oklahoma, to become reservations for the Arapahos, Caddos, Cheyennes, Comanches, Iowas, Kaws, Kickapoos, Pawnees, Potawatomis, Sauk and Foxes, and Shawnees. In addition, the tribes had to allow railroads to cut across their land.

The Tragedy of the Western Indians

It took white settlers a century and a half to expand as far west as the Appalachian Mountains, a few hundred miles from the Atlantic Coast. It took another 50 years to push the frontier to the Mississippi. By 1830, fewer than 100,000 American soldiers, missionaries, fur trappers, and traders had crossed the Mississippi.

By 1850, pioneers had pushed the edge of settlement all the way to the Pacific Ocean. When Americans ventured westward, they did not enter virgin land. Large parts of the West were already occupied by Indians and

Mexicans, who had lived in the region for hundreds of years and established their own distinctive ways of life.

In 1840, before large numbers of white pioneers and farmers crossed the Mississippi, at least 500,000 Indians lived in the Southwest, California, the Great Plains, and the Northwest Pacific Coast, divided into more than two hundred tribes. The single largest concentration of Indians was in California, where some 275,000 lived in the early nineteenth century.

The California Indians had little contact with Europeans before the late eighteenth century, when Spanish explorers, soldiers, and missionaries arrived from Mexico. Despite its proximity to Mexico, Spain did not begin to colonize the area until 1769, when it learned that Russian seal hunters and traders were moving south from Alaska.

The Spanish clergy played a critical role in colonization, using the mission system, which was designed to spread Christianity among, and establish control over, the indigenous western population. A Franciscan father, Junipero Serra, established the first California mission near the site of present-day San Diego. Between 1769 and 1823, Spain established twenty-one missions in California, extending from San Diego northward to Sonoma. By 1830, thirty thousand Indians lived in mission communities, where they toiled in workhouses, orchards, and fields for long hours. At least a quarter million other Indians lived outside of missions, occupying small villages during the winter, and moving during the rest of the year gathering wild plants and seeds, hunting small game, and fishing in the rivers.

The Mexican Revolution led to the demise of the mission system in California. In 1833–34, the missions were "secularized"—broken up and their property sold or given away to private citizens. By 1846, mission lands had fallen into the hands of eight hundred private landowners. The Indians who worked on these private estates had a status similar to that of slaves. Indeed, the death rate of Indians on these *ranchos* was twice as high as among southern slaves, and by 1848 a fifth of California's Indian population had died.

The acquisition of California by the United States resulted in further reductions in the number of Indians. In 1846, fifteen years before the United States was plunged into civil war, it fought a war against Mexico that increased the country's size by one third. On January 10, 1848, less than ten days before the signing of the peace treaty ending the war, gold was discovered in California. Within two years, California's non-Indian population soared from 14,000 to 100,000. For California's Indians, the results were catastrophic. Between 1849 and 1859, disease and deliberate campaigns of extermination killed 70,000 Indians. Many Indian women were forced into concubinage and many men into virtual slavery. By 1880, there were fewer than 20,000 Indians in California.

In California and northward the Indian population remained extremely vulnerable to European diseases. In the Oregon country of the Pacific Northwest, the arrival of Protestant missionaries, beginning in 1834, ignited

A Comanche village in Texas, painted by George Catlin in 1834. *(Courtesy, Smithsonian Institution)*

epidemics of measles and other diseases that killed tens of thousands of people. Many more died during the Cayuse War (1847–50) and the Rogue River wars of the 1850s.

A pervasive belief in white supremacy led to mass killings of Indians in Texas and the Great Basin, the harsh, barren region between the Sierra Nevada and the Rocky Mountains. A treatise of the 1850s provided a pseudo-scientific rationale for the extermination campaigns: "The *Barbarous* races of America ... are essentially untameable. Not merely have all attempts to civilize them failed, but also every endeavor to enslave them."

In Texas, settlers accused Indian warriors of impaling white women on fence posts and staking men under the sun with their eyelids removed, while heaping burning coals on their genitals. They retaliated with campaigns of extermination against the Karankawas and other peoples who inhabited the area. In the Great Basin, where food was so scarce that the Paiutes and Gosiutes subsisted on berries, pine nuts, roots, and rabbits, impoverished Indians were sometimes shot by trappers for sport.

Resistance on the Great Plains

Beyond the Mississippi River, stretching westward to the Rocky Mountains and south from Alberta and Saskatchewan to Texas, lies a dry, largely treeless region known as the Great Plains. Before European contact, the Plains

An 1834 sketch of funeral scaffold of a Sioux chief. *(Courtesy, Smithsonian Institution)*

Indians were relatively small in number, since it was difficult to cultivate the tough Plains sod. Many of the original inhabitants of the Plains were farmers who lived in villages along rivers and streams where the land was more easily cultivated. In the summer, these people would leave their villages to hunt antelope, bison, deer, and elk.

The introduction of the horse by the Spanish brought about a thorough transformation of life on the Plains. Population size, hunting, communication, transportation, and warfare—all greatly changed. Horses made the Plains Indians much more efficient hunters. Animals that were difficult to hunt on foot could easily be followed on horseback. As a result, many agricultural people, like the Cheyenne, became hunters.

During the eighteenth and early nineteenth centuries, many new peoples—including the Apaches, the Arapahos, the Blackfeet, the Cheyennes, the Comanches, and the Sioux—moved onto the Plains, tripling the population to approximately 360,000. As an increasing number of tribes were forced onto the Plains by advancing white settlement, intertribal conflict grew. These Indians developed sign language as an easily understood system of communication.

Not all Plains Indians, however, conformed to the Hollywood image of hunters on horseback. Many village dwellers continued to herd sheep and cultivate corn, beans, and squash. Semi-sedentary tribes, such as the Iowa, Kansas, Missouri, and Pawnee, lived in earth- or sod-covered lodges with log frames, while more nomadic peoples lived in portable tipis covered with buffalo hides.

A belief that the Great Plains was a dry, barren wasteland—a great American desert—delayed white settlement in that region. But the discovery of gold, silver, copper, and lead in Nevada and Colorado in the 1850s, Idaho and Montana in the 1860s, and the Black Hills of South Dakota in the 1870s touched off a rush of white prospectors into these areas. Ranchers soon arrived, bringing cattle and sheep to the Plains. Farmers followed, using windmills to draw water from wells, and shipping their goods on newly constructed railroads. As miners, ranchers, and land-hungry farmers moved onto the Plains, they violated treaties that guaranteed this land to the Indians "as long as the rivers shall run and the grass shall grow."

To find a way for Indians and white settlers to live peacefully federal officials introduced a policy known as "concentration." At Fort Laramie in Wyoming in 1851, representatives of the United States government and the Plains Indians met and Indian leaders agreed to restrict hunting to specified regions in exchange for yearly payments in money and goods. But this agreement quickly broke down, as railroad tracks disrupted the migration routes of buffalo herds and farms disrupted Indian lands.

Beginning in the 1860s, a thirty-year conflict arose as the government sought to concentrate the Plains tribes on reservations. Philip Sheridan, a Civil War general who led many campaigns against the Plains Indians, is famous for saying "the only good Indian is a dead Indian." But even he recognized the injustice that lay behind the late nineteenth-century warfare:

> We took away their country and their means of support, broke
> up their mode of living, their habits of life, introduced disease
> and decay among them, and it was for this and against this that
> they made war. Could anyone expect less?

Violence erupted first in Minnesota, where, by 1862, the Santee Sioux were confined to a territory 150 miles long and just ten miles wide. Denied a yearly payment and agricultural aid promised by treaty, these people rose up in August 1862 and killed five hundred white settlers at New Ulm. Lincoln appointed John Pope, who had commanded Union forces at the second Battle of Bull Run, to crush the uprising. The general announced that he would deal with the Sioux "as maniacs or wild beasts, and by no means as people with whom treaties or compromises can be made." When the Sioux surrendered in September 1862, about 1,800 were taken prisoner and 303 were condemned to death. Lincoln commuted the sentences of most, but he authorized the hanging of thirty-eight, the largest mass execution in American history.

In 1864, warfare spread to Colorado, after the discovery of gold led to an influx of whites. Because the regular army was fighting the Confederacy, the Colorado territorial militia was responsible for maintaining order. On November 29, 1864, a group of Colorado volunteers, under the command

An 1858 watercolor shows Plains people driving buffalo over a cliff. *(Courtesy, Walters Art Gallery, Baltimore)*

of Colonel John M. Chivington, fell on Chief Black Kettle's unsuspecting band of Cheyennes at Sand Creek in eastern Colorado, where they had gathered under the protection of the governor. "We must kill them big and little," he told his men. "Nits make lice" (nits are the eggs of lice). The militia slaughtered about 150 Cheyenne, mostly women and children.

Violence broke out on other parts of the Plains. Between 1865 and 1868, conflict raged in Utah. In 1866, the Teton Sioux tried to stop construction of the Bozeman Trail, leading from Fort Laramie, Wyoming, to the Virginia City, Wyoming, gold fields, by attacking and killing Captain William J. Fetterman and seventy-nine soldiers.

The Sand Creek and Fetterman massacres produced a national debate over Indian policy. In 1867, Congress created a Peace Commission to recommend ways to reduce conflict on the Plains. The commission recommended that Indians be moved to small reservations, where they would be Christianized, educated, and taught to farm.

At two conferences in 1867 and 1868, the federal government demanded that the Plains Indians give up their lands and move to reservations. In return for supplies and annuities, the southern Plains Indians were told to move to poor, unproductive lands in Oklahoma and the northern tribes to the Black Hills of the Dakotas. The alternative to acceptance was warfare. The commissioner of Indian Affairs, Ely S. Parker, himself a Seneca Indian, declared that any Indian who refused to "locate in permanent abodes provided for them, would be subject wholly to the control and supervision of military authorities." Many whites regarded the Plains Indian as an intolerable obstacle to westward expansion. They agreed with Theodore Roosevelt that the West was not meant to be "kept as nothing but a game reserve for squalid savages."

Leaders of several tribes—including the Apaches, Arapahos, Cheyennes, Kiowas, Navajos, Shoshones, and Sioux—agreed to move onto reservations. But many Indians rejected the land cessions made by their chiefs.

In the Southwest, war broke out in 1871 in New Mexico and Arizona with the massacre of more than one hundred Indians at Camp Grant. The Apache war did not end until 1886, when their leader Geronimo was captured. On the southern Plains, war erupted when the Cheyennes, Comanches, and Kiowas staged raids into the Texas panhandle. The Red River War ended only after federal troops destroyed Indian food supplies and killed a hundred Cheyenne warriors near the Sappa River in Kansas. This brought resistance on the southern Plains to a close. In the Pacific Northwest, the Nez Percé of Oregon and Idaho rebelled against the federal reservation policy and then attempted to escape to Canada, covering 1300 miles in just 75 days. They were forced to surrender in Montana, just forty miles short of the Canadian border. Chief Joseph, the Nez Percé leader, offered a poignant explanation for why he had surrendered:

> I am tired of fighting. . . . The old men are all killed. . . .
> The little children are freezing to death. . . . From where the sun
> now stands, I will fight no more forever.

After their surrender, the Nez Percé were taken to Oklahoma, where most died of disease.

The best-known episode of Indian resistance took place after miners discovered gold in the Black Hills—land that had been set aside as a reservation "in perpetuity." When thousands of miners staked claims on Sioux lands, war erupted, in which an Indian force led by Crazy Horse and Sitting Bull killed General George Custer and his 264 men at the Battle of the Little Big Horn. "Custer's Last Stand" was followed by five years of warfare in Montana that confined the Sioux to their reservations.

Several factors contributed to the defeat of the Plains Indians. One was a shift in the military balance of power. Before the Civil War, an Indian could shoot thirty arrows in the time it took a soldier to load and shoot his rifle once. The introduction of the Colt six-shooter and the repeating rifle after the Civil War, undercut this Indian advantage. During the 1870s, the army also introduced a military tactic—winter campaigning. The army attacked Plains Indians during the winter when they divided into small bands, making it difficult for Indians effectively to resist.

Another key was the destruction of the Indian food supply, especially the buffalo. In 1860, about thirteen million buffalo roamed the Plains. These animals provided Plains Indians with many basic necessities. They ate buffalo meat, made clothing and tipi coverings out of hides, used fats for grease, fashioned the bones into tools and fishhooks, made thread and bow-strings from the sinews, and even burned dried buffalo droppings ("chips") as fuel. Buffalo also figured prominently in Plains Indians' religious life. After the Civil War, the herds were cut down by professional hunters, who shot a hundred an hour to feed railroad workers, and by wealthy easterners who killed them for sport. By 1890, only about 1,000 bison remained alive. Government officials quite openly viewed the destruction of the buffalo as a tool for controlling the Plains Indians. Secretary of the Interior Columbus Delano explained in 1872, "as they become convinced that they can no longer rely upon the supply of game for their support, they will return to the more reliable source of subsistence. . . ."

Wounded Knee

The late nineteenth century marked the nadir of Indian life. Deprived of their homelands, their revolts suppressed, and their way of life besieged, many Plains Indians dreamed of restoring a vanished past, free of hunger, disease, and bitter warfare. Beginning in the 1870s, a religious movement known as the Ghost Dance arose among Indians of the Great Basin, and then spread, in the late 1880s, to the Great Plains. Beginning among the Paiute Indians of Nevada in 1870, the Ghost Dance promised to restore the way of life of their ancestors.

During the late 1880s, the Ghost Dance had great appeal among the Sioux, despairing over the death of a third of their cattle by disease and angry that the federal government had cut their food rations. In 1889, Wovoka, a Paiute holy man from Nevada, had a revelation. If only the Sioux would perform sacred dances and religious rites, then the Great Spirit would return and raise the dead, restore the buffalo to life, and cause a flood that would destroy the whites.

Wearing special Ghost Dance shirts, fabricated from white muslim and decorated with red fringes and painted symbols, dancers would spin in a circle until they became so dizzy that they entered into a trance. White settlers became alarmed: "Indians are dancing in the snow and are wild and crazy. . . . We need protection, and we need it now."

Fearful that the Ghost Dance would lead to a Sioux uprising, army officials ordered Indian police to arrest the Sioux leader Sitting Bull. When Sitting Bull resisted, he was killed. In the ensuing panic, his followers fled the Sioux reservation. Federal troops tracked down the Indians and took them to a cavalry camp on Wounded Knee Creek. There, on December 29, 1890, one of the most brutal incidents in American history took place. While soldiers disarmed the Sioux, someone fired a gun. The soldiers responded by using machine guns to slaughter over 200 Indian men, women, and children. The Oglala Sioux spiritual leader Black Elk summed up the meaning of Wounded Knee:

Wovoka, who brought the Ghost Dance to the Plains, photographed with the adjutant general of Wyoming. *(Courtesy, Smithsonian Institution)*

I can see that something else died there in the bloody mud, and was buried in the blizzard. A people's dream died there.

The Battle of Wounded Knee marked the end of three centuries of bitter warfare between Indians and whites. Indians had been confined to small reservations, where reformers would seek to transform them into Christian farmers. In the future, the Indian struggle to maintain an independent way of life and a separate culture would take place on new kinds of battlefields.

"Kill the Indian and Save the Man"

In 1879, an army officer named Richard H. Pratt opened a boarding school for Indian youth in Carlisle, Pennsylvania. His goal: to use education to uplift and assimilate them into the mainstream of American culture. That year, fifty Cheyenne, Kiowa, and Pawnee arrived at his school. Pratt trimmed their hair, required them to speak English, and prohibited any displays of tribal traditions, such as Indian clothing, dancing, or religious cere-monies. Pratt's motto was "kill the Indian and save the man."

The Carlisle Indian School became a model for Indian education. Not only were remote private boarding schools established, so too were reserva-tion boarding schools. The ostensible goal of such schools was to teach Indian children the skills necessary to function effectively in American soci-ety. But in the name of uplift, civilization, and assimilation, these schools took Indian children away from their families and tribes and sought to strip them of their cultural heritage.

By the late nineteenth century, there was a widespread sense that the removal and reservation policies had failed. No one had done a more effec-tive job of arousing public sentiment about the Indians' plight than Helen Hunt Jackson, a Massachusetts-born novelist and poet. Her classic book *A Century of Dishonor* (1881), recorded the country's sordid record of bro-ken treaty obligations, and did almost as much to stimulate public concern over the condition of Indians as Harriet Beecher Stowe's *Uncle Tom's Cabin* did to raise public sentiment against slavery or Rachel Carson's *Silent Spring* did to ignite outrage against environmental depradation. Ironically, reformers believed that the solution to the "Indian problem" was to erase a distinctive Indian identity.

During the late nineteenth century, humanitarian reformers repeatedly called for the government to support schools to teach Indian children "the white man's way of life," end corruption on Indian reservations, and eradi-cate tribal organizations. The federal government partly adopted the re-formers' agenda. Many reformers denounced corruption in the Indian Bureau, which had been set up in 1824 to provide assistance to Indians. In 1869, one member of the House of Representatives said, "No branch of the federal government is so spotted with fraud, so tainted with corruption . . . as this Indian Bureau." To end corruption, Congress established the Board of Indian Commissioners in 1869, which had the major Protestant religious denominations appoint agents to run Indian reservations. The agents were to educate and Christianize the Indians and teach them to farm. Dissatisfac-tion with bickering among church groups and the inexperience of church agents led the federal government to replace church-appointed Indian agents with federally-appointed agents during the 1880s.

To weaken the authority of tribal leaders, Congress in 1871 ended the practice of treating tribes as sovereign nations. To undermine older systems of tribal justice, Congress, in 1882, created a Court of Indian Offenses to try Indians who violated government laws and rules.

Native Americans at the Turn of the Century

As the nineteenth century ended, Native Americans seemed to be a disap-pearing people. The 1890 census recorded an Indian population of less than

225,000, and falling. The prevailing view among whites was that Indians should be absorbed as rapidly as possible into the dominant society: their reservations broken up, tribal authority abolished, traditional religions and languages eradicated. Late nineteenth-century federal policy embodied this attitude. In 1871 Congress declared that tribes were no longer separate, independent governments. It placed tribes under the guardianship of the federal government. The 1887 Dawes Act allotted reservation lands to individual Indians in units of 40 to 160 acres. Land that remained after allotment was to be sold to whites to pay for Indian education.

The Dawes Act was supposed to encourage Indians to become farmers. But most of the allotted lands proved unsuitable for farming owing to a lack of sufficient rainfall. The plots were also too small to support livestock.

Much Indian land quickly fell into the hands of whites. There was to be a twenty-five-year trust period to keep Indians from selling their land allotments, but an 1891 amendment did allow Indians to lease them, and a 1907 law let them sell portions of their property. A policy of "forced patents" took additional lands out of Indian hands. Under this policy, begun in 1909, government agents determined which Indians were "competent" to assume full responsibility for their allotments. Many of these Indians quickly sold their lands to white purchasers. Altogether, the severalty policy reduced Indian-owned lands from 155 million acres in 1881 to 77 million in 1900 and just 48 million acres in 1934. The most dramatic loss of Indian land and natural resources took place in Oklahoma. At the end of the nineteenth century, the Cherokee, Chickasaw, Choctaw, and Creek nations held half the territory's land. But by 1907, when Oklahoma became a state, much of this land, as well as its valuable asphalt, coal, natural gas, and oil resources, had passed into the possession of whites.

Revitalization and Renewal

During the 1920s, however, federal Indian policy began to shift away from its longstanding emphasis on assimilation. This shift was due in large measure to a reformer named John Collier, whose career illustrates in vivid terms the difference that one person's life can make. After conducting an investigation of Indian living conditions for the General Federation of Women's Clubs in 1922, Collier became a staunch advocate of preserving tribal cultures and lands. He helped convince the Rockefeller Foundation to fund the Meriam Commission, a comprehensive investigation of federal Indian policies. The commission found that half of all Indians owned less than $500 worth of property and that 71 percent lived on less than $200 a year. The commission blamed Indian poverty on misguided public policies.

When Franklin D. Roosevelt became president in 1933, he named Collier commissioner of the Bureau of Indian Affairs, a post he held until 1945. As commissioner, Collier led "the Indian New Deal"—wide-ranging efforts to extend New Deal relief and job programs to Native Americans and stop the sale of Indian reservation land. A special Indian Emergency Conservation work group was established which employed Indians in programs of soil erosion control, irrigation, and land development. The 1934 Johnson–O'Malley Act promoted cooperation between the federal and state governments in improving Indian agriculture, education, and health care. The Indian Reorganization Act, also passed in 1934, encouraged reservation Indians to take a more active role in managing their own affairs, by providing for the election of tribal councils to represent the tribes with state and federal governments. Funds were also allocated to provide scholarships for Indian students and help Indians establish their own businesses.

World War II brought profound changes to Indian lives, as tens of thousands left reservations to serve in the military and work in wartime industries. In 1943 alone, over 46,000 took jobs off reservations in shipyards, lumbering, canneries, mines, and farms. Over 24,000 served in the armed forces—over a third of all Indian men between eighteen and fifty. Unlike African Americans, Indians were not confined to separate military units, performing all kinds of military duties. This policy increased the integration of many Native Americans into the dominant currents of American society.

Perhaps the most unique Indian contribution to the war effort was the development of a secret military code. During the war, Navajo radio operators, including 350 in the Pacific theater, used Navajo words for military radio transmissions—a code that neither the Germans nor the Japanese were ever able to break.

Wartime experience intensified a sense of Indian identity, reinforced religious beliefs, and exposed many Indians to life outside the reservations. After the war, Indians became increasingly active politically, demanding equal voting rights and an end to discrimination. In Arizona and New Mexico, Indians who paid no United States taxes were denied the right to vote, in spite of the 1924 Indian Citizenship Act that granted Indians full citizenship. In 1948, both states ended this denial of voting rights. In other political activities, Indians resisted the construction of dams that threatened to flood reservation lands and destroy Indian fishing sites.

The major postwar innovation in Indian policy was the establishment by Congress in 1946 of the Indian Claims Commission to compensate Indians for fraud or unfair treatment by the federal government. The commission, operating from 1946 to 1978, heard 852 claims and awarded about $818 million in damages. Indian groups criticized the Claims Commission for basing awards on land values at the time of cession and refusing to pay interest or adjust awards for inflation.

A renewed sense of Indian nationalism emerged during the 1940s and 1950s. In 1944, Indian leaders from fifty tribes formed the National Congress of American Indians (NCAI), the first major intertribal organization. Among the group's primary concerns were protection of Indian land, mineral, and timber resources and improved economic opportunities, education, and health for Indians. During the 1950s, the organization led opposition to a congressional policy known as termination. In 1953, Congress passed a resolution that called for the government to transfer federal responsibilities for tribes to the states. It would also allow states to assert legal jurisdiction over Indian reservations without tribal consent. The NCAI effectively organized opposition to these measures. "Self-determination rather than termination" was the NCAI slogan. Earl Old Person, a Blackfoot leader, explained:

> It is important to note that in our Indian language the only translation for termination is to 'wipe out' or 'kill off' . . . how can we plan our future when the Indian Bureau threatens to wipe us out as a race?

Many Indians criticized another postwar government program—relocation—as termination in disguise. Under this policy, begun in 1948, the Bureau of Indian Affairs provided transportation, job placement, vocational training, and counseling to Indians who wanted to leave reservations. As a result of Indian protests, federal policies began to shift away from termination during the 1960s toward self-determination, the principle that Indians should exercise autonomy in matters affecting their welfare and economic well-being.

Indian Power

In 1970 American Indians were the nation's poorest minority group, worse off than any other group according to virtually every socio-economic measure. The Indian unemployment rate was ten times the national average, and 40 percent of the Native American population lived below the poverty line. In that year, Indian life expectancy was just forty-four years, a third less than that of the typical American. Deaths caused by pneumonia, hepatitis, dysentery, strep throat, diabetes, tuberculosis, alcoholism, suicide, and homicide were two to sixty times higher than among the whole United States population. Half a million Indian families lived in unsanitary, dilapidated dwellings, many in shanties, huts, or even abandoned automobiles.

Conditions on many of the nation's reservations were not unlike those found in underdeveloped areas of Africa, Asia, and Latin America. In one Apache town of 2,500 on the San Carlos reservation in Arizona, there were only twenty-five telephones and most houses had outdoor toilets and wood-burning stoves for heat. On the Navajo reservation in Arizona, which is roughly the size of West Virginia, most families lived in conditions of extreme poverty. The birth rate was two-and-a-half times the overall U.S. rate and the same as India's. The average family's purchasing power was about the same as a family in Malaysia. The typical house had two rooms; 60 percent had no electricity and 80 percent had no running water or sewers. The typical resident had just five years of schooling and fewer than one adult in six was graduated from high school.

During the 1960s, Native Americans began to revolt against such conditions. In 1961, a militant new Indian organization appeared, the National Indian Youth Council, which began to use the phrase "Red Power," and organized demonstrations, marches, and fish-ins to protest state efforts to abolish Indian fishing rights guaranteed by federal treaties. Native Americans in San Francisco in 1964 established the Indian Historical Society to present history from the Indian point of view, while the Native American Rights Fund brought legal suits against states that had taken Indian land and abolished Indian hunting, fishing, and water rights in violation of federal treaties. Many tribes took legal action to prevent strip mining or spraying of pesticides on Indian lands.

During the late 1960s and 1970s, Indian activists staged a series of dramatic demonstrations to dramatize the plight of the nation's Indians. In November 1969, two hundred Native Americans seized the abandoned federal penitentiary on Alcatraz Island in San Francisco Bay. For nineteen months, Indian activists occupied the island to draw attention to conditions on the nation's Indian reservations. Alcatraz, they said, symbolized conditions on reservations:

> It has no running water; it has inadequate sanitation facilities; there is no industry, and so unemployment is very great; there are no health care facilities; the soil is rocky and unproductive.

The activists offered to buy the island for "$24 in glass beads and red cloth"—the price that the Dutch had paid to buy Manhattan Island.

On Thanksgiving Day, 1970, the Wampanoag Indians, who had taken part in the first Thanksgiving 350 years before, held a National Day of Mourning at Plymouth, Massachusetts. A tribal representative declared:

> We forfeited our country. Our lands have fallen into the hands of the aggressor. We have allowed the white man to keep us on our knees.

Meanwhile, another group of Native Americans established a settlement at Mount Rushmore to demonstrate Indian claims to the Black Hills.

The best known of all Indian Power groups was AIM, formed in 1968 by two Chippewas, Dennis Banks and George Mitchell, to combat poverty and unemployment and protest police brutality. In the fall of 1972, AIM gained national visibility when it led urban Indians and traditionalists along the "Trail of Broken Treaties" to Washington, D.C., seized the offices of the Bureau of Indian Affairs, and occupied them for a week to dramatize Indian grievances. In the spring of 1973, two hundred Indians occupied the town of Wounded Knee, South Dakota, site of an 1890 massacre of 300 Sioux by the army cavalry, and occupied the town for seventy-one days to dramatize the injustices Indians suffered. They demanded the return of lands taken from Indians in violation of treaty agreements.

These militant protests paid off. The 1972 Indian Education Act gave Indian parents greater control over their children's schools. To address deficiencies in Indian health care, Congress passed the Indian Health Care Improvement Act in 1976, while the 1978 Indian Child Welfare Act gave tribes control over custody decisions involving Indian children. A 1978 congressional resolution on American Indian Religious Freedom directed federal agencies to respect traditional Indian religions.

During the 1970s, tribes asserted great control over their economic affairs. In 1975, twenty-five tribes with extensive oil and gas holdings formed the Council of Energy Resources Tribes to negotiate leases with energy companies.

A series of landmark Supreme Court decisions aided the cause of Indian sovereignty and tribal self-government. In a 1959 case, *Williams v. Lee*, the court upheld the authority of tribal courts to make decisions involving non-Indians. A 1968 case played a particularly important role in establishing the principle of Indian rights. In *Menominee Tribe v. United States*, the high court ruled that states could not invalidate fishing and hunting rights Indians had acquired through treaty agreements.

During the 1970s, a number of tribes initiated legal suits to recover land illegally seized by white settlers. In Maine, the Passamaquoddy and Penobscot tribes sued to recover twelve million acres, nearly two thirds of the state. In 1980, the Maine tribes agreed to drop the lawsuit in exchange for an $81.5 million settlement from the federal government. Also in 1980, the Supreme Court ordered the federal government to pay $105 million to the Sioux as payment for lands in South Dakota that the government seized illegally in 1877. Court decisions also permitted some tribal authorities to sell cigarettes, run gambling casinos, and levy taxes.

*   *   *

No longer are Indians a vanishing group of Americans. The 1990 census recorded an Indian population of over two million, five times the number recorded in 1950. About half of these people live on reservations, which cover 52.4 million acres in 27 states, while most others live in urban areas. As the Indian population has grown in size, individual Indians have claimed many accomplishments, including receipt of the Pulitzer Prize for fiction by N. Scott Momaday, a Kiowa.

Although Native Americans continue to face severe problems of employment, income, and education, they have demonstrated that they will not abandon their Indian identity and culture or be treated as dependent wards of the federal government.

PART I

FIRST CONTACTS

INTRODUCTION: Pocahontas

Hers is the one Indian name that every schoolchild knows. Today, Pocahontas is best remembered as a romantic heroine who rescued Captain John Smith, the leader of the colonists in Jamestown, Virginia, from execution by her father's people. But her brief life also illustrates the broader collision of cultures that occurred when English settlers arrived in colonial America.

She was born about 1595, the daughter of the Indian chief Powhatan, the leader of a powerful Indian confederacy. Comprised of some 30 tribes totaling about 20,000 people, the confederacy occupied much of what is now known as Virginia. She was about twelve years old when the English established their first permanent America settlement at Jamestown. During her life, she would play a pivotal role in maintaining friendly relations between the Indians and the English.

According to a story told by Captain John Smith in his book *True Relation of Virginia*, Smith was captured by local Indians while exploring the countryside. Powhatan, the Indian chief, was about to have him executed with a stone club. But Pocahontas, Smith claimed, placed her head upon his and begged her father to spare him. No one knows for sure if the story is true, because Smith did not mention the incident in the earliest edition of his book. But it appears that Pocahontas remained Smith's friend, warning him of at least one Indian plan to attack Jamestown.

When she was about fourteen, she reportedly married a chief in her tribe. Temporarily, she disappears from the colonial records only to reappear in 1613, when she is lured aboard an English ship and held captive. It is around this time that she is said to have fallen in love with her future husband.

Matoaks als Rebecka daughter to the mighty Prince
Powhatan Emperour of Attanoughkomouck als Virginia
converted and baptized in the Christian faith, and
Wife to the Wor.ll M.r Tho: Rolff.

Ætatis suæ 21. A.º 1616.

A portrait of
Pocahontas, painted in
1616, when she was 21.
(Courtesy, Smithsonian
Institution)

Her marriage in 1614 to John Rolfe, the Virginia settler who learned how to cure tobacco, helped bring peace between the the English and the Powhatan confederacy. In a letter to his patron, Rolfe addresses some of the concerns raised by his marriage, the first important English–Indian marriage in colonial American history:

> ... [I am] in no way led (so farre forth as mans weaknesse may permit) with the unbridled desire of carnall affection: but for the good of this plantation, for the honour of our countrie, for the glory of God, for my owne salvation, and for the converting to the true knowledge of God and Jesus Christ, an unbelieving creature, namely Pokahuntas. ...

This letter documents the mixture of motives that led him to marry someone (in his words) "whose education hath bin rude, her manners barbarous ... and so discrepant in all nurtriture from my selfe." After her marriage, Pocahontas converted to Christianity and adopted an English name, Rebecca.

Pocahontas's story ends tragically. In 1616 she went with her husband to London to help raise funds for the struggling colonists in Virginia. The English celebrated her as an Indian "princess," but while she was waiting to return to America, she contracted smallpox and died in 1617—one of countless Indians to die from European diseases.

Her husband's life also had an unhappy ending. After her death, he returned to Virginia, where he became a member of the Virginia council. But in 1622, he was one of several hundred colonists killed during an uprising led by Pocahontas's uncle.

An important cultural intermediary between two cultures, Pocahontas's life demonstrates the difficulty of achieving an accommodation between the Indian and English ways of life.

1.

NATIVE AMERICANS DISCOVER EUROPEANS

While most Americans are familiar with Columbus's initial impressions of the Indians, far fewer know how Indians perceived the arrival of European explorers. The following extracts offer readers a sense of the Indians' first impressions and reactions.

"They took the first ship they saw for a walking island"
William Wood (1634)

An English colonist who lived in Massachusetts Bay Colony from 1629 to 1633 describes the Indian reaction to the arrival of the first European ships.

These Indians being strangers to arts and sciences, and being unacquainted with the inventions that are common to a civilized people, are ravished with admiration at the first view of any such sight. They took the first ship they saw for a walking island, the mast to be a tree, the sail white clouds, and the discharging of ordnance for lightning and thunder, which did much trouble them, but this thunder being over and this moving-island steadied with an anchor, they manned out their canoes to go and pick strawberries there. But being saluted by the way with a broadside, they cried out, "What much hoggery, so big walk, and so big speak, and by and by kill"; which caused them to turn back, not daring to approach till they were sent for.

Source: William Wood, *New England's Prospect* (orig. 1634; Boston, 1897).

"Think . . . what must be the effect . . . of the sight of you"
A Gentleman of Elvas (1557)

A member of Hernando de Soto's expedition (perhaps Alvaro Fernandez) recorded the reaction of a Creek chief to de Soto's arrival at the village of Achese in Georgia.

Very high, powerful, and good master. The things that seldom happen bring astonishment. Think, then, what must be the effect, on me and mine, of the sight of you and your people, whom we have at no time seen, astride the fierce brutes, your horses, entering with such speed and fury into my country, that we had no tidings of your coming—things so altogether new, as to strike awe and terror into our hearts, which it was not our nature to resist, so that we should receive you with the sobriety due to so kingly and famous a lord. Trusting to your greatness and personal qualities, I hope no fault will be found in me, and that I shall rather receive favors, of which one is that with my person, my country, and my vassals, you will do as with your own things; and another, that you will tell me who you are, whence you come, whither you go, and what it is you seek, that I may the better serve you.

Source: A Relation of the Invasion and Conquest of Florida by the Spanish (London, 1686).

"They take . . . [our] hands in their own"
Joseph Nicolar (1893)

> Nicolar, a Penobscot, recorded a Penobscot oral tradition about the arrival of the first Europeans.

. . . [E]xciting news was brought from the extreme north to the effect that the white man's big canoe had come again, and had landed its people who are still remaining on the land . . . and have planted some heavy blocks of wood in the form of a cross. These people are white and the lower part of the faces of the elder ones are covered with hair, and the hair is in different colors, and the eyes are not alike, some have dark while others have light colored eyes, some have eyes the color of the blue sky. They have shown nothing only friendship, they take . . . [our] hands in their own and bow their heads down and make many signs in the direction of the stars; and their big canoe is filled with food which they eat and also give some to those that come to them and make signs of friendship.

Source: Joseph Nicolar, The Life and Traditions of the Red Man (Bangor, 1893), 128.

"The French have so little cleverness"
Chrestien Le Clercq (1676)

> A French missionary relates the response of a Micmac chief to French criticisms of his people's way of life.

. . . I am greatly astonished that the French have so little cleverness, as they seem to exhibit in the matter of which thou hast just told me on their behalf, in the effort to persuade us to convert our poles, our barks, and our wigwams into those houses of stone and of wood which are tall and lofty, according to their account, as these trees. Very well! But why now do men of five to six feet in height need houses which are sixty to eighty? . . . hast thou as much ingenuity and cleverness as the Indians, who carry their houses and their wigwams with them so they may lodge wheresoever they please, independently of any seignior whatsoever? . . . Thou sayest of us also that we are the most miserable and most unhappy of all men, living without religion, without manners, without honour, without social order, and, in a word, without any rules, like the beasts in our woods and our forests, lacking bread, wine, and a thousand other comforts which thou hast in superfluity in Europe. . . . I beg thee now to believe that, all miserable as we seem in thine eyes, we consider ourselves nevertheless much happier than thou in this, that we are very content with the little that we have; and believe also once for all, I pray, that thou deceivest thyself greatly if thou thinkest to persuade us that thy country is better than ours. For if France, as thou sayest, is a little terrestrial paradise, art thou sensible to leave it? . . . Now tell me this one thing, if thou hast any sense: Which of these two is the wisest and happiest—he who labours without ceasing and only obtains, and that with great trouble, enough to live on, or he who rests in comfort and finds all that he needs in the pleasure of hunting and fishing?

Source: Chrestien Le Clercq, *New Relation of Gaspesia, with the Customs and Religion of the Gaspesian Indians* (1691), translated and edited by William F. Ganong (Toronto, 1910), 103–6.

2.
THE DIVERSITY OF NATIVE AMERICA

THE SOUTHWEST
"Their government is one of complete freedom"
Juan de Oñate (1599)

> *In February 1598, Juan de Oñate, a Mexican mine owner, led 130 soldiers, many slaves, eight Franciscan missionaries, and 7,000 cattle north of Mexico into what is now the American Southwest. In this letter, he describes the people he encountered.*

The people are as a rule of good disposition, generally of the color of those of New Spain, and almost the same in customs, dress, grinding of meal, food, dances, songs, and in many other respects. This is not true

A mid-sixteenth century drawing of the wife of a chief of the Timucuas of Florida being carried to a ceremony. *(Courtesy, American Museum of Natural History)*

their languages, which here are numerous and different from those in Mexico. Their religion consists in worshipping of idols, of which they have many; in their temples they worship them in their own way with fire, painted reeds, feathers, and general offerings of almost everything: little animals, birds, vegetables, etc. Their government is one of complete freedom, for although they have some chieftains they obey them badly and in very few matters.

We have seen other nations, such as Querechos or Vaqueros, who live among the Cibola [Pueblo Indians] in tents of tanned hides. The Apaches, some of whom we also saw, are extremely numerous. Although I was told that they lived in rancherias, in recent days I have learned that they live in pueblos the same as the people here. . . . They are a people that has not yet publicly rendered obedience to his majesty. . . . Because of failure to exercise as much caution as was necessary, my maese de campo and twelve companions were killed at a fortress pueblo named Acoma, which must have contained three thousand Indians more or less. In punishment of their wickedness and treason to his majesty . . . and as a warning to others, I razed and burned their pueblo. . . .

Source: George P. Hammond and Agapito Rey, eds., *Don Juan de Oñate: Colonizer of New Mexico, 1595–1628* (Albuquerque: University of New Mexico, 1953), Vol. 1, 480–85.

THE PLAINS

"There was such a multitude of cows [buffalo] that they are numberless"
Pedro de Castañeda (1542)

This extract offers one of the earliest Spanish accounts of the Plains Indians.

... [I]n these plains there was such a multitude of cows that they are numberless. These cows are like those of Castile, and somewhat larger, as they have a little hump on the withers, and they are more reddish, approaching black. . . . Having proceeded many days through these plains, they came to a settlement of about 200 inhabited houses. The houses were made of the skins of cows, tanned white, like pavilions or army tents. The maintenance or sustenance of these Indians comes entirely from the cows, because they neither sow nor reap corn. With the skins they make their houses, with the skins they clothe and shoe themselves; of the skins they make rope, and also of the wool; from the sinews they make thread, with which they sew their clothes and also their houses; from the bones they make awls; the dung serves them for wood, because there is nothing else in that country; the stomachs serve them for pitchers and vessels from which they drink; they

Pueblo of Taos in New Mexico. *(Courtesy, Smithsonian Institution)*

live on the flesh. . . . These people have dogs like those in this country, except that they are somewhat larger, and they load these dogs like beasts of burden, and make saddles for them like our pack saddles; and they fasten them with their leather thongs, and these make their backs sore on the withers like pack animals. When they go hunting, they load these with their necessities, and when they move—for these Indians are not settled in one place, since they travel wherever the cows move, to support themselves—these dogs carry their houses and they have the sticks of their houses dragging along tied on to the pack-saddles besides the load which they carry on top, and the load may be, according to the dog, from thirty-five to fifty pounds.

Source: George P. Hammond and Agapito Rey, *Narratives of the Coronado Expedition, 1540–42* (Albuquerque: University of New Mexico, 1940), 208–9.

THE MIDDLE COLONIES
"In liberality they excel"
William Penn (1683)

> *Pennsylvania's founder offers a vivid description of the indigenous people of that area.*

The natives I shall consider in their persons, language, manners, religion and government. . . . For their persons, they are generally tall, straight, well-built, and of singular proportion; they tread strong and clever, and mostly walk with a lofty chin. . . . They grease themselves with bear's fat clarified, and, using no defense against sun or weather, their skins must needs be swarthy. . . .

Their language is lofty, yet narrow, but like the Hebrew; in signification full, like short-hand in writing; one word serveth in the place of three, and the rest are supplied by the understanding of the hearer. . . .

Of their customs and manners there is much to be said; I will begin with children. So soon as they are born, they wash them in water, and while very young and in cold weather to choose they plunge them in the rivers to harden and embolden them. Having wrapped them in a clout [cloth], they lay them on a straight, thin board, a little more than the length and breadth of the child, and swaddle it fast upon the board to make it straight. . . . The children will go [walk] very young, at nine months commonly; they wear only a small clout round their waist till they are big; if boys, they go fishing till ripe for the woods, which is about fifteen; then they hunt, and, after having given some proofs of their manhood by a good return of skins, they may marry. . . . The girls stay with their mothers and help to hoe the ground,

William Penn's treaty with the Delawares in 1682. *(Courtesy, Pennsylvania Academy of Fine Arts)*

plant corn, and carry burdens. . . . The age they marry at, if women, is about thirteen and fourteen; if men, seventeen and eighteen. . . .

Their houses are mats or barks of trees set on poles in the fashion of an English barn. . . .

Their diet is maize or Indian corn, divers ways prepared; sometimes roasted in the ashes, sometimes beaten and boiled with water, which they call "homine". . . .

But in liberality they excel; nothing is too good for their friends. Give them a fine gun, coat, or other thing, it may pass twenty hands before it sticks. . . . Wealth circulateth like the blood, all parts partake. . . .

If they die, they bury them with their apparel, be they man or woman, and the nearest of kin fling in something precious with them as a token of their love: their mourning is blacking of their faces, which they continue for a year. . . .

Their worship consists of two parts, sacrifice and cantico: their sacrifice is their first fruits; the first and fattest buck they kill goeth to the fire where he is all burnt. . . . The other part is their cantico, performed by round dances, sometimes words, sometimes songs, then shouts. . . . In the fall, when the corn cometh in, they begin to feast one another. . . .

Their government is by kings, which they call "Sachema" and those by succession, but always of the mother's side. . . .

Every king hath his council, and that consists of all the old and wise men of his nation, which perhaps is two hundred people. Nothing of moment is undertaken, be it war, peace, selling of land, or traffic, without advising with them, and which is more, with the young men too. . . .

The justice they have is pecuniary. In case of any wrong or evil fact, be it murder itself, they atone by feasts and presents of wampum, which is proportioned to the quality of the offence or person injured, or of the sex they are of: for in case they kill a woman they pay double. . . .

Source: William Penn, *A Letter from William Penn* (London, 1683).

THE NORTHEAST

"Amongst the Huron nations, the women name the counsellors"
Pierre de Charlevoix (1761)

> *Europeans expressed utter astonishment at women's important economic and political role within many Indian societies. A Jesuit priest describes life among Iroquoian-speaking Hurons whom he encountered.*

It must be agreed Madam, that the nearer we view our Indians, the more good qualities we discover in them: most of the principles which serve to regulate their conduct, the general maxims by which they govern themselves, and the essential part of their character, discover nothing of the barbarian. . . .

In the northern parts, and wherever the Algonquin tongue prevails, the dignity of chief is elective; and the whole ceremony of election and installation consists in some feasts, accompanied with dances and songs: the chief elect likewise never fails to make the panegyrick of his predecessor, and to invoke his genius. Amongst the Hurons, where this dignity is hereditary, the succession is continued through the women, so that at the death of a chief, it is not his own, but his sister's son who succeeds him; or, in default of which, his nearest relation in the female line. When the whole branch happens to be extinct, the noblest matron of the tribe or in the nation chuses the person she approves of most, and declares him chief. . . . These chiefs generally have no great marks of outward respect paid them, and if they are never disobeyed, it is because they know how to set bounds to their authority. It is true that they request or propose, rather than command; and never exceed the boundaries of that small share of authority with which they are vested. . . .

Nay more, each family has a right to chuse a counsellor of its own, and an assistant to the chief, who is to watch for their interest; and without whose consent the chief can undertake nothing.... Amongst the Huron nations, the women name the counsellors, and often chuse persons of their own sex....

The women have the chief authority amongst all the nations of the Huron language.... But if this be their lawful constitution, their practice is seldom agreeable to it. In fact, the men never tell the women anything they would have to be kept secret; and rarely any affair of consequence is communicated to them, though all is done in their name, and the chiefs are no more than their lieutenants....

Source: Pierre de Charlevoix, *Journal of a Voyage to North America* (London, 1761).

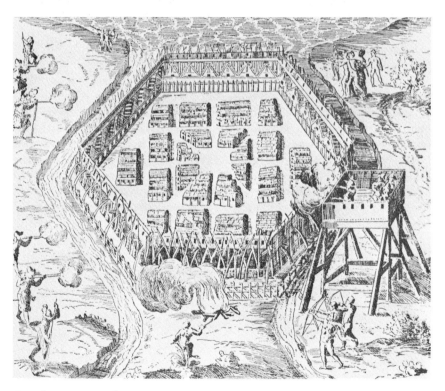

French troops attack an Onondaga village in 1615. *(Courtesy, Smithsonian Institution)*

3.

INDIGENOUS CUSTOMS

Childbirth and Infancy

"They depart . . . to a secluded place"
Adriaen Van der Donck (1655)

> *The legal officer of a Dutch estate in New Netherlands describes child-birth in that area.*

. . . [W]hen the time of their delivery is near . . . they depart alone to a secluded place near a brook, or stream of water, where they can be protected from the winds, and prepare a shelter for themselves with mats and covering, where, provided with provisions necessary for them, they await their delivery without the company or aid of any person. After their children are born, and if they are males, although the weather be ever so cold and freezing, they immerse them some time in the water, which, they say, makes them strong brave men and hardy hunters. After the immersion they wrap their children in warm clothing. . . .

The native Indian women of every grade always nurse their own children, nor do we know of any who have trusted that parental duty to others. . . . [W]hen they suckle or are pregnant, they in those cases practice the strictest abstinence, because, as they say, it is beneficial to their offspring, and to nursing children. In the meantime, their women are not precise or offended, if their husbands have foreign associations, but they observe the former custom so religiously, that they hold it to be disgraceful for a woman to recede from it before her child is weaned, which they usually do when their children are a year old, and those who wean their children before that period are despised. During a certain season, their women seclude themselves, and do not appear abroad or permit themselves to be seen of men.

Source: Adriaen Van der Donck, *Description of the New Netherlands* (1655), trans. by Jeremiah Johnson, *Collections of the New-York Historical Society*, 2nd series, Vol. 1 (1841).

"From their infant state they endeavor to promote an independent spirit"
John Long (1791)

> *A resident of North Carolina describes childrearing customs among the indigenous people of that area.*

A mother suckles her child till it attains the age of four or five years, and sometimes till it is six or seven. From their infant state they endeavor to promote an independent spirit. They are never known either to beat or scold them, lest the martial disposition which is to adorn their future life and character should be weakened; on all occasions they avoid everything compulsive, that the freedom with which they wish them to think and act may not be controlled. If they die, they lament their death with unfeigned tears, and even for months after their decease will weep at the graves of their departed children.

Source: John Long, *Voyages and Travels of an Indian Interpreter and Trader* (London, 1791).

"It is the duty of Waiyautitsa's mother-in-law, the child's paternal grandmother, to look after mother and child during the confinement"
Waiyautitsa (1922)

> *In 1922, Elsie Clews Parsons, one of the nation's leading anthropologists and sociologists, published a biography of a Zuni woman, which presents a vivid picture of the persistence of Zuni lifeways into the twentieth century.*

Waiyautitsa is now . . . an expectant mother. . . . On her husband fall a number of . . . pregnancy tabus. . . . If he hunts and maims an animal, the child will be similarly maimed—deformed or perhaps blind. If he joins in a masked dance, the child may have some mask-suggested misshape or some eruption like the paint on the mask. If he sings a great deal, the child will be a cry-baby. . . .

Perhaps Waiyautitsa has wished to determine the sex of the child. In that case she may have made a pilgrimage with a rain priest to Corn Mesa to plant a prayer stick which has to be cut and painted in one way for a boy, in another way for a girl. . . . Wanting a girl—and girls are wanted in Zuni quite as much as boys, if not more—Waiyautitsa need not make the trip to the mesa; instead her husband may bring her to wear in her belt scrapings from a stone in a phallic shrine near the mesa. When labor sets in and the pains are slight, indicating, women think, a girl, Waiyautitsa may be told by her mother, "Don't sleep, or you will have a boy." A nap during labor effects a change of sex. . . .

An 1808 drawing of a
Seneca woman and child
by the Baroness Hyde de
Neuville of France.

After the birth, Waiyautitsa will lie in for several days, four, eight, ten or twelve, according to the custom of her family. Whatever the custom, if she does not observe it, she runs the risk of "drying up" and dying. . . .

It is the duty of Waiyautitsa's mother-in-law, the child's paternal grandmother, to look after mother and child during the confinement, and at its close to carry the child outdoors at dawn and present him or her to the Sun. Had Waiyautitsa lost children, she might have invited a propitious friend, some woman who had had many children and lost none, to attend the birth and be the first to pick up the child and blow into his mouth. . . .

Left alone, a baby runs great risk—some family ghost may come and hold him, causing him to die within four days. And so a quasi-fetichistic ear of corn, a double ear thought of as mother and child, is left alongside the baby as a protector. That the baby may teethe promptly, his gums may be rubbed by one who has been bitten by a snake—"snakes want to bite." To make the child's hair grow long and thick, his grandfather or uncle may puff the smoke of native tobacco on his head. That the child may not be afraid in the dark, water-soaked embers are rubbed over his heart the first time he is taken out at night. . . .

Source: Elsie Clews Parsons, ed., *American Indian Life* (New York: B. W. Huebsch, 1922), 167–69.

Boyhood and Girlhood

"He will reply to her that this is a girl's work and will do none of it"
Gabriel Sagard (1632)

> *A French missionary describes boyhood and girlhood among the Huron.*

The usual and daily practice of the young boys is none other than drawing the bow and shooting the arrow, making it rise and glide in a straight line a little higher than the ground. They play a game with curved sticks, making them slide over the snow and hit a ball of light wood, just as is done in our parts; they learn to throw the prong with which they spear fish, and practice other little sports and exercises, and then they put in an appearance at the lodge at meal-times, or else when they feel hungry. But if a mother asks her son to go for water or wood or do some similar household service, he will reply to her that this is a girl's work and will do none of it. . . .

Just as the little boys have their special training and teach one another to shoot with the bow as soon as they begin to walk, so also the little girls, whenever they begin to put one foot in front of the other, have a little stick put into their hands to train them and teach them early to pound corn, and when they are grown somewhat they also play various little games with their companions, and in the course of these small frolics they are trained quietly to perform trifling and petty household duties, sometimes also to do the evil that they see going on before their eyes. . . . They vie with one another as to which shall have the most lovers. . . .

Source: Gabriel Sagard, *The Long Journey to the Country of the Hurons* (1632), ed. by George M. Wrong, trans. by H. H. Langston (Toronto: Champlain Society, 1939).

"A strong sentiment of respect for their elders"
John Heckewelder (1819)

A Moravian minister describes childrearing practices among the Indians of Pennsylvania.

The first step that parents take towards the education of their children, is to prepare them for future happiness, by impressing upon their tender minds, that they are indebted for their existence to a great, good and benevolent Spirit, who not only has given them life, but has ordained them for certain great purposes. That he has given them a fertile extensive country well stocked with game of every kind for their subsistence, and that by one of his inferior spirits he has also sent down to them from above corn, pumpkins, squashes, beans and other vegetables for their nourishment; all which blessings their ancestors have enjoyed for a great number of ages. That this great Spirit looks down upon the Indians, to see whether they are grateful to him and make him a due return for the many benefits he has bestowed, and therefore that it is their duty to show their thankfulness by worshipping him, and doing that which is pleasing to his sight. . . .

They are then told that their ancestors, who received all this from the hands of the great Spirit . . . must have been informed of what would be most pleasing to this good being . . . and they are directed to look up for instruction to those who know all this, to learn from them, and revere them for their wisdom and the knowledge which they possess; this creates in the children a strong sentiment of respect for their elders, and a desire to follow their advice and example. Their young ambition is then excited by telling them that they were made the superiors of all other creatures, and are to have power over them; great pains are taken to make this feeling take early root, and it becomes in fact their ruling passion through life; for no pains are spared to instil into them that by following the advice of the most admired and extolled hunter, trapper or warrior, they will at a future day acquire a degree of fame and reputation, equal to that which he possesses; that by submitting to the counsels of the aged, the chiefs, the men superior in wisdom, they may also rise to glory, and be called *Wisemen*, an honourable title, to which no Indian is indifferent. They are finally told that if they respect the aged and infirm, and are kind and obliging to them, they will be treated in the same manner when their turn comes to feel the infirmities of old age. . . .

When . . . instruction is given in the form of precepts, it must not be supposed that it is done in an authoritative or forbidding tone, but, on the contrary, in the gentlest and most persuasive manner: nor is the parent's

authority ever supported by harsh or compulsive means; no whips, no pun-
ishments, no threats are even used to enforce commands or compel obedience. The child's *pride* is the feeling to which an appeal is made, which
proves successful in almost every instance. A father needs only to say in
the presence of his children: "I want such a thing done; I want one of my
children to go upon such an errand; let me see who is the *good* child that
will do it!" The word *good* operates, as it were, by magic, and the children immediately vie with each other to comply with the wishes of their
parent. . . .

In this manner of bringing up children, the parents, as I have already
said, are seconded by the whole community. . . . The whole of the Indian
plan of education tends to elevate rather than depress the mind, and by that
means to make determined hunters and fearless warriors. . . .

They are to learn the arts of hunting, trapping, and making war, by lis-
tening to the aged when conversing together on those subjects, each, in his
turn, relating how he acted, and opportunities are afforded to them for that
purpose. By this mode of instructing youth, their respect for the aged is kept
alive. . . .

[Initiation ceremonies]

By certain methods which I shall presently describe, they put the mind
of a boy in a state of perturbation, so as to excite dreams and visions; by
means of which they pretend that the boy receives instructions from certain
spirits or unknown agents as to his conduct in life, and he is informed of his
future destination and of the wonders he is to perform in his future career
through the world.

When a boy is to be thus *initiated*, he is put under an alternate course of
physic and fasting, either taking no food whatever, or swallowing the most
powerful and nauseous medicines, and occasionally he is made to drink
decoctions of an intoxicating nature, until his mind becomes sufficiently
bewildered, so that he sees or fancies that he sees visions, and has extraordinary dreams, for which, of course, he has been prepared before hand. He
will fancy himself flying through the air, walking under ground, stepping
from one ridge or hill to the other across the valley beneath, fighting and
conquering giants and monsters, and defeating whole hosts by a single arm.
Then he has interviews with the Mannitto [Manitou] or with spirits, who
inform him of what he was before he was born and what he will be after his
death. His fate in this life is laid entirely open before him, the spirit tells him
what is to be his future employment, whether he will be a valiant warrior, a
mighty hunter, a doctor, a conjurer, or a prophet. There are even those who
learn or pretend to learn in this way the time and manner of their death.

When a boy has been thus initiated, a name is given to him analogous
to the visions that he has seen, and to the destiny that is supposed to be prepared for him. The boy, imagining all that happened to him while under

perturbation, to have been real, sets out in the world with lofty notions of himself, and animated with courage for the most desperate undertakings.

Source: John Heckewelder, *Account of the History, Manners, and Customs, of the Indian Natives who once Inhabited Pennsylvania and the Neighbouring States* in *Transactions of the American Philosophical Society* (1819), 98–103, 238–41.

"He is called the future defender of his people . . . She is . . . addressed as the future mother of a noble race"
Charles Eastman (1902)

> *Dr. Charles Eastman, a member of the Santee Sioux, was around forty years old when he wrote a book describing his boyhood in the Dakota Territory and Minnesota.*

It is commonly supposed that there is no systematic education of their children among the aborigines of this country. Nothing could be farther from the truth. All the customs of this primitive people were held to be divinely instituted, and those in connection with the training of children were scrupulously adhered to and transmitted from one generation to another.

The expectant parents conjointly bent all their efforts to the task of giving the new-comer the best they could gather from a long line of ancestors. A pregnant Indian woman would often choose one of the greatest characters of her family and tribe as a model for her child. This hero was daily called to mind. She would gather from tradition all of his noted deeds and daring exploits, rehearsing them to herself when alone. In order that the impression might be more distinct, she avoided company. . . .

The Indians believed, also, that certain kinds of animals would confer peculiar gifts upon the unborn, while others would leave so strong an adverse impression that the child might become a monstrosity. A case of hare-lip was commonly attributed to the rabbit. . . . Even the meat of certain animals was denied the pregnant woman, because it was supposed to influence the disposition or features of the child.

Scarcely was the embryo warrior ushered into the world, when he was met by lullabies that speak of wonderful exploits in hunting and war. . . . He is called the future defender of his people, whose lives may depend upon his courage and skill. If the child is a girl, she is at once addressed as the future mother of a noble race. . . .

Very early, the Indian boy assumed the task of preserving and transmitting the legends of his ancestors and his race. Almost every evening a myth, or a true story of some deed done in the past, was narrated by one of the parents or grandparents.... On the following evening, he was usually required to repeat it....

All the stoicism and patience of the Indian are acquired traits, and continual practise alone makes him master of the art of wood-craft. Physical training and dieting were not neglected. I remember that I was not allowed to have beef soup or any warm drink. The soup was for the old men. General rules for the young were never to take their food very hot, nor to drink much water.

Source: C. A. Eastman, *Indian Boyhood* (New York: McClure, Phillips, 1902), 49–60.

"A girl is rated by her ability in handicrafts and in providing food"
Cries-for-salmon (1922)

> *An Alaskan informant describes childbirth, childrearing, and girlhood in that culture area.*

When Cries-for-salmon was to be born, they called in ... Their-little-grandmother, an old woman of experience, to help. For three days after the birth Their-little-grandmother stayed by the side of the bed of skins, nor might the mother leave her bed without the permission of Their-little-grandmother.... [T]he boys and men do not stay in the house at this time; they go to the kadjim (the men's house). All I know is that the after-birth is wrapped in a cloth, and placed in the fork of a tree....

The baby's cord is tied around the wrist or the neck of the baby with sinew, and left on for two or three years. An ax head is placed on the body of a boy baby for a certain number of days....

For twenty days after Cries-for-salmon was born, her father had to stay at home, indoors, "under his smoke hole," as people used to say when they lived in igloos or underground houses.... During these twenty days a man is not to touch any object made by white people, more particularly things of steel or iron, knife or ax or ice pick. Copper, got in trade from the coast, which has been melted down and hand beaten, a man may use; and he would eat out of dishes of wood or bone. Work tools of any kind he would not handle....

As with work after a birth in his family, so with amusements—a man should not take part. He should sit quiet, with his head down, for at this time he is supposed to be in connection with his spirits....

A young man is rated by his ability in making snowshoes and in running down game, fox, deer and, before the portaging of the whites drove them out, caribou. A girl is rated by her ability in handicrafts and in providing food, but she is also esteemed for her household behavior. . . .

Cries-for-salmon was taught, like other little girls and boys, never to sing or whistle when eating, and never to imitate at any time in the winter the birds of summer—that would prolong the winter. . . .

Little girls and boys together play at fishing and housekeeping. The boys will gather willows and make them into a great bundle, a foot and a half thick and fifteen feet long. They choose a shallow place in the river where there are little fish, and they lay the willow trap in an oval. After the catch the girls take the fish to cook, and boys and girls pair off together to make fish camps like their elders. . . .

We go on now to when Cries-for-salmon is a big girl. When she first menstruated, she was placed in the corner of her father's house to be out of sight of young men, and to stay so for a year, as we count by moons. The space assigned to Cries-for-salmon was just long enough to lie down in. In this corner Cries-for-salmon had to keep all the things she used, more particularly her own cup and bucket of water. When no one was about, she went to fill the bucket, but, as with her other things, she had to be scrupulous about not leaving the bucket where young men could by any chance come in contact with it. Girls are supposed not to go outdoors at all; but if a girl has to go, she must walk with head bent so that if she passed by a young man her eyes would not get a direct line on his eyes, or his eyes on hers. . . .

In the corner, a girl wears continually a beaded forehead band to which bear claws are attached. Her behavior during this time determines whether or not she is to be a worthy woman for life, and how skilled she will be in the domestic arts. For at this time she makes everything she is going to use after she marries. . . . She learns to sew, to make beadwork and porcupine-quill work, to make baskets, and fish nets. The first few months she is not allowed to cook, but towards the close of the period the cooking, the bulk of the housework, indeed, is put upon her. And it is then that suitors take notice of her work and accomplishments. They notice whether the seams of the boots and mittens she has made look strong and durable; whether her bead embroidery is fine, whether she is industrious and competent, how she carries herself. A man knows how important to his welfare the character of his wife is. A man has to run his chase, but, after he marries, that is all; his wife does all the hard work. She gets wood and water, she snares grouse and rabbits, she sets fish traps, and she prepares all the clothing and all the food, not only for the family but for the ceremonies at which the man is called upon to contribute.

Source: T. B. Reed and Elsie Clews Parsons, "Cries-for-salmon, a Ten'a Woman" in E. C. Parsons, ed., *American Indian Life* (New York: B.W. Huebsch, 1922), 337–45.

Courtship and Marriage

"The girl will never approve the suit, unless it be agreeable to her father"

Chrestien Le Clercq (1676)

A French missionary describes courtship and marriage customs among the Micmac.

A boy has no sooner formed the design to espouse a girl than he makes for himself a proposal about it to her father, because he well knows that the girl will never approve the suit, unless it be agreeable to her father. The boy asks the father if he thinks it suitable for him to enter into his wigwam, that is to say, into relationship with him through marrying his daughter. . . . If the father does not like the suit of the young Indian, he tells him so without other ceremony than saying it cannot be; and this lover, however enamoured he may be, receives this reply with equanimity as the decisive decree of his fate and of his courtship, and seeks elsewhere some other sweetheart. . . . If the father finds that the suitor who presents himself is acceptable . . . he tells him to speak to his sweetheart. . . . For they do not wish . . . to force the inclinations of their children in the matter of marriage, or to induce them, whether by use of force, obedience, or affection, to marry men whom they cannot bring themselves to like. . . .

The boy, then, after obtaining the consent of the father, addresses himself to the girl, in order to ascertain her sentiments. He makes her a present from whatever important things he possesses; and the custom is such that if she is agreeable to his suit, she receives and accepts it with pleasure, and offers him in return some of her most beautiful workmanship. . . .

The presents having been received and accepted by both parties, the Indian returns to his home, takes leave of his parents, and comes to live for an entire year in the wigwam of his sweetheart's father, whom, according to the laws of the country, he is to serve, and to whom he is to give all the furs which he secures in hunting. . . . The girl, for her part, also does her best with that which concerns the housekeeping, and devotes herself wholly, during this year . . . to making snowshoes, sewing canoes, preparing barks, dressing skins of moose or of beaver, drawing the sled—in a word, to doing everything which can give her the reputation of being a good housewife. . . .

When, then, the two parties concur in disposition and tastes, at the end of the year the oldest men of the nation, and the parents and friends of the future married couple, are brought together to the feast which is to be made for the public celebration of their marriage. . . . If it turns out that the disposition of one is incompatible with the nature of the other, the boy or the girl retires without fuss, and everybody is as content and satisfied as if the marriage had been accomplished, because, say they, one ought not to marry only to be unhappy the remainder of one's days.

There is nevertheless much instability in these sorts of alliances, and the young married folks change their inclinations very easily when several years go by without their having children. . . . [I]t can be said with truth that the children are then the indissoluble bonds, and the confirmation, of the marriage of their father and mother, who keep faithful company without ever separating, and who live in so great a union with one another, that they seem not to have more than a single heart and a single will. . . .

One cannot express the grief of a Gaspesian when he loses his wife. It is true that outwardly he dissimulates as much as he can the bitterness which he has in his heart, because these people consider it a mark of weakness unworthy of a man, be he ever so little brave and noble, to lament in public.

Source: Chrestien Le Clercq, *New Relation of Gaspesia, with the Customs and Religion of the Gaspesian Indians* (1691), translated and edited by William F. Ganong (Toronto, 1910).

Marital Relations and Gender Roles

"The parties are not to live together any longer than they shall be pleased with each other"
John Heckewelder (1819)

A Moravian missionary discusses the division of labor within Indian families in colonial Pennsylvania.

There are many persons who believe, from the labour that they see the Indian women perform, that they are in a manner treated as slaves. These labours, indeed, are hard, compared with the tasks that are imposed upon females in civilised society; but they are no more than their fair share . . . of the hardships attendant on savage life. Therefore they are not only voluntarily, but cheerfully submitted to; and as women are not obliged to live with their husbands any longer than suits their pleasure or convenience, it cannot be supposed that they would submit to be loaded with unjust or unequal burdens.

Marriages among the Indians are not, as with us, contracted for life; it is understood on both sides that the parties are not to live together any longer than they shall be pleased with each other. The husband may put away his wife whenever he pleases, and the woman may in like manner abandon her husband. . . .

When a marriage takes place, the duties and labours incumbent on each party are well known to both. It is understood that the husband is to build a house for them to dwell in, to find the necessary implements of husbandry, as axes, hoes, &c. to provide a canoe, and also dishes, bowls, and other necessary vessels for house-keeping. The woman generally has a kettle or two, and some other articles of kitchen furniture, which she brings with her. . . .

When a couple is newly married, the husband . . . takes considerable pains to please his wife, and by repeated proofs of his skill and abilities in the art of hunting, to make her sensible that she can be happy with him, and that she will never want while they live together. . . .

[The wife's] principal occupations are to cut and fetch the fire wood, till the ground, sow and reap the grain, and pound the corn in mortars for their pottage, and to make bread which they bake in the ashes. . . .

The tilling of the ground at home, getting of the fire wood, and pounding of corn in mortars, is frequently done by female parties, much in the manner of those husking, quilting and other *frolics* (as they are called,) which are so common in some parts of the United States. . . .

When the harvest is in, which generally happens by the end of September, the women have little else to do than to prepare the daily victuals, and

A 1591 engraving shows men breaking up ground while women plant seeds in Florida. (*Courtesy, Library of Congress*)

get fire wood, until the latter end of February or beginning of March ...
when they go to their sugar camps, where they extract sugar from the maple
tree. The men having built or repaired their temporary cabin, and made all
the troughs of various sizes, the women commence making sugar, while the
men are looking out for meat, at this time generally fat bears, which are still
in their winter quarters. When at home, they will occasionally assist their
wives in gathering the sap, and watch the kettles in their absence, that the
syrup may not boil over. ...

The husband generally leaves the skins and peltry which he has procured by hunting to the care of his wife, who sells or barters them away to
the best advantage for such necessities as are wanted in the family; not for-
getting to supply her husband with what he stands in need of. ...

Source: John Heckewelder, *Account of the History, Manners, and Customs, of the
Indian Natives who once Inhabited Pennsylvania and the Neighbouring States* in
Transactions of the American Philosophical Society (1819), 142–52.

"Just as the men have their special occupation ... so also the women and girls keep their place"
Gabriel Sagard (1632)

*A French missionary describes the economic activities of Huron men
and women.*

The occupations of the savages are fishing, hunting, and war; going off
to trade, making lodges and canoes, or contriving the proper tools for doing
so. The rest of the time they pass in idleness, gambling, sleeping, singing,
dancing, smoking, or going to feasts, and they are reluctant to undertake
any other work that forms part of the women's duty except under strong
necessity. ...

During winter with the twine twisted by the women and girls they make
nets and snares for fishing and catching fish in summer, and even in winter
under the ice by means of lines or the seine-net, through holes cut in several
places. They make also arrows with the knife, very straight and long, and
when they have no knives they use sharp-edged stones; they fledge them
with feathers from the tails and wings of eagles, because these are strong
and carry well in the air, and at the point with strong fish-glue they attach
sharp-pointed stones or bones, or iron heads obtained in trade with the
French. They also make wooden clubs for warfare, and shields which cover
the whole body, and with animals' guts they make bow-strings and rackets
for walking on the snow when they go for wood and to hunt. ...

A 1585 painting by John White shows Indians fishing with traps, spears, and nets. (*Courtesy, British Museum*)

Just as the men have their special occupation and understand wherein a man's duty consists, so also the women and girls keep their place and perform quietly their little tasks and functions of service. They usually do more work than the men, although they are not forced or compelled to do so. They have the care of the cooking and the household, of sowing and gathering corn, grinding flour, preparing hemp and tree-bark, and providing the necessary wood. And because there still remains plenty of time to waste, they employ it in gaming, going to dances and feasts, chatting and killing time, and doing just what they like with their leisure. . . .

They make pottery, especially round pots without handles or feet, in which they cook their food, meat or fish. When winter comes they make mats of reeds, which they hang in the doors of their lodges, and they make others to sit upon, all very neatly. . . . They dress and soften the skins of beaver and moose and others, as well as we could do it here, and of these they make their cloaks and coverings. . . . Likewise they make reed baskets, and others out of birchbark, to hold beans, corn, and peas . . . meat, fish, and other small provender. . . . They employ themselves also in making bowls of bark for drinking and eating out of, and for holding their meats and soups. Moreover, the sashes, collars, and bracelets that they and the men wear are of their workmanship; and in spite of the fact that they are more occupied than the men, who play the noblemen among them and think only of hunting, fishing, or fighting, still they usually love their husbands better than the women here. . . .

Clearing [land] is very troublesome for them, since they have no proper tools. They cut down the trees at the height of two or three feet from the ground, then they strip off all the branches, which they burn at the stump of the same trees in order to kill them, and in course of time they remove the roots. Then the women clean up the ground between the trees thoroughly, and at distances a pace apart dig round holes or pits. In each of these they sow nine or ten grains of maize, which they have first picked out, sorted, and soaked in water for a few days, and so they keep on until they have sown enough to provide food for two or three years, either for fear that some bad season may visit them or else in order to trade it to other nations for furs and other things they need. . . .

The grain ripens in four months, or in three in some places. After that they gather it, and turning the leaves up and tying them round the ears arrange it in bundles hung in rows, the whole length of the lodge from top to bottom, on poles which they put up as a sort of rack. . . . When the grain is quite dry and fit for storing the women and girls shell it, clean it, and put it into their great vats or casks made for the purpose and placed in the porch or some corner of the lodge.

Source: Gabriel Sagard, *The Long Journey to the Country of the Hurons* (1632) ed. by George M. Wrong, trans. by H. H. Langton (Toronto: Champlain Society, 1939).

PART II

CULTURES IN CONFLICT

INTRODUCTION: Tecumseh and the Shawnee Prophet

During the last years of the eighteenth century, defeat, disease, and death were the lot of Indians living in the Old Northwest. In 1794, an American force crushed an opposing Indian army at the Battle of Fallen Timbers near present-day Toledo, Ohio. This victory forced Native Americans to give up 25,000 square miles of land north of the Ohio River.

Some 45,000 land-hungry white settlers poured into the Ohio country during the next six years. They spread a variety of killer diseases, including smallpox, influenza, and measles. Aggressive frontier settlers infringed on Indian hunting grounds, and rapidly killed off the game that provided Indians with subsistence. Deprived of their homelands, faced with severe food shortages and a drastic loss of population, Native Americans in the Old Northwest saw the fabric of their society torn apart.

One of the Native Americans who suffered from the breakdown of Indian society was a Shawnee youth named Laulewasika. A few months before he was born, white frontiersmen, who crossed into Indian territory in violation of a recent treaty, killed his father. Shortly thereafter, his despondent mother, a Creek, fled westward, leaving behind her children to be raised by relatives.

As a young man Laulewasika lacked direction. Then in 1805 he underwent a powerful transformation. Overcome by images of his own wickedness, he fell into a deep trance during which he met the Indian Master of Life. On the basis of this mystical experience, he embarked on a crusade "to reclaim the Indians from bad habits." Adopting a new name, Tenskwatawa ("the open door"), he called on Indians to stop drinking alcohol. Then, like other Indian prophets before and after, he demanded an end to intertribal fighting and a return to ancestral ways. His central message was Indian unity as the key to blocking white encroachment on tribal lands.

His older brother, the famed Shawnee war chief Tecumseh (1768–1813), also advocated a broad-based Indian alliance. In 1808, he and his brother relocated their tribal village in northwestern Indiana along the shoreline of the Tippecanoe River. William Henry Harrison, the territorial governor, challenged the growing influence of the Shawnee brothers. He conducted negotiations with local chiefs, and forced them to turn over title to three million acres in Indiana for $7000 and an annuity of $1750.

Tecumseh needed time to build his alliance. Before he set off on a journey to the South to rally support, he warned Tenskwatawa to avoid any conflict with Harrison. Tenskwatawa did not listen. Harrison approached the Indian village with a 1,000 man army. Tenskwatawa authorized 450 warriors to attack the Americans. What followed was a rout. Harrison's troops drove off the Indians and burned their village, destroying Tenskwatawa's power and prestige.

When Tecumseh returned home from his trip, he was shocked and enraged, and "swore . . . eternal hatred" against white settlers. When the War of 1812 broke out, he allied himself to the British. In October 1813, after U.S. troops forced the British to retreat from Detroit, the Shawnee warrior tried to halt an American advance along the Thames River in eastern Ontario in Canada. The day before the climactic encounter, Tecumseh told his followers: "Brother warriors, we are about to enter an engagement from which I will not return." His premonition was correct. He died the next afternoon from multiple wounds. His vision of pan-Indian resistance to white encroachment into the Old Northwest likewise perished.

4.

COEXISTENCE AND CONFLICT IN
THE SPANISH SOUTHWEST

The Pueblo Revolt of 1680

"Why they burned the images, temples, crosses, rosaries, and things of divine worship"

Pedro Naranjo (1680)

> *In 1680, the Pueblo Indians of New Mexico rose up against the Spanish missionaries and soldiers, destroying every Catholic church in the region. Pedro Naranjo, an Indian prisoner, explains the reasons behind the revolt.*

Asked whether he knows the reason or motives which the Indians of this kingdom had for rebelling . . . and why they burned the images, temples, crosses, rosaries, and things of divine worship, committing such atrocities as killing priests, Spaniards, women, and children . . . he said . . . they have planned to rebel on various occasions through conspiracies of the Indian sorcerers. . . . Finally, in the past years, at the summons of an Indian named Popé who is said to have communication with the devil, it happened that in an estufa [Indian temple] of the pueblo of Los Taos there appeared to the said Popé three figures of Indians who never came out of the estufa. They gave the said Popé to understand that they were going underground to the lake of Copala. He saw these figures emit fire from all the extremities of their bodies. . . . They told him to make a cord of maguey fiber and tie some knots in it which would signify the number of days that they must wait before the rebellion. He said that the cord was passed through all the pueblos of the kingdom so that the ones which agreed to it [the rebellion] might untie one knot in sign of obedience, and by the other knots they would know the days which were lacking. . . . The said cord was taken from pueblo to pueblo by the swiftest youths under the penalty of death if they revealed the secret. Everything being thus arranged, two days before the time set for its execution, because his lordship had learned of it and had imprisoned two Indian accomplices . . . it was carried out prematurely that night, because it seemed to them that they were now discovered; and they killed religious, Spaniards, women, and children. This being done, it was proclaimed in all the pueblos that everyone in common should obey the commands of their father whom they did not know, which would be given through . . . Popé. . . . [A]s soon as the Spaniards had left the kingdom an order came from the said Indian, Popé, in which he commanded all the Indians to break

A 1545 painting of a Spanish attack on a Southwestern pueblo. *(Courtesy, Frans Halsmuseum, Haarlem)*

the lands and enlarge their cultivated fields, saying that now they were as they had been in ancient times, free from the labor they had performed for the religious and the Spaniards, who could not now be alive. He said that this is the legitimate cause and the reason they had for rebelling. . . .

Asked for what reason they so blindly burned the images, temples, crosses, and other things of divine worship, he stated that the said Indian, Popé . . . ordered in all the pueblos through which he passed that they instantly break up and burn the images of the holy Christ, the Virgin Mary and the other saints, the crosses, and everything pertaining to Christianity, and that they burn the temples, break up the bells, and separate from the wives whom God had given them in marriage and take those whom they desired. In order to take away their baptismal names, the water, and the holy oils, they were to plunge into the rivers and wash themselves with amole, which is a root native to the country, washing even their clothing, with the understanding that there would thus be taken from them the character of the holy sacraments. . . . [T]hey thereby returned to the state of their antiquity . . . that this was the better life and the one they desired, because the God of the Spaniards was worth nothing and theirs was very strong, the Spaniard's God being rotten wood. . . . [Popé] saw to it that they at once erected and rebuilt their houses of idolatry which they call estufas, and made very ugly masks in imitation of the devil . . . ; and he said likewise that the devil had given them to understand that living thus in accordance with the law of their ancestors, they would harvest a great deal of maize, many beans, a great abundance of cotton, calabashes, and very large watermelons and cantaloupes; and that they could erect their houses and enjoy abundant health and leisure.

Source: Charles Wilson Hackett, *Revolt of the Pueblo Indians of New Mexico and Otermin's Attempted Reconquest, 1680–1682* (Albuquerque: University of New Mexico, 1942), 245–49.

THE CALIFORNIA MISSIONS

"Some of these means [of obtaining converts] go far beyond the bounds of legitimate persuasion"
Alexander Forbes (1839)

> *In California, the most important Spanish colonial institution was the religious mission. As Alexander Forbes, an English traveler explains, the mission was not only supposed to convert the Indians to Christianity, but also to teach them the skills of "civilization."*

This 1786 drawing is the earliest known view of an Indian mission in California. *(Courtesy, Museo Naval, Madrid)*

Each mission has allotted to it . . . a tract of land of about fifteen miles square, which is generally fertile and well-suited for husbandry. This land is set apart for the general uses of the mission, part being cultivated, and part left in its natural condition and occupied as grazing ground. . . . The Indian population generally live in huts at about two hundred yards distant from the principal edifices; these huts are sometimes made of *adobes*, but the Indians are often left to raise them on their own plan; viz. of rough poles erected into a conical figure, of about four yards in circumference at the base, covered with dry grass and a small aperture for the entrance. When the huts decay, they set them on fire, and erect new ones. . . . In these huts the married part of the community live, the unmarried of both sexes being kept, each sex separate, in large barn-like apartments, where they work under strict supervision. . . .

The object of the whole of the Californian or missionary system being the conversion of the Indians and the training of them up, in some sort, to a civilized life, the constant care of the fathers is and ever has been directed towards these ends. . . . There can be no doubt that some of these means [of obtaining converts] go far beyond the bounds of legitimate persuasion. . . . It must be admitted that with their particular views of the efficacy of baptism and ceremonial profession of Christianity in saving souls, the conversion of the Indians even by force, can hardly be otherwise regarded by them as the greatest of benefits conferred on these people and therefore justifying some severity in effecting it.

_____

Source: Alexander Forbes, *California* (London, 1839).

5.

CONFLICT AND ACCOMMODATION IN THE NORTHWEST

OPENING OF THE FRENCH FUR TRADE

"They might in the future more than ever before engage in hunting beavers"
Samuel de Champlain (1604)

Although Jacques Cartier established France's claim in the St. Law-rence Valley in 1534, it would not be until the early seventeenth cen-

tury that France founded its first permanent settlements. Here, the explorer Samuel de Champlain describes how he encouraged Indians to participate in the fur trade.

. . . I went on shore with my companions and two of our savages who served as interpreters. I directed the men in our barque to approach near the savages, and hold their arms in readiness to do their duty in case they notice any movement of these people against us. Bessabez [the chief], seeing us on land, bade us sit down, and began to smoke with his companions. . . . They presented us with venison and game.

I directed our interpreter to say to our savages that . . . Sieur de Monts [Champlain's patron] had sent me to see them, and . . . that he desired to inhabit their country and show them how to cultivate it, in order that they might not continue to lead so miserable a life as they were doing. . . . They expressed their great satisfaction, saying that no greater good could come to them than to have our friendship, and that they desired to live in peace with their enemies, and that we should dwell in their land, in order that they might in the future more than ever before engage in hunting beavers, and give us a part of them in return for our providing them with things which they wanted. . . .

_____

Source: William L. Grant, ed., *The Voyages of Samuel De Champlain* (New York, 1907), 49–50.

THE PILGRIMS FROM THE INDIAN PERSPECTIVE

"Without asking liberty from anyone, they possessed themselves of a portion of the country"
William Apes (1836)

In a speech, William Apes, a Pequot, offers an Indian perspective on the early history of relations between the English colonists and the native peoples of New England.

December, 1620, the Pilgrims landed at Plymouth, and without asking liberty from anyone, they possessed themselves of a portion of the country, and built themselves houses, and then made a treaty, and commanded them [the Indians] to accede to it. . . . And yet for their kindness and resignation towards the whites, they were called savages, and made by God on purpose for them to destroy. . . .

This 1651 engraving, the earliest known view of Manhattan Island, shows Indians bringing beaver pelts to sell to the Dutch.

The next we present before you are things very appalling. We turn our attention to dates, 1623, January and March, when Mr. Weston['s] Colony, came very near to starving to death; some of them were obliged to hire themselves to the Indians, to become their servants, in order that they might live. Their principal work was to bring wood and water; but not being contented with this, many of the whites sought to steal the Indians' corn; and because the Indians complained of it, and through their complaint, some one of their number being punished, as they say, to appease the savages. Now let us see who the greatest savages were; the person that stole the corn was a stout athletic man, and because of this, they wished to spare him, and take an old man who was lame and sickly . . . and because they thought he would not be of so much use to them, he was, although innocent of any crime, hung in his stead. . . . Another act of humanity for Christians, as they call themselves, that one Capt. Standish, gathering some fruit and provisions, goes forward with a black and hypocritical heart, and pretends to prepare a feast for the Indians; and when they sit down to eat, they seize the Indians' knives hanging around their necks, and stab them in the heart. . . .

The Pilgrims promised to deliver up every transgressor of the Indian treaty, to them, to be punished according to their laws, and the Indians were to do likewise. Now it appears that an Indian had committed treason, by conspiring against the king's [Massasoit's] life, which is punishable with death . . . and the Pilgrims refused to give him up, although by their oath of alliance they had promised to do so. . . .

In this history of Massasoit we find that his own head men were not satisfied with the Pilgrims; that they looked upon them to be intruders, and had a wish to expel those intruders out of their coast. A false report was made respecting one Tisquantum, that he was murdered by an Indian. . . . Upon this news, one Standish, a vile and malicious fellow, took fourteen of his lewd Pilgrims with him . . . at midnight. . . . At that late hour of the night, meeting a house in the wilderness, whose inmates heard—Move not, upon the peril of your life. At the same time some of the females were so frightened, that some of them undertook to make their escape, upon which they were fired upon. . . . These Indians had not done one single wrong act to the whites, but were as innocent of any crime, as any beings in the world. But if the real sufferers say one word, they are denounced, as being wild and savage beasts. . . .

We might suppose that meek Christians had better gods and weapons than cannon. But let us again review their weapons to civilize the nations of this soil. What were they: rum and powder, and ball, together with all the diseases, such as the small pox, and every other disease imaginable; and in this way sweep off thousands and tens of thousands.

Source: William Apes, *Eulogy on King Philip* (Boston, 1836), 10 ff.

DESTRUCTION OF THE PEQUOTS
"Horrible was the stinck and sente"
William Bradford (1636)

> *In this extract, William Bradford, a leader in the founding of Plymouth and the colony's longtime governor, describes the destruction by fire of the Pequots' major village, in which at least 400 Indians were burned to death. In his epic novel* Moby Dick, *Herman Melville called his doomed whaling ship* The Pequod, *which was sacrificed by its captain, Ahab, out of greed and pride—a clear reference to earlier events in New England.*

Those that scaped the fire were slaine with the sword; some hewed to peeces, other rune throw with their rapiers, so as they were quickly dispatchte, and very few escaped. It was conceived they thus destroyed about 400, at this time. It was a fearful sight to see them thus frying in the fyer, and the streams of blood quenching the same, and horrible was the stinck and sente there of; but the victory seemed a sweete sacrifice, and they gave the prayers thereof to God, who had wrought so wonderfully for them, thus to inclose their enemise in their hands, and give them so speedy a victory over so proud and insulting an enimie.

Source: William Bradford, *History of Plymouth Plantation* (Boston, 1856).

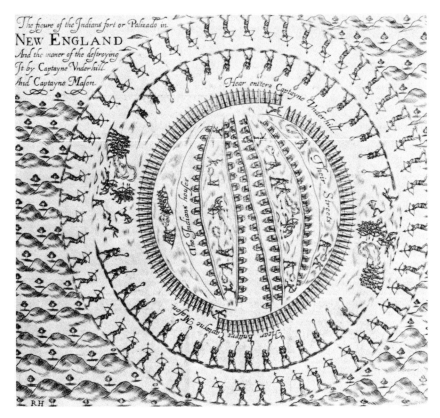

New Englanders destroy the Pequots' major village. *(Courtesy, Rare Book Room, New York Public Library)*

A NARRAGANSETT PLEA FOR UNITY

"We must be as one as the English are"
Miantonomo (1642)

A Narragansett chief calls on other Indian tribes to join him in repulsing the English colonists. Note his observations about the ways that the English had transformed the natural environment.

Brothers, we must be as one as the English are, or we shall all be destroyed. You know our fathers had plenty of deer and skins and our plains were full of game and turkeys, and our coves and rivers were full of fish.

But, brothers, since these Englishmen have seized our country, they have cut down the grass with scythes, and the trees with axes. Their cows and horses eat up the grass, and their hogs spoil our bed of clams; and finally we shall all starve to death; therefore, stand not in your own light, I ask you, but resolve to act like men. All the sachems both to the east and the west have joined with us, and we are resolved to fall upon them at a day appointed, and therefore I come secretly to you, cause you can persuade your Indians to do what you will.

Source: Herbert Milton Sylvester, *Indian Wars of New England* (Cleveland, 1910), I, 386.

KING PHILIP'S WAR

"There having been about 1200 houses burned"
Edward Randolph (1675)

> *The last major Indian war in New England, King Philip's War was the most destructive conflict, relative to the size of the population, in American history. England dispatched Edward Randolph to determine the conflict's causes and assess the damage.*

Various are the reports and conjectures of the causes of the present Indian warre. Some impute it to an imprudent zeal in the magistrates of Boston to christianize those heathen before they were civilized and injoyning them the strict observation of their lawes, which, to a people so rude and licentious, hath proved even intollerable, and that the more, for that while the magistrates, for their profit, put the lawes severely in execution against the Indians, the people, on the other side, for lucre and gain, intice and provoke the Indians to the breach thereof, especially to drunkennesse, to which those people are so generally addicted that they will strip themselves to their skin to have their fill of rume and brandy. . . .

Some beleeve there have been vagrant and jesuiticall priests, who have made it their businesse, for some yeares past, to goe from Sachim to Sachim, to exasperate the Indians against the English and to bring them into a confederacy, and that they were promised supplies from France and other parts to extirpate the English nation out of the continent of America. Others impute the cause to some injuries offered to the Sachim Philip; for he being possessed of a tract of land called Mount Hope . . . some English had a mind to dispossesse him thereof, who never wanting one pretence or other to attain their end, complained of injuries done by Philip and his Indians to their stock and cattle, whereupon Philip was often summoned before the magistrate, sometimes imprisoned, and never released but upon parting with a considerable part of his land.

But the government of the Massachusets . . . do declare these are the

King Philip. *(Courtesy, Smithsonian Institution)*

great evills for which God hath given the heathen commission to rise against them. . . . For men wearing long hayre and perewigs made of womens hayre; for women . . . cutting, curling and laying out the hayre. . . . For profanesse in the people not frequenting their meetings. . . .

With many such reasons . . . the English have contributed much to their misfortunes, for they first taught the Indians the use of armes, and admitted them to be present at all their musters and trainings, and shewed them how to handle, mend and fix their muskets, and have been furnished with all sorts of armes by permission of the government. . . .

The losse to the English in the severall colonies, in their habitations and stock, is reckoned to amount to 150,000*l.* there having been about 1200 houses burned, 8000 head of cattle, great and small, killed, and many thousand bushels of wheat, pease and other grain burned . . . and upward of 3000 Indians men women and children destroyed. . . .

Source: Albert B. Hart, ed., *American History Told by Contemporaries* (New York, 1897), Vol. 1, 458–60.

6.

CONFLICT AND COOPERATION IN THE SOUTHEAST

"I knowe the difference of peace and warre better then any in my Countrie"
Powhatan (1609)

> *Responding to rumors that the English were intent on destroying his confederacy, Powhatan, Virginia's leading chief, asked the English to cease threatening to use force against the Indians. Otherwise, Powhatan threatened to cut off the food supply that the English depended on for subsistence.*

Captaine Smith, you may understand that I, having seene the death of all my people thrice, and not one living of those 3 generations but my selfe, I knowe the difference of peace and warre better then any in my Countrie. But now I am old, and ere long must die. My brethren, namely Opichapam, Opechankanough, and Kekataugh, my two sisters, and their two daughters, are distinctly each others successours. I wish their experience no lesse then mine, and your love to them, no less then mine to you: but this brute [rumor] from Nansamund, that you are come to destroy my Countrie, so

Scenes of life in late sixteenth century Virginia. *(Courtesy, Engravings by de Bry)*

A 1590 drawing of life in Secota, a village in Virginia, by John White. *(Courtesy, Virginia State Library)*

much affrighteth all my people, as they dare not visit you. What will it availe you to take that perforce you may quietly have with love, or to destroy them that provide you food? What can you get by war, when we can hide our provision and flie to the woodes, whereby you must famish, by wronging us your friends? And whie are you thus jealous of our loves, seeing us unarmed, and both doe, and are willing still to feed you with that you cannot get but by our labours? Think you I am so simple not to knowe it is better to eate good meate, lie well, and sleepe quietly with my women and children, laugh, and be merrie with you, have copper, hatchets, or what I want being your friend; then bee forced to flie from all, to lie cold in the woods, feed upon acorns roots and such trash, and be so hunted by you that I can neither rest eat nor sleepe, but my tired men must watch, and if a twig but breake, everie one crie, there comes Captaine Smith: then must I flie I knowe not whether and thus with miserable feare end my miserable life, leaving my pleasures to such youths as you, which, through your rash unadvisednesse, may quickly as miserably ende, for want of that you never knowe how to find? Let this therefore assure you of our loves, and everie yeare our friendly trade shall furnish you with corn; and now also if you would come in friendly manner to us, and not thus with your gunnes and swords, as to invade your foes.

Source: Samuel G. Drake, *Biography and History of the Indians of North America* (Boston, 1841), 353.

BEGINNINGS OF THE FUR TRADE IN THE CAROLINAS
"They presented mee diverse deare skins"
Dr. Henry Woodward (1674)

> *In 1674, Dr. Henry Woodward, an early Carolina colonist, began to trade furs with the Westos Indians. Here he describes how European traders reached accommodation with the area's Indian population. Note that much of the initiative for establishing the fur trade comes from the Indians.*

As we travelled . . . I saw . . . where these Indians had drawne uppon trees (the barke being hewed away) the effigies of a bever, a man, on horseback and guns. Intimating thereby . . . their desire for freindship and comerse with us. . . . Wee met two Indians with their fowling peeces, sent by their cheife to congratulate my arrivale into their parts, who himself awaited my comeing with diverse others at the Westoe River. . . . I was carried to the Captains hutt, who courteously entertained mee with a good repast of those

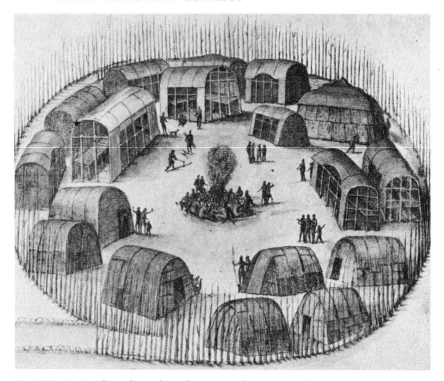

A 1585 painting by John White shows an Algonquian village in North Carolina. *(Courtesy, British Museum)*

things they counte rarietys amonge them. . . . The cheife of the Indians made long speeches intimating their own strength (and as I judged their desire of freindship with us). This night first haveing oyled my eyes and joynts with beares oyl, they presented mee diverse deare skins, setting befoore me suffi-cient of their food to satisfy at least half a dozen of their own appetites. Here taking my first nights repose, the next day I veiwed the Towne, which is built in a confused maner, consisting of many long houses whose sides and tops are both artifitially done with barke, upon the tops of most whereof fastened to the ends of long poles hang the locks of haire of Indians they have slain. . . . [Nearby] seldom ly less than one hundred faire canoes ready uppon all occasions. They are well provided with arms, amunition, tradeing cloath and other trade from the northward for which at set times of the year they truck drest deare skins furrs and young Indian slaves.

_____

Source: Alexander S. Salley, ed., *Narratives of Early Carolina* (New York, 1911), 130–34.

7.

NATIVE AMERICANS AND THE GREAT WARS FOR EMPIRE

Between 1680 and 1763, the French and English waged repeated wars to control the Indian trade. The struggle between the rival powers was motivated not only by the prospects of economic profit, but also by religion, national honor, and dreams of empire. A major battleground in this contest for empire took place in upstate New York, where the English formed an alliance with the Iroquois in order to disrupt French trade in the interior.

THE IROQUOIS AND ENGLISH FORM AN ALLIANCE

"You must Protect us against the French, which if you dont we shall loose all our Hunting & Bevers"
A Speech of the Onnondages & Cajouga Sachems (1684)

You are a Mighty Sachem & we but a Small People. When the English first came to New York to Virginia & Maryland, they were but a small People & we a large Nation; & we finding they were good People gave them Land & dealt Civilly by them; Now that you are grown Numerous & we decreased, you must Protect us against the French, which if you dont we shall loose all our Hunting & Bevers: The French want all the Bevers & are Angry that we bring any to the English.

Source: Charles H. McIlain, ed., *Wraxall's Abridgement of the New York Indian Affairs, 1678–1751* (Cambridge, Mass., 1915), 10–17.

France and England, and their Indian allies, fought four major wars between 1689 and 1763. King William's War (1689–1697) erupted when England's Indian allies raided French settlements near Montreal. France and its allies retaliated by attacking the Iroquois and English in New York and frontier New England. British attempts to seize Quebec in 1690 and 1691 failed. The Treaty of Ryswick restored the prewar boundaries.

A new struggle, Queen Anne's War (1702–1713) broke out when the French and their Indian allies raided English settlements on the New England frontier. Fighting then spread to the southern frontier, where English colonists in the Carolinas attacked Spanish territory in Florida. An English invasion of Quebec in 1710 failed, but in the Treaty of Utrecht ending the war, France ceded Newfoundland, Nova

Scotia, and French territory around Hudson Bay to England and abandoned its claim to sovereignty over the Iroquois. Following the war conflict persisted in the South, where English settlers in the Carolinas destroyed the Yamassee Indians, who were allies of the French, while the French brutally put down an uprising by the Natchez Indians and their Chickasaw allies.

The third war for empire, King George's War (1744–1748) began when France attempted to recapture Nova Scotia. With France forced to concentrate its military powers in Canada, English traders were able to move into western Pennsylvania and eastern Ohio.

The stage was now set for the climactic conflict, the French and Indian War (1754–1763), which ended France's colonial empire in North America. The war grew out of French efforts to control the fur trade north of the Ohio River by expelling English traders from the region and building a chain of forts along the Allegheny River. British victories in the war led many Indian tribes to shift their affiliations to the English. The following speech by a Cherokee chief illustrates this change in allegiances.

SHIFTING LOYALTIES

"The bloody tommahawke . . . must now be buried"
Ostenaco (1765)

The bloody tommahawke, so long lifted against our brethren the English, must now be buried deep, deep in the ground, never to be raised again; and whoever shall act contrary to any of these articles, must expect a punishment equal to his offence. Should a strict observance of them be neglected a war must necessarily follow, and a second peace may not be so easily obtained. I therefore once more recommend to you, to take particular care of your behavior towards the English whom we must now look upon as ourselves, they have the French and Spaniards to fight, and we enough of our own colour, without medling with either nation. I desire likewise, that the white warrior, who has ventured himself here with us, may be well used and respected by all, wherever he goes amongst us.

Source: Henry Timberlake, The Memoirs of Lieut. Henry Timberlake (London, 1765), 28–41.

France's defeat at the Battle of Quebec in 1759 crippled the French war effort, and led to the Treaty of Paris (1763), which gave French territory east of the Mississippi River to Britain. The French defeat led to a rapid influx of traders, land speculators, and frontier farmers into *the region west of the Allegheny Mountains. Instigated in part by French traders, a group of Ottawa Indians led by Pontiac tried to stop this intrusion onto their lands by laying siege to Detroit. A frontier war followed, and within ninety days, Indians had driven English settlers out of much of the Old Northwest. Without the support of French arms, however, Pontiac was forced to make peace in 1764.*

"Although you have conquered the French, you have not yet conquered us!"
Minavavana (1761)

In this address to an English trader named Alexander Henry, Minavavana, a Chippewa or Ojibwa chief, warns the English that France's defeats during the French and Indian War do not mean that England can assert sovereignty over Indian lands.

Englishman!—You know that the French King is our father. He promised to be such; and we, in return, promised to be his children. This promise we have kept.

Englishman!—It is you that have made war with this our father. You are his enemy; and how then could you have the boldness to venture among us, his children? You know that his enemies are ours. . . .

Englishman!—Although you have conquered the French, you have not yet conquered us! We are not your slaves. These lakes, these woods and mountains, were left to us by our ancestors. They are our inheritance, and we will part with them to none. . . .

Englishman!—Our father, the king of France, employed our young men to make war upon your nation. In this warfare, many of them have been killed; and it is our custom to retaliate, until such time as the spirits of the slain are satisfied. Now the spirits of the slain are to be satisfied in either of two ways. The first is by the spilling of the blood of the nation by which they fell; the other, by *covering the bodies of the dead*, and thus allaying the resentment of their relations. This is done by making presents.

Englishman!—Your king has never sent us any presents, nor entered into any treaty with us. Wherefore he and we are still at war; and, until he does these things, we must consider that we have no other father, nor friend, among the white men, than the king of France. But, for you, we have taken into consideration, that you have ventured your life among us, in the expectation that we should not molest you. You do not come armed, with an intention to make war. You come in peace, to trade with us, and supply us with necessaries, of which we are much in want. We shall regard you, therefore, as a brother; and you may sleep tranquilly, without fear of the Chippe-was. As a token of our friendship, we present you with this pipe, to smoke.

Source: B. B. Thatcher, *Indian Biography* (New York, 1841), Vol. II, 76–77.

ADVICE FROM THE MASTER OF LIFE
"Drive them out, make war on them"
Pontiac (1763)

> *In this speech, Pontiac tells a number of assembled tribes that the Indian Master of Life has commanded them to stop drinking the white traders' alcohol, to take no more than one wife, and overcome their dependency on whites. Here he repeats the Indian Master's words.*

I am the Master of Life, whom thou desirest to know and to whom thou wouldst speak. Listen well to what I am going to say to thee and all thy red brethren. I am he who made heaven and earth, the trees, lakes, rivers, all men, and all that thou seest, and all that thou hast seen on earth. Because [I have done this and because] I love you, you must do what I say and [not do] what I hate. I do not like that you drink until you lose your reason, as you do; or that you fight with each other; or that you take two wives, or run after the wives of others; you do not well; I hate that. You must have but one wife, and keep her until death. When you are going to war, you juggle, join the medicine dance, and believe that I am speaking. You are mistaken, it is to Manitou to whom you speak; he is a bad spirit who whispers to you nothing but evil, and to whom you listen because you do not know me well. This land, where you live, I have made for you and not for others. How comes it that you suffer the whites on your lands? Can you not do without them? I know that those whom you call the children of your Great Father supply your wants, but if you were not bad, as you are, you would well do without them. You might live wholly as you did before you knew them. Before those whom you call your brothers come on your lands, did you not live by bow and arrow? You had no need of gun nor powder, nor the rest of their things, and nevertheless you caught animals to live and clothe your-selves with their skins, but when I saw that you inclined to the evil, I called back the animals into the depths of the woods, so that you had need of your brothers to have your wants supplied and cover you. You have only to become good and do what I want, and I shall send back to you the animals to live on. I do not forbid you, for all that, to suffer amongst you the chil-dren of your father. I love them, they know me and pray to me, and I give them their necessities and all that they bring to you, but as regards those who have come to trouble your country, drive them out, make war on them.

I love them not, they know me not, they are my enemies and the enemies of your brothers. Send them back to the country which I made for them. There let them remain.

Source: Pioneer Society of the State of Michigan, Collections, 8 (1907), 268 ff.

8.
SURVIVAL STRATEGIES

During the late eighteenth and early nineteenth centuries, the Indian peoples of eastern North America adopted a variety of survival strategies, ranging from armed resistance to cultural adaptation and revitalization. One of the most important Native American revitalization prophets was a Seneca named Handsome Lake.

"Three things that our younger brethren [the Americans] do are right to follow"
Handsome Lake (1799)

At the end of the eighteenth century, Handsome Lake, a Seneca religious leader, experienced a series of visions and began to preach a new religion that blended Quaker and Iroquois beliefs. The Handsome Lake religion helped the Iroquois adapt to a changing social environment, while maintaining many traditional practices and religious tenets.

Four words tell a great story of wrong, and the Creator is sad because of the trouble they bring, so go and tell your people.

The first word is One'ga [alcohol]. It seems that you never have known that this word stands for a great and monstrous evil and has reared a high mound of bones. [Other circumscribed practices included abortion and witchcraft.] . . .

Three things that our younger brethren [the Americans] do are right to follow.

Now, the first. The white man works on a tract of cultivated ground and harvests food for his family. . . .

Now, the second thing. It is the way a white man builds a house. . . .

Now the third. The white man keeps horses and cattle . . . there is no evil in this for they are a help to his family.

Source: Arthur C. Parker, *The Code of Handsome Lake* (Albany, 1913), 27, 38.

"We ought to consider ourselves as one man"
Tenskwatawa (1808)

> *Tenskwatawa, the Shawnee Prophet, describes his teachings to William Henry Harrison, the territorial governor of Indiana.*

Father:—It is three years since I first began with that system of religion which I now practice. The white people and some of the Indians were against me; but I had no other intention but to introduce among the Indians, those good principles of religion which the white people profess. I was spoken badly of by the white people, who reproached me with misleading the Indians; but I defy them to say that I did anything amiss.

Father, I was told that you intended to hang me. When I heard this, I intended to remember it, and tell my father, when I went to see him, and relate to him the truth. . . .

The Great Spirit told me to tell the Indians that he had made them, and made the world—that he had placed them on it to do good, and not evil.

I told all the red skins, that the way they were in was not good, and that they ought to abandon it.

That we ought to consider ourselves as one man; but we ought to live agreeably to our several customs, the red people after their mode, and the white people after theirs; particularly, that they should not drink whiskey; that it was not made for them, but the white people, who alone knew how to use it; and that it is the cause of all the mischief which the Indians suffer; and that they must always follow the directions of the Great Spirit, and we must listen to him, as it was he that made us: determine to listen to nothing that is bad: do not take up the tomahawk, should it be offered by the British, or by the long knives: do not meddle with any thing that does not belong to you, but mind your own business, and cultivate the ground, that your women and your children may have enough to live on. . . .

You have promised to assist us: I now request you, in behalf of all the red people, to use your exertions to prevent the sale of liquor to us. . . .

Source: Benjamin Drake, *Life of Tecumseh, and of His Brother, the Prophet* (New York, 1841), 107–9.

Tecumseh rescues white prisoners. Tecumseh was well known for his revulsion at senseless cruelty. *(Courtesy, Henry E. Huntington Library and Art Gallery)*

"When Jesus Christ came upon the earth you killed Him and nailed Him to the cross"
Tecumseh (1810)

> *Told by Governor Harrison to place his faith in the good intentions of the United States, Tecumseh offers a bitter retort. He calls on Native Americans to revitalize their societies so that they can regain life as a unified people and put an end to legalized land grabs.*

You wish to prevent the Indians from doing as we wish them, to unite and let them consider their lands as the common property of the whole. You take the tribes aside and advise them not to come into this measure. . . . You want by your distinctions of Indian tribes, in allotting to each a particular, to make them war with each other. You never see an Indian endeavor to make the white people do this. You are continually driving the red people, when at last you will drive them onto the great lake, where they can neither stand nor walk.

Since my residence at Tippecanoe, we have endeavored to leave all distinctions, to destroy village chiefs, by whom all mischiefs are done. It is they who sell the land to the Americans. Brother, this land that was sold, and the

Tecumseh *(Courtesy, Chicago Natural History Museum)*

goods that was given for it, was only done by a few. . . . In the future we are prepared to punish those who propose to sell land to the Americans. If you continue to purchase them, it will make war among the different tribes, and at last I do not know what will be the consequences among the white people. Brother, I wish you would take pity on the red people and do as I have requested. If you will not give up the land and do cross the boundary of our present settlement, it will be very hard, and produce great trouble between us.

The way, the only way to stop this evil is for the red men to unite in claiming a common and equal right in the land, as it was at first, and should be now—for it was never divided, but belongs to all. No tribe has the right to sell, even to each other, much less to strangers. . . . *Sell a country! Why not sell the air, the great sea, as well as the earth?* Did not the Great Spirit make them for all the use of his children?

How can we have confidence in the white people?

When Jesus Christ came upon the earth you killed Him and nailed Him to the cross. You thought He was dead and you were mistaken. . . .

Source: Benjamin B. Thatcher, *Indian Biographies* (New York, 1832), 234 ff.

"Shall we, without a struggle, give up our homes"
Tecumseh (1811)

Tecumseh calls on his native brethren to join together to resist white encroachments on their lands.

Where today are the Pequot? Where are the Narragansett, the Mohican, the Pocanet, and other powerful tribes of our people? They have vanished before the avarice and oppression of the white man, as snow before the summer sun. . . . Will we let ourselves be destroyed in our turn, without making an effort worthy of our race? Shall we, without a struggle, give up our homes, our lands, bequeathed to us by the Great Spirit? The graves of our dead and everything that is dear and sacred to us? . . . I know you will say with me, Never! Never! . . .

Sleep not longer, O Choctaws and Chickasaws, in false security and delusive hopes. . . . Will not the bones of our dead be plowed up, and their graves turned into plowed fields?

Source: H. B. Cushman, *History of the Choctaw, Chickasaw and Natchez Indians* (Greenville, Texas, 1899), 310 ff.

"You now have no just cause to declare war against the American people"
Pushmataha (1811)

In a speech to the Choctaws and the Chickasaws, the Choctaw chief rejects Tecumseh's call for a pan-Indian alliance against the Americans. In 1814, Pushmataha fought with Andrew Jackson against the Creeks, the Spanish, and the English. But in the end, Pushmataha's strategy of cooperation proved no more successful than Tecumseh's of armed resistance. In 1820, Pushmataha's people were forced to surrender five million acres of land in Mississippi for barren lands in Oklahoma and southwestern Arkansas.

The question before us now is not what wrongs they have inflicted upon our race, but what measures are best for us to adopt in regard to them; and though our race may have been unjustly treated and shamefully wronged by them [the whites], yet I shall not for that reason alone advise you to destroy them unless it was just and wise for you so to do; nor would I advise you to forgive them, though worthy of your commiseration, unless I believe it would be to the interest of our common good. . . .

My friends and fellow countrymen! you now have no just cause to declare war against the American people, or wreak your vengeance upon them as enemies, since they have ever manifested feelings of friendship towards you. It is ... a disgrace to the memory of your forefathers, to wage war against the American people merely to gratify the malice of the English.

The war, which you are now contemplating against the Americans ... forbodes nothing but destruction to our entire race. It is a war against a people whose territories are now far greater than our own, and who are far better provided with all the necessary implements of war, with men, guns, horses, wealth, far beyond that of all our race combined, and where is the necessity or wisdom to make war upon such a people?

Source: H. B. Cushman, *History of the Choctaw, Chickasaw and Natchez Indians* (Greenville, Texas, 1899), 315–18.

Although insignificant in a global sense, the War of 1812 had critical consequences for Native Americans, effectively destroying their ability to resist American expansion east of the Mississippi. With Tecumseh's demise, Indian power in the Old Northwest was broken. Another group, the Creeks, suffered stinging defeat in the South. In 1813, the Creek Indians, encouraged by the British, had attacked American settlements in what are now Alabama and Mississippi. Frontiersmen from Georgia, Mississippi, and Tennessee, led by Major General Andrew Jackson, retaliated and succeeded in defeating the Creeks in March 1814 at the battle of Horseshoe Bend in Alabama.

"I can do no more than weep over the misfortunes of my nation"
William Weatherford (1814)

In the following extract, the Creek leader, William Weatherford (1780–1824), surrenders to Andrew Jackson. The Creek defeat at the battle of Horseshoe Bend not only stripped the Creeks of half their land, it also dramatically weakened their capacity to resist white encroachments into what would become the Old South's richest cotton growing regions.

I am in your power: do with me what you please. I am a soldier. I have done the white people all the harm I could. I have fought them, and fought them bravely. If I had an army, I would yet fight, and contend to the last. But I have done—my people are all gone—I can do no more than weep over the misfortunes of my nation. Once I could animate my warriors to battle: but I cannot animate the dead.... Whilst there were chances of success, I never left my post, nor supplicated peace. But my people are gone, and now I ask it for my nation, and for myself.

On the miseries and misfortunes brought upon my country, I look back with the deepest sorrow, and wish to avert still greater calamities. . . . But your people have destroyed my nation. You are a brave man. I rely upon your generosity. You will exact no terms of a conquered people, but such as they should accede to. Whatever they may be, it would now be madness and folly to oppose them. If they are opposed, you shall find me among the sternest enforcers of obedience.

Source: W. H. G. Kingston, *Adventures Among the Indians* (Chicago, 1884), 17–18.

PART III

REMOVAL AND THE TRAIL OF TEARS

INTRODUCTION: James L. McDonald and John Ross

Two early nineteenth-century Native Americans followed different paths, one assimilation, the other resistance. Both ended in tragedy. James L. McDonald, a Choctaw, was to serve as a model for the Indians' capacity for full integration into American society. As a boy, he was raised by Thomas L. McKenney, the nation's first commissioner of the Bureau of Indian Affairs, and learned to read Greek and Latin. Later, he studied law under John McLean, a future Supreme Court justice, and became the country's first Indian lawyer. But he began to drink, and after a white woman spurned his marriage proposal, he fell off a cliff to his death. McKenney would later claim that McDonald's sad story would make him an advocate of removing eastern Indians west of the Mississippi River.

John Ross, a Cherokee chief, led his peoples' resistance to removal from their homelands. The son of a Scottish trader and a Cherokee woman of mixed background, he, like McDonald, was exceptionally well educated, first by a tutor and later in a white academy. During the War of 1812, he took part in the battle of Horseshoe Bend, assisting Andrew Jackson to defeat the Creek Indians. A planter who owned some twenty slaves, he owned a plantation worth $20,000 and served for a time as a U.S. postmaster. Ross's dream, however, was to establish a separate Cherokee nation or state within the United States. In 1827, he led the effort to draft a Cherokee constitution modeled on the United States Constitution. When Andrew Jackson tried to remove his people from their homelands, he organized

103

staunch resistance, leading a series of legal battles against the policy. But he found himself thrown in jail and in 1839 he and his family were forced to walk the "Trail of Tears," with his wife, Quatie, dying along the way. He served as his peoples' principal chief until his death in 1866.

The Trail of Tears, by Robert Lindneux. *(Courtesy, Woolaroc Museum)*

9.

INDIAN HATERS AND SYMPATHIZERS

During the late eighteenth and early nineteenth centuries, white attitudes toward Indians were sharply divided. On the one hand, white hatred of Indians persisted, an attitude exemplified by the quotation from H. H. Brackenridge. But the rise of the romantic movement in art and literature, with its emphasis on the emotional and the spiritual, also bred other images. Rejecting the image of the "barbaric savage" or "devil in the flesh," romantic literature often expressed a bitter distaste for the costs of "civilization" and a deep nostalgia for the rapidly disappearing world of nature.

Between 1830 and 1836 and then again from 1852 to 1857, George Catlin (1796–1872) traveled among many Indian peoples, and painted Indian portraits and lifeways in order to document a vanishing culture.

"They have the shapes of men . . . but . . . approach nearer the character of Devils"
H. H. Brackenridge (1782)

On what is their claim founded? —Occupancy. A wild Indian with his skin painted red, and a feather through his nose, has set foot on the broad continent of North and South America; a second wild Indian with his ears cut in ringlets, or his nose slit like a swine or a malefactor, also sets his foot on the same extensive tract of soil. Let the first Indian make a talk to his brother, and bid him take his foot off the continent, for he being first upon it, has occupied the whole, to kill buffaloes, and tall elks with long horns. . . .

What use do these . . . streaked, spotted and speckled cattle make of the soil? Do they till it? Revelation said to man, "Thou shalt till the ground." . . . I would as soon admit a right in the buffalo to grant lands, as . . . the ragged wretches that are called chiefs and sachems. . . .

With regard to forming treaties or making peace with this race, there are many ideas:

They have the shapes of men and may be of the human species, but certainly in their present state they approach nearer the character of Devils. . . .

The tortures which they exercise on the bodies of their prisoners, justify extermination. . . . If we could have any faith in the promises they make we could suffer them to live, provided they would only make war amongst themselves, and abandon their hiding or lurking on the pathways of our citizens . . . and murdering men, women and children in a defenceless situation. . . .

—————————

Source: H. H. Brackenridge, *Indian Atrocities: Narratives of the Perils and Sufferings of Dr. Knight and John Slover Among the Indians* (Cincinnati, 1867), 62–72.

"Victims and dupes of white man's cupidity"
George Catlin (1841)

The Indians of North America . . . were once a happy and flourishing people . . . were sixteen millions in numbers. . . . Their country was entered by white men . . . and thirty millions of these are now scuffling for the goods and luxuries of life, over the bones and ashes of twelve millions of red men; six millions of whom have fallen victims to the small-pox, and the remainder to the sword, the bayonet, and whiskey. . . . Of the two millions remaining alive at this time, about 1,400,000 are already the miserable living victims and dupes of white man's cupidity, degraded, discouraged, and lost in the bewildering maze that is produced by the use of whiskey and its concomitant vices; and the remaining number are yet unaroused and unenticed from their wild haunts or their primitive modes, by the dread or love of white man and his allurements.

—————————

Source: George Catlin, *North American Indians* (New York, 1841), I, 6–7.

10.
THE MISSIONARY IMPULSE

By the early nineteenth century, there was a growing consensus among humanitarian reformers that Indian survival depended on "civilization and Christianization." By this, they meant education in white ways of life, adoption of single family farms, and acceptance of Protestant religious tenets.

"There is no place on earth to which they can migrate, and live in the savage and hunter state"
American Board of Commissioners for Foreign Missions (1824)

... A prominent object of the board we represent is to extend the blessing of civilization and Christianity, in all their variety, to the Indian tribes within the limits of the United States. In carrying on this work of benevolence and charity, we are happy to acknowledge, with much gratitude, the aid received from the government, in making and supporting the several establishments for accomplishing this purpose....

The history of our intercourse with Indians, from the first settlement of this country, contains many facts honorable to the character of our ancestors, and of our nation—many, also, too many, which are blots on this character.... We here allude to the neglect with which the aboriginal tribes have been treated in regard to their civil, moral, and religious improvement—to the manner in which we have, in many, if not most instances, come into possession of their lands, and of their peltry: also, to the provocations we have given, in so many instances, to those cruel, desolating, and exterminating wars, which have been successively waged against them; and to the corrupting vices, and fatal diseases, which have been introduced

Sequoyah (1770?–1843) invented the Cherokee written alphabet. (*Courtesy, Library of Congress*)

among them, by wicked and unprincipled white people.... The only way, we humbly conceive, to ... secure the forgiveness and favor of Him whom we have offended ... is happily, that which has been already successfully commenced, and which the government of our nation, and Christians of nearly all denominations, are pursuing. ...

We are aware of the great and only objection, deserving notice, that is made to our project ... that "it is *impracticable*; that Indians, like some species of birds and beasts ... are *untameable*; and that no means, which we can employ, will prepare them to enjoy with us the blessings of civilization." In answer to this objection, we appeal to facts ... which cannot be doubted ... as furnish indubitable evidence of the practicability of educating Indians in such manner, as to prepare them to enjoy all the blessings, and to fulfill all the duties, of civilized life. ...

It *is* desirable that our Indians should receive such an education as has been mentioned, we conceive, because the civilized is preferable to the savage state; because the Bible, and the religion therein revealed to us, with its ordinances, are blessings of infinite and everlasting value and which the Indians do not now enjoy. It is also desirable as an act of common humanity. The progress of the white population, in the territories which were lately the hunting grounds of the Indians, is rapid, and probably will continue to increase. Their game, on which they principally depend for subsistence, is diminishing, and is already gone from those tribes who remain among us. In the natural course of things, therefore, they will be compelled to obtain their support in the manner we do ours. They are, to a considerable extent, sensible of this already. But they cannot thus live, and obtain their support, till they receive the education for which we plead. There is no place on earth to which they can migrate, and live in the savage and hunter state. The Indian tribes must, therefore, be *progressively civilized*, or *successively* perish.

Source: American Board of Commissioners for Foreign Missions, "Memorial to the Senate and the House of Representatives," in American Society for Improving Indian Tribes, *First Annual Report*, 1824, 66–68.

"That the government shall occupy a paternal character, treating the Indians as their wards"
Henry Benjamin Whipple (1860)

> *In a letter to President James Buchanan, Whipple, the first Episcopal Bishop of Minnesota, calls on the government to embrace a paternalistic scheme to uplift the Chippewas, Sioux, and Winnebagoes.*

The only hope for the Indians is in civilization and Christianization. They understand this, and I believe would welcome any plan which will save them from destruction.

The curse of the Indian country is the firewater which flows through its borders. Although every treaty pledges to them protection against its sale and use, and the government desires to fulfil this pledge, thus far all efforts have proved ineffectual.

The difficulties in the way are these: First, the policy of our government has been to treat the red man as an equal. Treaties are then made. The annuities are paid in gross sums annually; from the Indian's lack of providence and the influence of traders, a few weeks later every trace of the payment is gone. Secondly, the reservations are scattered and have a widely extended border of ceded lands. As the government has no control over the citizens of the state, traffic is carried on openly on the border. Third, the Indian agents have no police to enforce the laws of Congress, and cannot rely upon the officers elected by a border population to suppress a traffic in which friends are interested. Fourth, the army, being under the direction of a separate department, has no definite authority to act for the protection of the Indians. Fifth, if arrests are made, the cases must be tried before some local state officer, and often the guilty escape. Sixth, as there is no distinction made by the government between the chief of temperate habits and the one of intemperate, the tribe loses one of the most powerful influences for good—that of pure official example.

With much hesitation I would suggest to those who have Indian affairs in charge. . . .

First, whether, in future, treaties cannot be made so that the government shall occupy a paternal character, treating the Indians as their wards. . . .

Fourth, whether the department has the power to strike from the roll of chiefs, the name of any man of intemperate habits, and thus make a pure, moral character the ground of government favor.

Fifth, whether the department has authority to issue a medal on one side of which should be a pledge to abstain from intoxicating drinks for one year. . . .

Seventh, whether some plan cannot be devised to create in the Indians an interest in securing themselves homes where they can live by the cultivation of the soil.

Eighth, whether practical Christian teachers cannot be secured to teach the Indians the peaceful pursuits of agriculture and the arts of civilization.

Source: Henry Benjamin Whipple, *Lights and Shadows of a Long Episcopate* (New York, 1899), 50–53.

"For the purpose of providing against . . . further decline"
Civilization Fund Act (1819)

> *To assist reform and missionary societies in their efforts to establish schools for Indians, the federal government established a "Civilization Fund." In 1824, the federal government created a Bureau of Indian Affairs in the War Department to administer the fund.*

. . . [F]or the purpose of providing against the further decline and final extinction of the Indian tribes, adjoining the frontier settlements of the United States, and for introducing among them the habits and arts of civilization, the President of the United States shall be, and he is hereby authorized, in every case where he shall judge improvement in the habits and condition of such Indians practicable, and that the means of instruction can be introduced with their own consent, to employ capable persons of good moral character, to instruct them in the mode of agriculture suited to their situation; and for teaching their children in reading, writing and arithmetic. . . .

Source: U.S. Statutes at Large, 3:516–17.

"Our mental powers are not by nature inferior to yours"
To-Cha Lee and Chu Li-Oa (1813)

> *In this document, two Cherokee chiefs describe the great strides that their people had made in acculturation. Yet despite this tangible proof that their people could meet the "test of civilization," they would be removed from their homelands during the 1830s.*

By the rapid progress of settlements in the western part of the United States, our country is now nearly surrounded by our white brothers. . . . It is for the interest of all that harmony and good neighborhood should be preserved between us—and when from misunderstanding, or the disorderly conduct of individuals on either side, our harmony may have been temporarily interrupted, it gives you and us concern and uneasiness, because we cannot control the passions of men. . . .

In former years we were of *necessity* under the influence of your enemies. We spilled our blood in their cause; they were finally compelled by your arms to leave us; they made no stipulation for our security. When those years of distress had passed away, we found ourselves in the power of a generous nation; past transactions were consigned to oblivion; our boundaries were established by compact, and liberal provision was made for our future security and improvement, for which we placed ourselves under the protection of the United States. Under these provisions, our nation has prospered, our population has increased.—The knowledge and practice of agriculture and some of the useful arts, have kept pace with time. Our stocks of cattle and other domestic animals fill the forests, while the wild animals have disappeared. Our spinning wheels and looms now in use by the ingenious hands of our wives and our daughters, enable us to clothe ourselves principally in decent habits, from the production of materials . . . of our soil. In addition to these important acquisitions, many of our youth of both sexes have acquired such knowledge of letters and figures as to show to the most incredulous that our mental powers are not by nature inferior to yours— and we look forward to a period of time, when it may be said, this artist, this mathematician, this astronomer, is a Cherokee. . . .

Source: *Niles Weekly Register*, April 10, 1813, 96–97.

11.
"JUSTIFYING" REMOVAL

"Removal . . . would . . . promote their welfare and happiness"
President James Monroe (1825)

> *In a message to Congress, President Monroe describes the removal of Indians to lands west of the Mississippi River as a providential solution to a series of problems: the United States' need to solidify control over its southeastern border, the desire of land-hungry settlers for new lands to cultivate, the goal of protecting Indians from white encroachments, and the aim of "civilizing" Native Americans at their own pace.*

Being deeply impressed with the opinion that the removal of the Indian tribes from the lands which they now occupy within the limits of the several States and Territories . . . is of very high importance to our Union, and may be accomplished on conditions and in a manner to promote the interest and happiness of those tribes, the attention of the Government has been long drawn with great solicitude to the object. For the removal of the tribes within the limits of the State of Georgia the motive has been peculiarly strong, arising from the compact with that State whereby the United States are bound to extinguish the Indian title to the lands within it whenever it may be done peaceably and on reasonable conditions. . . . The removal of the tribes from the territory which they now inhabit . . . would not only shield them from impending ruin, but promote their welfare and happiness. Experience has clearly demonstrated that in their present state it is impossible to incorporate them in such masses, in any form whatever, into our system. It has also demonstrated with equal certainty that without a timely anticipation of and provision against the dangers to which they are exposed, under causes which it will be difficult, if not impossible to control, their degradation and extermination will be inevitable.

Source: James D. Richardson, *Messages and Papers of the Presidents*, Vol. 2, 280–83.

"The fate of the Mohegan, the Narragansett, and the Delaware is fast overtaking the Choctaw, the Cherokee, and the Creek"
President Andrew Jackson (1829)

> *President Jackson offers his rationale for removing Indians to lands west of the Mississippi River.*

It has long been the policy of Government to introduce among them the arts of civilization, in the hope of gradually reclaiming them from a wandering life. This policy has, however, been coupled with another wholly incompatible with its success. Professing a desire to civilize and settle them, we have at the same time lost no opportunity to purchase their lands and thrust them farther into the wilderness. By this means they have not only been kept in a wandering state, but been led to look upon us as unjust and indifferent to their fate. . . . A portion, however, of the Southern tribes, having mingled much with the whites and made some progress in the arts of civilized life, have lately attempted to erect an independent government within the limits of Georgia and Alabama. These States, claiming to be the only sovereigns within their territories, extended their laws over the Indians, which induced the latter to call upon the United States for protection. . . .

I informed the Indians inhabiting parts of Georgia and Alabama that their attempt to establish an independent government would not be countenanced by the Executive of the United States, and advised them to emigrate beyond the Mississippi or submit to the laws of those States. . . .

An 1834 sketch by George Catlin of the Choctaw in Oklahoma after removal.

Our ancestors found them the uncontrolled possessors of these vast regions. By persuasion and force they have been made to retire from river to river and from mountain to mountain, until some of the tribes have become extinct and others have left but remnants to preserve for a while their once terrible names. Surrounded by the whites with their arts of civilization, which by destroying the resources of the savage doom him to weakness and decay, the fate of the Mohegan, the Narragansett, and the Delaware is fast overtaking the Choctaw, the Cherokee, and the Creek. That this fate surely awaits them if they remain within the limits of the States does not admit of a doubt. Humanity and national honor demand that every effort should be made to avert so great a calamity. . . .

As a means of effecting this end I suggest for your consideration the propriety of setting apart an ample district west of the Mississippi, and without the limit of any State or Territory now formed, to be guaranteed to the Indian tribes as long as they shall occupy it. . . . There they may be secured in the enjoyment of governments of their own choice, subject to no other control from the United States than such as may be necessary to preserve peace on the frontier and between the several tribes. There the benevolent may endeavor to teach them the arts of civilization. . . .

This emigration should be voluntary, for it would be as cruel as unjust to compel the aborigines to abandon the graves of their fathers and seek a home in a distant land. But they should be distinctly informed that if they remain within the limits of the States they must be subject to their laws. . . .

_____

Source: James D. Richardson, *Messages and Papers of the Presidents*, Vol. 2, 456–59.

"Nations of dependent Indians . . . are driven from their homes into the wilderness"
Edward Everett (1830)

> *One of the staunchest Congressional opponents of removal was the famous orator Edward Everett. Here he vehemently attacks Andrew Jackson's removal policy.*

The evil, Sir, is enormous; the inevitable suffering incalculable. Do not stain the fair fame of the country. . . . Nations of dependent Indians, against their will, under color of law, are driven from their homes into the wilderness. You cannot explain it; you cannot reason it away. . . . Our friends will view this measure with sorrow, and our enemies alone with joy. And we ourselves, Sir, when the interests and passions of the day are past, shall look back upon it, I fear, with self-reproach, and a regret as bitter as unavailing.

_____

Source: Jeremiah Evarts, ed., *Speeches on the Passage of the Bill for the Removal of the Indians Delivered in the Congress of the United States* (Boston, 1830), 299.

"In vain did the Indians implore the government to protect them"
Thomas L. McKenney (1830)

> *Thomas L. McKenney was the first Commissioner of Indian Affairs, holding the office from 1824 to 1830, when he was dismissed by President Jackson. Here, he attacks the federal government for failing to keep whites off of Cherokee land as required by treaty.*

The fifth article of the treaty [between the Cherokee Nation and the United States] . . . contains this provision: "—And all white people who *have* intruded, or may *hereafter* intrude, on the lands reserved for the Cherokees, *shall be removed by the United States*". . . .

But this law was destined, at last, though unrepealed, to become a dead letter! The solemn compacts with the Indians, guaranteeing to them "protection," were treated as things obsolete, or regarded as mockeries. In the face, and in violation of the provisions ... surveyors were permitted to penetrate the Indian territory, roam over it, lay it off into counties, and to proceed, in all things, for its settlement, as though no Indians occupied it, and no laws existed, demanding the interference of the government to prevent it! In vain did the Indians implore the government to protect them; in vain did they call the attention of the Executive to the provisions of treaties, and to the pledges of the law.

Source: Thomas L. McKenney, *Sketches of Travels among the Northern & Southern Indians* (3rd ed.; New York, 1854), Vol. I, 256–62.

"Cause them gradually ... to cast off their savage habits and become an interesting, civilized, and Christian community"
Andrew Jackson (1830)

> *Jackson defends the removal policy in his second annual message to Congress.*

It gives me pleasure to announce to Congress that the benevolent policy of the government, steadily pursued for nearly thirty years, in relation to the removal of the Indians beyond the white settlements is approaching to a happy consummation. Two important tribes have accepted the provision made for their removal ... and it is believed that their example will induce the remaining tribes also to seek the same obvious advantages.

The consequences of a speedy removal will be important to the United States, to individual States, and to the Indians themselves. ... It puts an end to all possible danger of collision between the authorities of the General and State governments on account of the Indians. It will place a dense and civilized population in large tracts of country now occupied by a few savage hunters. By opening the whole territory between Tennessee on the north and Louisiana on the south to the settlement of the whites it will incalculably strengthen the southwestern frontier and render the adjacent States strong enough to repel future invasions without remote aid. It will relieve the whole State of Mississippi and the western part of Alabama of Indian occupancy, and enable those States to advance rapidly in population, wealth and power. It will separate the Indians from immediate contact with settlements of whites; free them from the power of the States; enable them to pursue happiness in their own way and under their own rude institutions; will retard the progress of decay, which is lessening their numbers, and perhaps cause them gradually ... to cast off their savage habits and become an interesting, civilized, and Christian community. ...

Toward the aborigines of the country no one can indulge a more friendly feeling than myself, or would go further in attempting to reclaim them from their wandering habits and make them a happy, prosperous people. . . .

Humanity has often wept over the fate of the aborigines of this country. . . . To follow to the tomb the last of his race and to tread on the graves of extinct nations excite melancholy reflections. But true philanthropy reconciles the mind to these vicissitudes as it does to the extinction of one generation to make room for another. In the monuments and fortresses of an unknown people, spread over the extensive regions of the West, we behold the memorials of a once powerful race, which was exterminated or has disappeared to make room for the existing savage tribes. . . . What good man would prefer a country covered with forests and ranged by a few thousand savages to our extensive Republic, studded with cities, towns, and prosperous farms . . . and filled with all the blessings of liberty, civilization, and religion? . . .

Doubtless it will be painful to leave the graves of their fathers; but what do they more than our ancestors did or than our children are now doing? To better their condition in an unknown land our forefathers left all that was dear in earthly objects. . . . Can it be cruel in this Government when, by events which it can not control, the Indian is made discontented in his ancient home, to purchase his lands, to give him a new and extensive territory, to pay the expense of his removal, and support him a year in his new abode? How many thousands of our own people would gladly embrace the opportunity of removing to the West on such conditions!

Source: Second Annual Message, December 6, 1830, in James Richardson, ed., Messages and Papers of the Presidents (New York, n.d.), Vol. III, 1082–85.

"Manual-labor schools are what the Indian condition calls for"
T. Hartley Crawford (1838)

> The Commissioner of Indian Affairs spells out the directions of post-removal Indian policy: allotment of land to individual Indians, training in farming and handicrafts, and education in basic literacy.

The principal lever by which the Indians are to be lifted out of the mire of folly and vice in which they are sunk is education. The learning of the already civilized and cultivated man is not what they want now. . . . In the present state of their social existence, all they could be taught, or would learn, is to read and write, with a very limited knowledge of figures. . . . To teach a savage man to read, while he continues a savage in all else, is to

throw a seed on a rock. . . . If you would win an Indian from the wayward-
ness and idleness and vice of his life, you must improve his morals, as well
as his mind, and that not merely by precept, but by teaching him how to
farm, how to work in the mechanic arts, and how to labor profitably. . . .
Manual-labor schools are what the Indian condition calls for. . . .

Unless some system is marked out by which there shall be a separate
allotment of land to each individual whom the scheme shall entitle to it, you
will look in vain for any general casting off of savagism. Common property
and civilization cannot co-exist. . . . If . . . the large tracts of land set apart
for them shall continue to be joint property, the ordinary motive to industry
(and the most powerful one) will be wanting. . . . A few acres of badly cultivated corn about their cabins will be seen, instead of extensive fields, rich
pastures, and valuable stock. . . .

Source: *Senate Document No. 1, 25th Cong., 3rd. sess., serial 338, 450–56.*

"When compelled to face the stern necessities of life . . . he in a very short time becomes a changed being"
William Medill (1848)

*Already by 1848 it was clear to the Commissioner of Indian Affairs
that the area west of the Mississippi would not remain reserved for
Indians. He calls for a new policy: concentrating Indians on distinct
reservations.*

Stolid and unyielding in his nature, and inveterately wedded to the savage habits, customs, and prejudices in which he has been reared and trained,
it is seldom that the full blood Indian of our hemisphere can, in immediate
juxtaposition with the white population, be brought farther within the pale
of civilization than to adopt its vices; under the corrupting influences of
which, too indolent to labor, and too weak to resist, he soon sinks into misery and despair. . . . Cannot this sad and depressing tendency of things be
checked, and the past be at least measurably repaired by better results in the
future? . . .

The policy already begun and relied on to accomplish objects so momentous and so desirable to every Christian and philanthropist is, as rapidly
as it can safely and judiciously be done, to colonize our Indian tribes beyond
the reach, for some years, of our white population; confining each within a
small district of country, so that, as the game decreases and becomes scarce,
the adults will gradually be compelled to resort to agriculture and other
kinds of labor to obtain subsistence. . . . To establish, at the same time, a
judicious and well devised system of manual labor schools for the education

of the youth of both sexes in letters—the males in practical agriculture and the various necessary and useful mechanic arts, and the females in the different branches of housewifery, including spinning and weaving. . . .

The strongest propensities of an Indian's nature are his desire for war and his love of the chase. These lead him to display tact, judgment, and energy, and to endure great hardships, privation, and suffering; but in all other respects he is indolent and inert, physically and mentally. . . . But anything like labor is distasteful and utterly repugnant to his feelings and natural prejudices. He considers it a degradation. His subsistence and dress are obtained principally by means of the chase; and if this resource is insufficient, and it be necessary to cultivate the earth or to manufacture materials for dress, it has to be done by the women, who are their "hewers of wood and drawers of water." . . . When compelled to face the stern necessities of life and resort to labor for a maintenance, he in a very short time becomes a changed being. . . . Such is the experience in the cases of several of the tribes not long since colonized, who a few years ago were mere nomads and hunters. . . . The most marked change, however, when this transition takes place, is in the condition of the females. She who had been the drudge and the slave then begins to assume her true position as an equal; and her labor is transferred from the field to her household—to the care of her family and children. . . .

Source: House Executive Document No. 1, 30th Cong., 2d sess., serial 537, 385–89.

12.
RESISTANCE IN THE COURTS

The Cherokee people did not respond passively to President Andrew Jackson's efforts to evict them from their lands. They challenged the removal policy in court.

In 1828, the Cherokee living in Georgia tried to secure their lands by adopting a constitution. Georgia refused to recognize the document and declared that the Cherokee were subject to state laws. The Cherokee appealed to the Supreme Court, but in the case of Cherokee Nation v. Georgia, *the court ruled that it lacked jurisdiction, since the Cherokee were not a foreign nation as defined by the United States Constitution.*

"The motion for an injunction is denied"
Cherokee Nation v. Georgia (1831)

Though the Indians are acknowledged to have an unquestionable, and, heretofore, unquestioned right to the lands they occupy, until that right shall be extinguished by a voluntary cession to our government; yet it may well be doubted whether those tribes which reside within the acknowledged boundaries of the United States can, with strict accuracy, be denominated foreign nations. They may, more correctly, perhaps, be denominated domestic dependent nations. They occupy a territory to which we assert a title independent of their will, which must take effect in point of possession when their right of possession ceases. Meanwhile they are in a state of pupilage. Their relation to the United States resembles that of a ward to his guardian.

They look to our government for protection; rely upon its kindness and its power; appeal to it for relief to their wants; and address the president as their great father. They and their country are considered by foreign nations, as well as by ourselves, as being so completely under the sovereignty and dominion of the United States, that any attempt to acquire their lands, or to form a political connexion with them, would be considered by all as an invasion of our territory, and an act of hostility. . . .

If it be true that the Cherokee nation have rights, this is not the tribunal in which those rights are to be asserted. If it be true that wrongs have been inflicted, and that still greater are to be apprehended, this is not the tribunal which can redress the past or prevent the future.

The motion for an injunction is denied.

Source: 5 Peters 15–20 (1831).

"The Cherokee nation, then, is a distinct community . . . in which the laws of Georgia can have no force"
Worcester v. Georgia (1832)

In 1832, the year after Cherokee Nation v. Georgia, *the Cherokees won a legal victory in the Supreme Court. The state of Georgia had imprisoned Samuel A. Worcester, a religious missionary, for residing on Cherokee land in violation of a state law, which required him to obtain a permit and swear allegiance to the state. The court ruled on Worcester's behalf, declaring that the Cherokees were a distinct community "in which the laws of Georgia can have no force" and that the federal government had an obligation to enforce its treaty obligations.*

President Jackson refused to enforce the decision, and the state of Georgia began to distribute Cherokee lands to whites.

The treaties and laws of the United States contemplate the Indian territory as completely separated from that of the states; and provide that all intercourse with them shall be carried on exclusively by the government of the Union.

The Indian nations had always been considered as distinct, independent, political communities, retaining their original natural rights, as the undisputed possessors of the soil, from time immemorial. . . . The constitution, by declaring treaties already made, as well as those to be made, to be the supreme law of the land, has adopted and sanctioned the previous treaties with the Indian nations, and consequently, admits their rank among those powers who are capable of making treaties. . . .

The Cherokee nation, then, is a distinct community, occupying its own territory, with boundaries accurately described, in which the laws of Georgia can have no force, and which the citizens of Georgia have no right to enter, but with the assent of the Cherokees themselves, or in conformity with treaties, and with the acts of Congress. . . .

The act of the state of Georgia, under which the plaintiff in error was prosecuted, is consequently void, and the judgment a nullity.

Source: 315 U.S. 515 (1832).

13.
RESPONSES TO REMOVAL

"Shall . . . [we] live, or . . . be swept from the earth?"
Elias Boudinot (1826)

A Cherokee leader educated in white schools in North Carolina and Connecticut, Boudinot served as the first editor of the first Cherokee newspaper, the Cherokee Phoenix. *Initially, he was a bitter opponent of removal, but when the state of Georgia began distributing Cherokee lands to whites, he began to view removal as the only way for the Cherokee to survive as a unified people. In 1832 and 1835 he signed treaties of removal, and was assassinated in 1839 for alienating Cherokee lands.*

1843 painting of a gathering, attended by 10,000 delegates, in the new Cherokee capital in Oklahoma. *(Courtesy, Smithsonian Institution)*

What is an Indian? Is he not formed of the same materials with yourself? For "of one blood God created all the nations that dwell on the face of the earth." Though it be true that he is ignorant, that he is a heathen, that he is a savage; yet he is no more than all others have been under similar circumstances. Eighteen centuries ago what were the inhabitants of Great Britain?

You here behold an *Indian*, my kindred are *Indians*, and my fathers sleeping in the wilderness grave—they too were *Indians*. But I am not as my fathers were. . . . I have had greater advantages than most of my race; and I now stand before you delegated by my native country to seek her interest . . . and by my public efforts to assist in raising her to an equal standing with other nations of the earth. . . .

My design is to offer a few disconnected facts relative to the present improved states, and to the ultimate prospects of that particular tribe called Cherokees to which I belong. . . . At this time there are 22,000 cattle; 7,600 horses; 46,000 swine; 2,500 sheep; 762 looms; 2,488 spinning wheels; 172 waggons; 2,943 ploughs . . . 18 schools [in my nation]. . . . Yes, methinks I can view my native country, rising from the ashes of her degradation, wearing her purified and beautiful garments, and taking her seat with the nations of the earth. . . .

I ask you, shall red men live, or shall they be swept from the earth? With you and this public at large, the decision chiefly rests. Must they perish? Must they all, like the unfortunate Creeks, (victims of the unchristian policy of certain persons,) go down in sorrow to their grave?

They hang upon your mercy as to a garment. Will you push them from you, or will you save them? Let humanity answer.

Source: An Address to the Whites (Philadelphia, 1826).

"We must go forth as wanderers in a strange land!"
George W. Harkins (1832)

In a farewell letter to the American people, George Harkins, a Choctaw leader, denounces the evils of the removal policy.

But having determined to emigrate west of the Mississippi River this fall, I have thought proper in bidding you farewell, to make a few remarks of my views and the feelings that actuate me on the subject of our removal. . . .

We were hedged in by two evils, and we chose that which we thought least. Yet we could not recognize the right that the state of Mississippi had assumed to legislate for us. . . . Admitting that they understood the people, could they remove that mountain of prejudice that has ever obstructed the streams of justice, and prevented their salutary influence from reaching my devoted countrymen? We as Choctaws rather chose to suffer and be free, than live under the degrading influence of laws, where our voice could not be heard in their formation. . . .

Taking an example from the American government, and knowing the happiness which its citizens enjoy, under the influence of mild republican institutions, it is the intention of our countrymen to form a government assimilated to that of our white brethren in the United States, as nearly as their condition will permit. . . .

Friends, my attachment to my native land is strong—that cord is now broken; and we must go forth as wanderers in a strange land! . . .

Here is the land of our progenitors, and here are their bones; they left them as a sacred deposit, and we have been compelled to venerate its trust; it is dear to us yet we cannot stay. . . .

Source: American Indian (December, 1926).

"We have been . . . treated like dogs"
John Ross (1834)

John Ross, the principal Cherokee chief, was a leading opponent of removal.

Ever since [the whites came] we have been made to drink of the bitter cup of humiliation; treated like dogs . . . our country and the graves of our Fathers torn from us . . . through a period of upwards of 200 years, rolled back, nation upon nation [until] we find ourselves fugitives, vagrants and strangers in our own country. . . .

The existence of the Indian Nations as distinct independent communities within the limits of the United States seems to be drawing to a close. . . . You are aware that our Brethren, the Choctaws, Chickasaws and Creeks of the South have severally disposed of their country to the United States and that a portion of our own Tribe have also emigrated West of the Mississippi—but that the largest portion of our Nation still remain firmly upon our ancient domain. . . . Our position there may be compared to a solitary tree in an open space, where all the forest trees around have been prostrated by a furious tornado.

Source: Ross to Senecas, Apr. 14, 1834 in Gary E. Moulton, ed., *The Papers of John Ross* (Norman: University of Oklahoma, 1985), 1: 284–87.

"When taught to think and feel as the American citizen . . . they were to be *despoiled by their guardian*"
Memorial and Protest of the Cherokee Nation (1836)

In 1836, Chief John Ross submitted this memorial and protest to Congress, declaring that the treaties that supposedly justified Cherokee removal had been obtained by fraud.

. . . [T]he United States solemnly guaranteed to said nation all their lands not ceded, and pledged the faith of the government, that "all white people who have intruded, or may hereafter intrude on the lands reserved for the Cherokees, shall be removed by the United States. . . . " The Cherokees were happy and prosperous under a scrupulous observance of treaty stipulations by the government of the United States, and from the fostering hand extended over them, they made rapid advances in civilization, morals, and in the arts and sciences. Little did they anticipate, that when taught to think and feel as the American citizen, and to have with him a common interest, they were to be *despoiled by their guardian*, to become strangers and wanderers in the land of their fathers, forced to return to the savage life, and to seek a new home in the wilds of the far west, and that without their consent. An instrument purporting to be a treaty with the Cherokee people, has recently been made public by the President of the United States, that will have such an operation if carried into effect. This instrument, the delegation aver before the civilized world, and in the presence of Almighty God, is fraudulent, false upon its face, made by unauthorized individuals, without the sanction, and against the wishes, of the great body of the Cherokee people. Upwards of fifteen thousand of those people have protested against it, solemnly declaring they will never acquiesce.

_____

Source: House Executive Document No. 286, 24th Cong., 1st sess., 1–2.

14.
THE BLACK HAWK AND SEMINOLE WARS

The removal policy led to violence in the Old Northwest and in Florida. In 1829, the Fox and Sauk were removed to Iowa from their farms in northern Illinois. When a number of these people returned in 1832 to harvest their crops, the Black Hawk war erupted, named after a Sauk leader. The four month long conflict resulted in the deaths of some 70 white settlers and soldiers and between 400 and 500 Indians.

When the Seminoles were informed in 1835 that they must move from Florida to lands west of the Mississippi, or be forcibly removed, a faction led by Osceola (1800?–1838) refused to emigrate. A war erupted, which would last until 1842, and cost the United States approximately $30 million and 3,000 casualties. The conflict pitted a 10,000 man American force against about 1,000 Seminole warriors. The war's key event took place in the summer of 1837, when the Seminole leader was captured while attending a conference under a flag of truce. He died a prisoner in 1838.

"What *right* had these people to our village and our fields"
Black Hawk (1833)

Black Hawk (1767–1838), a Sauk leader, refused to accept a treaty that removed his people from their lands in Illinois. Mistakenly convinced that British Canada would support an attack on American settlements, he led a group of his people back into northern Illinois. In

A sketch of a battle during the Seminole War. *(Courtesy, Public Archives of Canada)*

his autobiography, he describes the causes of the Black Hawk War—and the conflict's gruesome conclusion, when many of his people were killed as they tried to flee across the Mississippi River.

The whites were settling the country fast. I was out one day hunting in a bottom, and met three white men. They accused me of killing their hogs. I denied it, but they would not listen to me. One of them took my gun out of my hand and fired it off—then took out the flint . . . and commenced beating me with sticks, and ordered me off. I was so much bruised that I could not sleep for several nights.

Some time after this occurrence, one of my camp cut a bee-tree, and carried the honey to his lodge. A party of white men soon followed, and told him that the bee-tree was theirs. . . . He pointed to the honey, and told them to take it. They were not satisfied with this, but took all the packs of skins that he had collected during the winter, to pay his trader and clothe his family in the spring, and carried them off! . . .

This summer our agent came to live at Rock Island. The trader explained to me the terms of a treaty that had been made, and said we would be obliged to leave the Illinois side of the Mississippi. . . .

During the winter, I received information that three families of whites had arrived at our village, and destroyed some of our lodges, and were making fences and dividing our cornfields for their own use. . . .

What *right* had these people to our village and our fields, which the

An 1833 painting, by John Jarvis, of Black Hawk (right) and his son as a prisoner of war. *(Courtesy, Gilcrease Institute)*

Great Spirit had given us to live upon? My reason teaches me that land cannot be sold. . . .

The white people brought whisky into our village, made our people drunk, and cheated them out of their horses, guns, and traps! . . .

It was ascertained that a great war chief [General E. P. Gaines], with a large number of soldiers, was on his way to Rock River. The war chief arrived, and convened a council at the agency. He said: "I hope you will consult your own interest and leave the country you are occupying, and go to the other side of the Mississippi."

I replied: "That we had never sold our country. We never received any annuities from our American father! And we are determined to hold on to our village!"

The war chief said: "I came here, neither to beg nor hire you to leave your village. My business is to remove you, peaceably if I can, but forcibly if I must! I will now give you two days to remove. . . ."

We crossed the Mississippi during the night. . . . The great war chief convened another council for the purpose of making a treaty with us. In this treaty, he agreed to give us corn in place of that we had left growing in our fields. I touched the goose quill to this treaty, and was determined to live in peace.

The corn that had been given us was soon found to be inadequate to our wants; when loud lamentations were heard in the camp, by our women and children, for their roasting-ears, beans, and squashes. To satisfy them, a small party of braves went over, in the night, to steal corn from their own fields. They were discovered by the whites and fired upon. Complaints were again made of the depredations committed by some of my people, *on their own corn fields!*

[Black Hawk's people returned to the Illinois side of the Mississippi to plant corn on Winnabago land; several clashes occurred between the Fox and Sauk and the Americans.]

I had resolved upon giving up the war—and sent a flag of peace to the American war chief, expecting, as a matter of right, reason, and justice that our flag would be respected. Yet instead I was forced into war, with about five hundred warriors, to contend against three or four thousand....

A party of whites, being in advance of the army, came upon our people, who were attempting to cross the Mississippi. They tried to give themselves up—the whites paid no attention to their entreaties—but commenced *slaughtering* them! In a little while the whole army arrived. Our braves, but few in number, finding that the enemy paid no regard to age or sex, and seeing that they were murdering helpless women and little children, determined to *fight until they were killed.* As many women as could, commenced swimming the Mississippi, with their children on their backs. A number of them were drowned, and some shot, before they could reach the opposite shore.

The massacre, which terminated the war, lasted about two hours. Our loss in killed, was about sixty, besides a number that were drowned.

Source: *Life of Ma-ka-tai-me-she-kia-kiak or Black Hawk, Dictated by Himself* (Cincinnati, 1833), 83–136.

"That was the last sun that shone on Black-hawk"
Black Hawk (1835)

After his capture, Black Hawk surrendered and delivered the following speech.

You have taken me prisoner with all my warriors. I am much grieved, for I expected, if I did not defeat you, to hold out much longer, and give you more trouble before I surrendered. I tried hard to bring you into ambush, but your last general understands Indian fighting. The first one was not so wise. When I saw that I could not beat you by Indian fighting, I determined to rush on you, and fight you face to face. I fought hard. But your guns were well aimed.... My warriors fell around me; it began to look dismal. I saw my evil day at hand. The sun rose dim on us in the morning, and at night it sunk in a dark cloud. . . . That was the last sun that shone on Black-hawk. His heart is dead. . . . He is now a prisoner to the white men; they will do with him as they wish. But he can stand torture, and is not afraid of death. He is no coward. Black-hawk is an Indian. . . .

Farewell, my nation! Black-hawk tried to save you, and avenge your wrongs. He drank the blood of some of the whites. He has been taken prisoner, and his plans are stopped. He can do no more. He is near his end. His sun is setting, and he will rise no more. Farewell to Black-hawk.

Source: Samuel G. Drake, *Biography and History of the Indians of North America* (Boston, 1841), 657.

"His tongue was forked; he lied and stung us"
Coacooche (1841)

> *Coacooche, a son of a major Seminole leader, was taken captive, along with Osceola, in 1837, during negotiations with the U.S. military. He and nineteen others escaped from an American prison in St. Augustine. He was finally forced to surrender in 1841, when he made the following statement.*

The Indians held out in the swampy Everglades of Florida in villages such as the one depicted here.

Oceola refuses to cede Seminole land. *(Courtesy, Public Archives of Canada)*

I saw the white man, and was told he was my enemy. I could not shoot him as I would a wolf or a bear; yet like these he came upon me; horses, cattle, and fields, he took from me. He said he was my friend; he abused our women and children, and told us to go from the land. Still he gave me his hand in friendship; we took it; whilst taking it, he had a snake in the other; his tongue was forked; he lied and stung us. I asked but for a small piece of these lands, enough to plant and to live upon, far south, a spot where I could place the ashes of my kindred, a spot only sufficient upon which I could lay my wife and child. This was not granted me. I was put in prison; I escaped. I have been again taken; you have brought me back; I am here; I feel the irons in my heart.... I wish now to have my band around me and go to Arkansas. You say I *must* end this war! Look at these irons! can I go to my warriors? Coacooche chained! No; do not ask me to see them. I never wish to tread upon my land unless I am free. If I can go to them *unchained,* they will follow me in ... they will surrender and emigrate.

Source: John T. Sprague, *The Origin, Progress, and Conclusion of the Florida War* (New York, 1848), Chapter 6.

Oceola, chief of the
Seminoles.

PART IV

RESISTANCE ON THE PLAINS

INTRODUCTION: Sitting Bull

Even in death he was the symbol of resistance to white authority. His name was Sitting Bull, and he was a chief and holy man of the Hunkpapa people, one of the tribes forming the Teton Sioux. During the 1840s and 1850s, his people engaged in intertribal warfare with the Shoshoni, Assiniboin, and Crow as each group sought to expand its hunting grounds. But in 1863 and 1864, federal troops sought to assert control over the Sioux following an uprising in Minnesota, and Sitting Bull participated in repeated clashes with these forces.

After some of the Teton Sioux made peace with the whites in 1868 in exchange for a reservation in the Black Hills, Sitting Bull was selected leader of those determined to maintain Sioux independence. To resist federal efforts to open the Black Hills to miners, he created a coalition of Plains tribes, and in the winter of 1875 repulsed an American force of 1,000 soldiers led by General George Crook. Ten days later, his warriors overwhelmed George Armstrong Custer and his men at the Battle of the Little Big Horn. Fearing federal retaliation, the Indian alliance broke into bands, and Sitting Bull led his people into Canada. Facing starvation, however, Sitting Bull surrendered in 1881. He traveled with Buffalo Bill's Wild West Show in 1885, then returned to his reservation. There, he opposed land sales—angering many whites.

Convinced that he was responsible for the spread of a religious revitalization movement, known as the Ghost Dance, Major James McLaughlin ordered Sitting Bull arrested. Early in the morning of December 15, 1890, during the arrest, gunfire erupted. Sitting Bull, his seventeen-year-old son, six of his followers, and six Indian police officers died.

Sitting Bull. *(Courtesy, Smithsonian Institution)*

15.

THE RESERVATION POLICY

"They be placed in positions where they can be controlled, and finally compelled by stern necessity to resort to agricultural labor or starve"
Luke Lea (1850)

> *In 1850, Indian Commissioner Luke Lea recommended that the government concentrate the Plains Indians on specific reservations. By reducing the amount of land available for hunting, he hoped to force these people to adopt a farming economy.*

Experience ... has conclusively shown that there is but one course of policy by which the great work of regenerating the Indian race may be effected. ... It is indispensably necessary that they be placed in positions where they can be controlled, and finally compelled by stern necessity to resort to agricultural labor or starve. Considering, as the untutored Indian does, that labor is a degradation, and there is nothing worthy of his ambition but prowess in war, success in the chase, and eloquence in council, it is only under such circumstances that his haughty pride can be subdued, and his wild energies trained to the more ennobling pursuits of civilized life. There should be assigned to each tribe, for a permanent home, a country adapted to agriculture, of limited extent and well-defined boundaries; within which all, with occasional exceptions, should be compelled constantly to remain until such time as their general improvement and good conduct may supersede the necessity of such restrictions. In the meantime the government should cause them to be supplied with stock, agricultural implements, and useful materials for clothing; encourage and assist them in the erection of comfortable dwellings, and secure to them the means and facilities of education, intellectual, moral, and religious. The application of their own funds to such purposes would be far better for them than the present system of paying their annuities in money, which does substantial good to but few, while to the great majority it only furnishes the means and incentive to vicious and depraving indulgence, terminating in destitution and misery, and too frequently in premature death.

Source: Senate Executive Document No. 1, 31st Cong., 2d sess, serial 587, 35–37.

16.
GREAT SIOUX UPRISING OF 1862

"All these things made many Indians dislike the whites"
Big Eagle (1894)

> *During the summer of 1862, Indian warfare broke out in southern*
> *Minnesota that left between 400 and 800 settlers and soldiers dead,*
> *and provoked military action against the Sioux in the Dakota Terri-*
> *tory. In this extract, Big Eagle describes the uprising's causes, includ-*
> *ing hunger, official corruption, and delayed annuity payments.*

The Indians bought goods of them [traders] on credit, and when the
government payments came the traders were on hand with their books,
which showed that the Indians owed so much and so much, and as the Indians kept no books they could not deny their accounts, but had to pay them,
and sometimes the traders got all their money. . . .

Then many of the white men often abused the Indians and treated them
unkindly. . . . Then some of the white men abused the Indian women in a
certain way and disgraced them, and surely there was no excuse for that.

All these things made many Indians dislike the whites. Then a little
while before the outbreak there was trouble among the Indians themselves.
Some of the Indians took a sensible course and began to live like white men.
The government built them houses, furnished them tools, seed, etc., and
taught them to farm. . . . Others stayed in their tepees. There was a white
man's party and an Indian party. . . .

As the summer advanced, there was great trouble among the Sioux—
troubles among themselves, troubles with the whites. . . . The war with the
South was going on then, and a great many men had left the state and had
gone down there to fight. . . . We understood that the South was getting the
best of the fight, and it was said that the North would be whipped. . . .

It began to be whispered about that now would be a good time to go to
war with the whites and get back the lands. It was believed that the men
who had enlisted last had all left the state, and that before help could be sent
the Indians could clean out the country, and that the Winnebagoes, and
even the Chippewas, would assist the Sioux. It was also thought that a war
with the whites would cause the Sioux to forget the troubles among themselves and enable many of them to pay off some old scores. . . .

But after the first talk of war the counsels of the peace Indians prevailed,
and many of us thought the danger had all blown over. The time of the government payment was near at hand, and this may have had something to do
with it. . . . The crops that had been put in by the "farmer" Indians were

Sioux tipis captured after the 1862 uprising. *(Courtesy, Minnesota Historical Society)*

looking well, and there seemed to be a good prospect for a plentiful supply of provisions for them the coming winter without having to depend on the game of the country or without going far out to the west on the plains for buffalo. . . . The "farmers" were favored by the government in every way. They had houses built for them, some of them even had brick houses, and they were not allowed to suffer. The other Indians did not like this. They were envious of them and jealous, and disliked them because they had gone back on the customs of the tribe and because they were favored. They called them "farmers," as if it was disgraceful to be a farmer. They called them "cut-hairs," because they had given up the Indian fashion of wearing the hair, and "breeches men," because they wore pantaloons. . . .

At last the time for the payment came and the Indians came in to the agencies to get their money. But the paymaster did not come, and week after week went by and still he did not come. . . . Somebody told the Indians that the payment would never be made. The government was in a great war, and gold was scarce, and paper money had taken its place, and it was said the gold could not be had to pay us. . . . Still, most of us thought the trouble would pass. . . .

You know how the war started—by the killing of some white people [three men and two women] near Acton, in Meeker County. . . . [W]ar was now declared. Blood had been shed, the payment would be stopped, and the whites would take a dreadful vengeance because women had been killed. . . . [S]oon the cry was "Kill the whites and kill all these cut-hairs who will not join us." . . . Little Crow gave orders to attack the agency early next morning and to kill all the traders. . . .

Source: "A Sioux Story of the War," Minnesota Historical Society, Collections, 6 (1894).

17.
THE SAND CREEK MASSACRE

"The soldiers scalped the dead"
George Bent (1864)

> The discovery of gold in the Pike's Peak region of Colorado ignited a rush of tens of thousands of miners onto Indian lands. The Arapaho and Cheyenne retaliated by raiding white settlements from 1861 to 1864. By the end of 1864, the Indian raids had been suppressed, and a group of Cheyenne sought government protection. The Third Colorado Volunteers under Colonel John Chivington attacked the Cheyenne November 29, 1864, killing between 200 and 450 Indians. George Bent offers an eyewitness account of the massacre.

When I looked toward the chief's lodge, I saw that Black Kettle had a large American flag up on a long lodgepole as a signal to the troops that the camp was friendly. . . . Black Kettle kept calling out not to be frightened; that the camp was under protection and there was no danger. Then suddenly the troops opened fire on this mass of men, women, and children, and all began to scatter and run.

The main body of Indians rushed up the bed of the creek, which was dry, level sand with only a few little pools of water here and there. . . . As we went along we passed many Indians, men, women, and children, some wounded, others dead, lying on the sand and in pools of water. Presently we came to a place where the main party had stopped, and were now hiding in pits that they had dug in the high bank of the stream. . . .

The soldiers concentrated their fire on the people in the pits, and we fought back as well as we could with guns and bows, but we had only a few guns. The troops did not rush in and fight hand to hand, but once or twice after they had killed many of the men in a certain pit, they rushed in and finished up the work, killing the wounded and the women and children that had not been hurt. The fight here was kept up until nearly sundown, when at last the commanding officer called off the men. . . . As they went back, the soldiers scalped the dead lying in the bed of the stream and cut up the bodies. . . .

Source: George Bird Grinnell, *The Fighting Cheyennes* (Norman: University of Oklahoma, 1956), 177–80.

"Men, women, and children were indiscriminately slaughtered"
Joint Committee on the Conduct of the War (1864)

A joint congressional committee conducted an investigation of the Sand Creek massacre and issued its report in 1864. This extract describes the events that occurred at Sand Creek.

In the summer of 1864 Governor Evans, of Colorado Territory, . . . sent notice to the various bands and tribes of Indians within his jurisdiction that such as desired to be considered friendly to the whites should at once repair to the nearest military post in order to be protected from the soldiers who were to take the field against the hostile Indians. . . .

Upon observing the approach of the soldiers, Black Kettle, the head chief, ran up to the top of his lodge an American flag . . . with a small white flag under it, as he had been advised to do in case he met with any troops on the prairies. Mr. Smith, the interpreter, supposing that they might be strange

The Sand Creek Massacre. *(Courtesy, Minnesota Historical Society)*

troops, unaware of the character of the Indians encamped there, advanced from his lodge to meet them, but was fired upon, and returned to his lodge.

And then the scene of murder and barbarity began—men, women, and children were indiscriminately slaughtered. In a few minutes all the Indians were flying over the plain in terror and confusion. A few who endeavored to hide themselves under the bank of the creek were surrounded and shot down in cold blood, offering but feeble resistance. From the sucking babe to the old warrior, all who were overtaken were deliberately murdered. Not content with killing women and children, who were incapable of offering any resistance, the soldiers indulged in acts of barbarity of the most revolting character; such, it is to be hoped, as never before disgraced the acts of men claiming to be civilized. No attempt was made by the officers to restrain the savage cruelty of the men under their command, but they stood by and witnessed these acts without one word of reproof, if they did not incite their commission. For more than two hours the work of murder and barbarity was continued, until more than one hundred dead bodies, three fourths of them women and children, lay on the plain as evidences of the fiendish malignity and cruelty of the officers who had so sedulously and carefully plotted the massacre, and of the soldiers who had so faithfully acted out the spirit of their officers. . . .

It is true that there seems to have existed among the people inhabiting that region of country a hostile feeling towards the Indians. Some of the Indians had committed acts of hostility towards the whites; but no effort seems to have been made by the authorities there to prevent these hostilities, other than by the commission of even worse acts. The hatred of the whites to the Indians would seem to have been inflamed and excited to the utmost; the bodies of persons killed at a great distance—whether by Indians or not, is not certain—were brought to the capital of the Territory and exposed to the public gaze for the purpose of inflaming still more the already excited feeling of the people. Their cupidity was appealed to, for the governor in a proclamation calls upon all, "either individually or in such parties as they may organize," "to kill and destroy as enemies of the country, wherever they may be found, all such hostile Indians," authorizing them to "hold to their own private use and benefit all the property of said hostile Indians that they may capture."

Source: 39th Congress, 2nd Session, U.S. Senate, Reports of Committees, No. 156.

18.
NEW DIRECTIONS IN GOVERNMENT POLICY

"The irrepressible conflict between a superior and an inferior race"
The Doolittle Committee (1867)

A joint congressional committee assesses the causes of the many outbreaks of violence between whites and Indians on the Great Plains.

The committee have arrived at the following conclusions:
First. The Indians everywhere, with the exception of the tribes within the Indian Territory, are rapidly decreasing in numbers from various causes: By disease; by intemperance; by wars, among themselves and with whites; by the steady and resistless emigration of white men into the territories of the west, which, confining the Indians to still narrower limits, destroys that game which, in their normal state, constitutes their principal means of subsistence; and by the irrepressible conflict between a superior and an inferior race when brought in presence of each other. . . .
Second. The committee are of opinion that in a large majority of cases Indian wars are to be traced to the aggressions of lawless white men, always

Fort Laramie, Wyoming, which served as a trading center. *(Courtesy, University of Oklahoma)*

to be found upon the frontier, or boundary line between savage and civilized life. . . .

From whatever cause wars may be brought on, either between different Indian tribes or between the Indians and the whites, they are very destructive, not only of the lives of the warriors engaged in it, but of the women and children also, often becoming a war of extermination. . . .

Third. Another potent cause of their decay is to be found in the loss of their hunting grounds and in the destruction of that game upon which the Indian subsists. This cause, always powerful, has of late greatly increased. . . . The discovery of gold and silver in California, and in all the mountain territories, poured a flood of hardy and adventurous miners across those planes. . . .

Two lines of railroad are rapidly crossing the plains. . . . They will soon reach the Rocky Mountains, crossing the centre of the great buffalo range in two lines from east to west. It is to be doubted if the buffalo in his migrations will many times cross a railroad where trains are passing and repassing, and with the disappearance of the buffalo from this immense region, all the powerful tribes of the plains will inevitably disappear. . . .

Source: Senate Report No. 156, 39th Cong., 2d sess, serial 1279, 3–10.

"Nobody pays any attention to Indian matters"
Report of the Indian Peace Commission (1868)

To combat the white–Indian warfare on the Plains, Congress created a special peace commission. The commission deplored public ignorance and apathy toward the Indian problem and denounced settlers and railroad companies for failing to recognize the Indians' humanity.

... Nobody pays any attention to Indian matters. This is a deplorable fact. Members of Congress understand the Negro question, and talk learnedly of finance, and other problems of political economy, but when the progress of settlement reaches the Indian's home, the only question considered is, "how best to get his lands." When they are obtained the Indian is lost sight of. While our missionary societies and benevolent associations have annually collected thousands of dollars from the charitable, to be sent to Asia and Africa for purposes of civilization, scarcely a dollar is expended or a thought bestowed on the civilization of Indians at our very doors. Is it because the Indians are not worth the effort at civilization? Or is it because

The signing of a treaty at Fort Laramie in 1868, which promised that the Sioux could keep the Black Hills. *(Courtesy, U.S. Signal Corps)*

our people, who have grown rich in the occupation of their former lands—too often taken by force or procured by fraud—will not contribute? . . .

The white and Indian must mingle together and jointly occupy the country, or one of them must abandon it. If they could have lived together, the Indian by this contact would soon have become civilized and war would have been impossible. . . . What prevented their living together? First. The antipathy of race. Second. The difference of customs and manners arising from their tribal or clannish organization. Third. The difference in language, which, in a great measure, barred intercourse and a proper understanding each of the other's motives and intentions.

Now by educating the children of these tribes in the English language these differences would have disappeared, and civilization would have followed at once. Nothing then would have been left but the antipathy of race, and that too is always softened in the beams of a higher civilization. . . .

To maintain peace with the Indian, let the frontier settler treat him with humanity, and railroad directors see to it that he is not shot down by employees in wanton cruelty. In short, if settlers and railroad men will treat Indians as they would treat whites under similar circumstances, we apprehend but little trouble will exist.

Source: House Executive Document No. 97, 49th Cong., 2d sess, serial 1337, 15–17.

"A shameful record of broken treaties and unfulfilled promises"
Report of the Board of Indian Commissioners (1869)

> *In this report, the Indian commissioners issued a stinging indictment of previous government policies toward Indians. The commissioners then recommended that tribal lands be allotted to individual Indians, that Indian children be educated to become American citizens, and that the government no longer make treaties with Indian tribes— recommendations that would be put into effect later in the century.*

The history of the government's connections with the Indians is a shameful record of broken treaties and unfulfilled promises.

The history of the border white man's connection with the Indians is a sickening record of murder, outrage, robbery, and wrongs committed by the former as the rule, and occasional savage outbreaks and unspeakably barbarous acts of retaliation by the latter as the exception. . . .

The testimony of some of our highest military officers of the United States is on record to the effect that, in our Indian wars, almost without exception, the first aggressions have been made by the white man. . . . In addition to the class of robbers and outlaws who find impunity in their nefarious pursuits upon the frontiers, there is a large class of professedly reputable men who use every means in their power to bring on Indian wars, for the sake of the profit to be realized from the presence of troops and the expenditure of government funds in their midst. They proclaim death to the Indians at all times, in words and publications, making no distinction between the innocent and the guilty. . . .

Paradoxical as it may seem, the white man has been the chief obstacle in the way of Indian civilization. . . . The soldiers, sent for their protection, too often carried demoralization and disease into their midst. The agent, appointed to be their friend and counsellor, business manager, and the almoner of the government bounties, frequently went among them only to enrich himself in the shortest possible time, at the cost of the Indians, and spend the largest available sum of the government money with the least ostensible beneficial result. . . .

The policy of collecting the Indian tribes upon small reservations . . . seems to be the best that can be devised. . . . When upon the reservation they should be taught as soon as possible the advantage of individual ownership of property; and should be given land in severalty as soon as it is desired by any of them, and the tribal relations should be discouraged. . . . The titles should be inalienable from the family of the holder for at least two or three generations. The civilized tribes now in the Indian territory should be taxed, and made citizens of the United States as soon as possible.

The treaty system should be abandoned, and as soon as any just method can be devised to accomplish it, existing treaties should be abrogated.

The legal status of the uncivilized Indians should be that of wards of the government; the duty of the latter being to protect them, to educate them in industry, the arts of civilization, and the principles of Christianity; elevate them to the rights of citizenship, and to sustain and clothe them until they can support themselves.

The payment of money annuities to the Indians should be abandoned, for the reason that such payments encourage idleness and vice, to the injury of those whom it is intended to benefit. Schools should be established, and teachers employed by the government to introduce the English language in every tribe. It is believed that many of the difficulties with Indians occur from misunderstanding as to the meaning and intention of either party. The teachers employed should be nominated by some religious body having a mission nearest to the location of the school. The establishment of Christian missions should be encouraged, and their schools fostered. The pupils should at least receive the rations and clothing they would get if remaining with their families. The religion of our blessed Saviour is believed to be the most effective agent for the civilization of any people.

Source: Annual Report of the Board of Indian Commissioners (Washington, 1869), 5–11.

"They have become falsely impressed with the notion of national independence"
Ely S. Parker (1869)

> *Ely S. Parker, the first Indian to serve as United States Commissioner of Indian Affairs, was a member of the Seneca. He served as General Ulysses S. Grant's secretary during the Civil War and as a brigadier general after the war. Grant named him Indian Commissioner in 1869. In this report, Parker calls for an end to treaty-making with Indian tribes because the two parties are unequal in power. Two years later, Congress ceased making treaties with Indian tribes.*

. . . It has become a matter of serious import whether the treaty system in use ought longer to be continued. In my judgment it should not. A treaty involves the idea of a compact between two or more sovereign powers, each possessing sufficient authority and force to compel a compliance with the obligations incurred. The Indian tribes of the United States are not sovereign nations, capable of making treaties. . . . They are held to be the wards of the government, and the only title the law concedes to them to the lands they occupy or claim is a mere possessory one. But, because treaties have been made with them, . . . they have become falsely impressed with the notion of national independence. It is time that this idea should be dispelled, and the government cease the cruel farce of thus dealing with its helpless and ignorant wards.

Source: House Executive Document No. 1, 41st Cong., 2d sess., serial 1414, 448.

19.
THE BATTLE OF THE LITTLE BIG HORN

"One whose cruel and ferocious nature far exceeds that of any wild beast of the desert"
Colonel George Armstrong Custer (1874)

> *Even though he graduated last in his class at the United States Military Academy, George Armstrong Custer quickly rose through the military ranks during the Civil War, becoming a brigadier general at 23 and a major general at 25 [after the war, many soldiers saw their ranks reduced]. He achieved fame as an Indian fighter when he joined the Seventh Cavalry in 1866. In this quotation from his autobiography, Custer expresses his view of Indians.*

Stripped of the beautiful romance with which we have been so long willing to envelope him, transferred from the inviting pages of the novelist to the localities where we are compelled to meet with him, in his native village, on the war path, and when raiding our frontier settlements and lines of travel, the Indian forfeits his claim to the appellation of the *"noble* red man." We see him as he is, and, so far as all knowledge goes, as he ever has been, a savage in every sense of the word; not worse, perhaps than his white brother would be similarly born and bred, but one whose cruel and ferocious nature far exceeds that of any wild beast of the desert.

Source: George Armstrong Custer, *My Life on the Plains* (New York, 1874), 163–65.

"All the soldiers were now killed"
Two Moons (1876)

> *A Cheyenne participant offers a firsthand account of the Battle of the Little Big Horn, where Colonel George Armstrong Custer was killed along with about 264 of his men.*

We traveled far, and one day we met a big camp of Sioux at Charcoal Butte. We camped with the Sioux, and had a good time, plenty grass, plenty game, good water. Crazy Horse was head chief of the camp. Sitting Bull was camped a little ways below, on the Little Missouri River.

Crazy Horse said to me, "I'm glad you are come. We are going to fight the white man again."

The camp was already full of wounded men, women, and children.

I said to Crazy Horse, "All right. I am ready to fight. I have fought already. My people have been killed, my horses stolen; I am satisfied to fight."...

About May, when the grass was tall and the horses strong, we broke camp and started across the country to the mouth of the Tongue River. Then Sitting Bull and Crazy Horse and all went up the Rosebud. There we had a big fight with General Crook, and whipped him. Many soldiers were killed—few Indians. It was a great fight, much smoke and dust.

From there we all went over the divide, and camped in the valley of Little Horn. Everybody thought, "Now we are out of the white man's country. He can live there, we will live here." After a few days, one morning when I was in camp north of Sitting Bull, a Sioux messenger rode up and said, "Let everybody paint up, cook, and get ready for a big dance."

Cheyennes then went to work to cook, cut up tobacco, and get ready. We all thought to dance all day. We were very glad to think we were far away from the white man.

Custer's Last Stand. *(Courtesy, Anheuser-Busch, Inc.)*

I went to water my horses at the creek, and washed them off with cool water, then took a swim myself. I came back to the camp afoot. When I got near my lodge, I looked up the Little Horn towards Sitting Bull's camp. I saw a great dust rising. It looked like a whirlwind. Soon Sioux horseman came rushing into camp shouting, "Soldiers come! Plenty white soldiers."...

I got on my horse, and rode out into my camp. I called out to the people all running about: "I am Two Moons, your chief. Don't run away. Stay here and fight. You must stay and fight the white soldiers. I shall stay even if I am to be killed."...

While I was sitting on my horse I saw flags come up over the hill to the east.... Then the soldiers rose all at once, all on horses.... They formed into three bunches with a little ways between. Then a bugle sounded, and they all got off horses, and some soldiers led the horses back over the hill.

Then the Sioux rode up the ridge on all sides, riding very fast. The Cheyennes went up the left way. Then the shooting was quick, quick. Pop-pop-pop very fast. Some of the soldiers were down on their knees, some standing. Officers all in front. The smoke was like a great cloud, and everywhere the Sioux went the dust rose like smoke. We circled all round him— swirling like water round a stone. We shoot, we ride fast, we shoot again. Soldiers drop, and horses fall on them. Soldiers in line drop, but one man rides up and down the line—all the time shouting. He rode a sorrel horse with white face and white fore-legs. I don't know who he was. He was a brave man.

Indians kept swirling round and round, and the soldiers killed only a few. Many soldiers fell. At last all horses killed but five. Once in a while some man would break out and run toward the river, but he would fall. At last about a hundred men and five horsemen stood on the hill all bunched together. All along the bugler kept blowing his commands. He was very brave too. Then a chief was killed. I hear it was Long Hair [George Armstrong Custer], I don't know; and then the five horsemen and the bunch of men, maybe so forty, started toward the river. The man on the sorrel horse led them, shouting all the time. He wore a buckskin shirt, and had long black hair and mustache. He fought hard with a big knife. His men were all covered with white dust. I couldn't tell whether they were officers or not. One man all alone ran far down toward the river, then round up over the hill. I thought he was going to escape, but a Sioux fired and hit him in the head. . . .

All the soldiers were now killed, and the bodies were stripped. After that no one could tell which were officers. The bodies were left where they fell. We had no dance that night. We were sorrowful.

Next day four Sioux chiefs and two Cheyennes and I, Two Moons, went upon the battlefield to count the dead. One man carried a little bundle of sticks. When we came to dead men, we took a little stick and gave it to another man, so we counted the dead. There were 388. There were thirty-nine Sioux and seven Cheyennes killed, and about a hundred wounded.

Some white soldiers were cut with knives, to make sure they were dead; and the war women had mangled some. Most were left just where they fell.

Source: McClure's Magazine (September, 1898).

20.
CHIEF JOSEPH

"I could not bear to see my wounded men and women suffer any longer"
Chief Joseph (1879)

> *His is one of the most heart wrenching stories in all of American history. Ordered to move from the Wallowa Valley of Oregon to a reservation in Idaho, Chief Joseph, a leader of the Nez Percé, decided to flee to Canada. He and his followers—55 warriors and about 300 women, children, and aged, traveled for four months across 1200 miles, through Idaho and Montana, before being forced to surrender just 40 miles from the Canadian border. Here, he describes his retreat.*

Chief Joseph of the
Nez Percés. *(Courtesy,
Smithsonian Institution)*

For a short time we lived quietly. But this could not last. White men had found gold in the mountains around the land of winding water. They stole a great many horses from us, and we could not get them back because we were Indians. The white men told lies for each other. They drove off a great many of our cattle. Some white men branded our young cattle so they could claim them. . . .

On account of the treaty made by the other bands of the Nez Percés, the white men claimed my lands. We were troubled greatly by white men crowding over the line. . . .

Nearly every year the agent came over from Lapwai and ordered us on to the reservation. We always replied that we were satisfied to live in Wallowa. We were careful to refuse the presents or annuities which he offered. . . .

Year after year we have been threatened, but no war was made upon my people until General [Oliver Otis] Howard came to our country two years ago and told us that he was the white war-chief of all that country. . . .

I said to General Howard: . . . "I do not believe that the Great Spirit Chief gave one kind of men the right to tell another kind of men what they must do."

General Howard replied: "You deny my authority, do you? You want to dictate to me, do you?" . . .

[Several days later] General Howard informed me, in a haughty spirit, that he would give my people *thirty days* to go back home, collect all their stock, and move on to the reservation, saying, "If you are not here in that time, I shall consider that you want to fight, and will send my soldiers to drive you on."

I said: "War can be avoided, and it ought to be avoided. I want no war. . . . I can not get ready to move in thirty days. Our stock is scattered, and Snake River is very high. Let us wait until fall, then the river will be low. We want time to hunt up our stock and gather supplies for winter." . . .

General Howard refused to allow me more than thirty days to move my people and their stock. . . .

We gathered all the stock we could find, and made an attempt to move. We left many of our horses and cattle in Wallowa, and we lost several hundred in crossing the river. . . . Many of the Nez Percés came together in Rocky Canyon to hold a grand council. . . . This council lasted ten days. There was a great deal of war-talk, and a great deal of excitement. There was one young brave present whose father had been killed by a white man five years before. . . . He left the council calling for revenge. . . .

I was leaving the council . . . when news came that the young man whose father had been killed had gone out with several other hot-blooded young braves and killed four white men. . . . I saw that the war could not then be prevented. The time had passed. I counseled peace from the begin-

Chief Joseph sat for this portrait while he was on his way to Oklahoma after his surrender. *(Courtesy, Smithsonian Institution)*

ning. I knew that we were too weak to fight the United States. We had many grievances, but I knew that war would bring more. . . .

We moved over to White Bird Creek, sixteen miles away, and there encamped, intending to collect our stock before leaving; but the soldiers attacked us, and the first battle was fought. We numbered in the battle sixty men, and the soldiers a hundred. The fight lasted but a few minutes. . . . They lost thirty-three killed, and had seven wounded. When an Indian fights, he only shoots to kill; but soldiers shoot at random. . . .

Seven days after the first battle, General Howard arrived in the Nez Percés country, bringing seven hundred more soldiers. It was now war in earnest. . . .

[Several days later] he attacked us with three hundred and fifty soldiers and settlers. We had two hundred and fifty warriors. The fight lasted twenty-seven hours. We lost four killed and several wounded. General Howard's loss was twenty-nine men killed and sixty wounded. . . .

Finding that we were outnumbered, we retreated to Bitter Root Valley.

Here another body of soldiers came upon us and demanded our surrender. We refused. . . . We then made a treaty with these soldiers. We agreed not to molest any one, and they agreed that we might pass through the Bitter Root country in peace. We bought provisions and traded stock with white men there.

We understood that there was to be no more war. We intended to go peaceably to the buffalo country, and leave the question of returning to our country to be settled afterward. . . .

[A few days later] the soldiers surrounded our camp. About daybreak one of my men went out to look after his horses. The soldiers saw him and shot him down like a coyote. . . . We had a hard fight. . . . In the fight . . . we lost fifty women and children and thirty fighting men. . . .

Several days passed. . . . We had repulsed each [army] in turn, and began to feel secure, when another army, under General Miles, struck us. This was the fourth army, each of which outnumbered our fighting force, that we encountered within sixty days.

We had no knowledge of General Miles's army until a short time before he made a charge upon us, cutting our camp in two, and capturing nearly all of our horses. About seventy men, myself among them, were cut off. . . .

I thought of my wife and children, who were now surrounded by soldiers, and I resolved to go to them or die. With a prayer in my mouth to the Great Spirit Chief who rules above, I dashed unarmed through the line of soldiers . . . but I was not hurt. . . .

My people were divided about surrendering. We could have escaped from Bear Paw Mountain if we had left our wounded, old women, and children behind. We were unwilling to do this. . . .

I could not bear to see my wounded men and women suffer any longer; we had lost enough already. General Miles had promised that we might return to our own country with what stock we had left. . . . I believed General Miles, or *I never would have surrendered*. I have heard that he has been censured for making the promise to return us to Lapwai. . . .

On the fifth day I went to General Miles and gave up my gun, and said, "From where the sun now stands I will fight no more." . . .

We gave up all our horses—over eleven hundred—and all our saddles—over one hundred—and we have not heard from them since. . . .

You might as well expect the rivers to run backward as that any man who was born a free man should be contented when penned up and denied liberty to go where he pleases. . . . If you pen an Indian up on a small spot of earth, and compel him to stay there, he will not be contented, nor will he grow and prosper.

Source: North American Review (April, 1879).

"I will fight no more forever"
Chief Joseph (1877)

According to General Oliver Otis Howard, Chief Joseph announced his surrender with the following poignant words.

I am tired of fighting. Our chiefs are killed. . . . The old men are all dead. . . . It is cold and we have no blankets. The little children are freezing to death. My people, some of them, have run away to the hills, and have no blankets, no food; no one knows where they are—perhaps freezing to death. I want to have time to look for my children and see how many of them I can find. Maybe I shall find them among the dead. Hear me, my chiefs. I am tired; my heart is sick and sad. From where the sun now stands I will fight no more forever.

Source: Annual Report of the Secretary of War . . . for the Fiscal Year Ending June 30, 1877, 630–31.

21.
THE GHOST DANCE AND THE WOUNDED KNEE MASSACRE

WOVOKA AND THE GHOST DANCE
"He told us . . . that all our dead were to be resurrected"
Porcupine (1896)

In 1889, a Paiute named Wovoka began to preach a religious doctrine that combined elements of Christianity and traditional Indian beliefs. He promised that if the Indians followed a special ritual whites would disappear and the dead would return. In this extract, Porcupine, a member of the Cheyenne nation, describes Wovoka's teachings.

He said: "I am the man who made everything you see around you. I am not lying to you, my children. I made this earth and everything on it. I have been to heaven and seen your dead friends and have seen my own father and mother. In the beginning, after God made the earth, they sent me back to teach the people, and when I came back on earth the people were afraid of me and treated me badly. This is what they did to me [showing his scars]. I did not try to defend myself. I found my children were bad, so went back to heaven and left them. My father told me the earth was getting old and worn out, and the people getting bad, and that I was to renew everything as it used to be, and make it better."

He told us also that all our dead were to be resurrected; that they were all to come back to earth, and that as the earth was too small for them and us, he would do away with heaven, and make the earth itself large enough to contain us all; that we must tell all the people we meet about these things. He spoke to us about fighting, and said that was bad, and we must keep from it; that the earth was to be all good hereafter, and we must all be friends with one another. He said that in the fall of the year the youth of all the good people would be renewed, so that nobody would be more than 40 years old, and that if they behaved themselves well after this the youth of everyone would be renewed in the spring. He said if we were all good he would send people among us who could heal all our wounds and sickness by mere touch, and that we would live forever. . . .

Source: *Fourteenth Annual Report of the Bureau of American Ethnology* (1896), Part 2, 793–96.

"Even our little ponies were taken away"
Red Cloud (1891)

A member of the Oglala Sioux describes the pattern of conflict be-tween Indians and the government that contributed to the rise of the Ghost Dance religion.

Everybody seems to think that the belief in the coming of the Messiah has caused all the trouble. This is a mistake. I will tell you the cause.

When we first made treaties with the Government . . . the Government promised us all the means necessary to make our living out of our land, and to instruct us how to do it, and abundant food to support us until we could take care of ourselves. We looked forward with hope to the time when we could be as independent as the whites, and have a voice in the Government.

The officers of the army could have helped us better than any others, but we were not left to them. An Indian Department was made, with a large number of agents and other officials drawing large salaries, and these men were supposed to teach us the ways of the whites. Then came the beginning of trouble. These men took care of themselves but not of us. It was made very hard to deal with the Government except through them. . . . We did not get the means to work our land. . . . Our rations began to be reduced. . . .

Remember that even our little ponies were taken away under the prom-

The Ghost Dance. *(Courtesy, Library of Congress)*

ise that they would be replaced by oxen and large horses, and that it was long before we saw any, and then we got very few. . . . Great efforts were made to break up our customs, but nothing was done to introduce the customs of the whites. Everything was done to break the power of the real chiefs, who really wished their people to improve, and little men, so-called chiefs, were made to act as disturbers and agitators. Spotted Tail wanted the ways of the whites, and a cowardly assassin was found to remove him. . . .

Rations were further reduced, and we were starving. . . . The people were desperate from starvation—they had no hope. They did not think of fighting. What good would it do? They might die like men, but what would all the women and children do? Some say they saw the son of God. All did not see Him. I did not see Him. . . . We doubted it, because we saw neither Him nor His works. . . .

We were faint with hunger and maddened by despair. We held our dying children, and felt their little bodies tremble as their souls went out and left only a dead weight in our hands. . . . There was no hope on earth, and God seemed to have forgotten us. Some one had again been talking of the Son of God, and said He had come. The people did not know; they did not care. They snatched at the hope. They screamed like crazy men to Him for mercy. They caught at the promises they heard He had made.

The white men were frightened, and called for soldiers. . . . We heard that soldiers were coming. We did not fear. We hoped that we could tell them our troubles and get help. A white man said the soldiers meant to kill us. We did not believe it, but some were frightened and ran away to the Bad

The Ghost Dance ritual among the Arapahos. *(Courtesy, Smithsonian Institution)*

Lands. The soldiers came. They said: "Don't be afraid; we come to make peace, and not war." It was true. They brought us food, and did not threaten us.

Source: W. Fletcher Johnson, *Life of Sitting Bull and History of the Indian War* (Philadelphia, 1891), 460–67.

"The code of morals as practiced by the white race will not compare with the morals of the Indians"
Masse Hadjo (1890)

> *In the* Chicago Tribune, *Masse Hadjo, a member of the Sioux, defended the Ghost Dance religion.*

You say, "If the United States army would kill a thousand or so of the dancing Indians there would be no more trouble." I judge by the above language you are a "Christian," and are disposed to do all in your power to advance the cause of Christ. You are doubtless a worshiper of the white man's Saviour, but are unwilling that the Indians should have a "Messiah" of their own.

The Indians have never taken kindly to the Christian religion as preached and practiced by the whites. Do you know why this is the case? Because the Good Father of all has given us a better religion—a religion that is all good and no bad, a religion that is adapted to our wants. You say if we are good, obey the Ten Commandments and never sin any more, we may be permitted eventually to sit upon a white rock and sing praises to God forevermore, and look down upon our heathen fathers, mothers, brothers and sisters who are howling in hell.

It won't do. The code of morals as practiced by the white race will not compare with the morals of the Indians. We pay no lawyers or preachers, but we have not one-tenth part of the crime that you do. If our Messiah does come we shall not try to force you into our belief. We will never burn innocent women at the stake or pull men to pieces with horses because they refuse to join in our ghost dances. . . . You are anxious to get hold of our Messiah, so you can put him in irons. This you may do—in fact, you may crucify him as you did that other one, but you cannot convert the Indians to the Christian religion until you contaminate them with the blood of the white man. The white man's heaven is repulsive to the Indian nature, and if the white man's hell suits you, why, you keep it. I think there will be white rogues enough to fill it.

Source: "An Indian on the Messiah Craze," *Chicago Tribune,* December 5, 1890.

WOUNDED KNEE MASSACRE

"Women and children of course were strewn all along the circular village"
Turning Hawk, Spotted Horse, and American Horse (1896)

> *On December 29, 1890, at Wounded Knee Creek on the Pine Ridge Reservation, the Seventh Cavalry began to disarm a group of Miniconjou Sioux, who had fled from their own reservation following Sitting Bull's death. A shot rang out; bitter hand to hand fighting ensued; then the soldiers opened fire with an early kind of machine gun. At least 146 Indians died, including 44 women and 18 children. In a poem entitled "American Names," Stephen Vincent Benet wrote these haunting words about the massacre that took place at Wounded Knee Creek:*
>
> > *You may bury my body in Sussex grass,*
> > *You may bury my tongue at Champmedy.*
> > *I shall not be there. I shall rise and pass.*
> > *Bury my heart at Wounded Knee.*

The Wounded Knee Massacre, 1890. *(Courtesy, Smithsonian Institution)*

TURNING HAWK: These people were coming toward Pine Ridge agency, and when they were almost on the agency they were met by the soldiers and surrounded and finally taken to the Wounded Knee creek, and there at a given time their guns were demanded. When they had delivered them up, the men were separated from their families, from their tipis, and taken to a certain spot. When the guns were thus taken and the men thus separated, there was a crazy man, a young man of bad influence and in fact a nobody, among that bunch of Indians [who] fired his gun, and of course the firing of a gun must have been the breaking of a military rule of some sort, because immediately the soldiers returned fire and indiscriminate killing followed.

SPOTTED HORSE: This man shot an officer in the army.... As soon as this shot was fired the Indians immediately began drawing their knives, and they were exhorted from all sides to desist, but this was not obeyed. Consequently the firing began immediately on the part of the soldiers.

TURNING HAWK: All the men who were in a bunch were killed right there, and those who escaped that first fire got into the ravine, and as they went along the ravine for a long distance they were pursued on both sides by the soldiers and shot down, as the dead bodies showed afterwards.

Burial of the dead following the Wounded Knee Massacre. *(Courtesy, Minnesota Historical Society)*

AMERICAN HORSE: There was a woman with an infant in her arms who was killed as she almost touched the flag of truce, and the women and children of course were strewn all along the circular village until they were dispatched. Right near the flag of truce a mother was shot down with her infant; the child not knowing that its mother was dead was still nursing, and that especially was a very sad sight. The women as they were fleeing with their babes were killed together, shot right through, and the women who were heavy with child were also killed. All the Indians fled in these three directions, and after most all of them had been killed a cry was made that all those who were not killed or wounded should come forth and they would be safe. Little boys who were not wounded came out of their places of refuge, and as soon as they came in sight a number of soldiers surrounded them and butchered them there.

Source: Fourteenth Annual Report of the Bureau of American Ethnology (1896), Part 2, 884–86.

An Indian killed in the Wounded Knee Massacre, 1890. *(Courtesy, Smithsonian Institution)*

"The Sioux tribes are naturally warlike and turbulent"
President Benjamin Harrison (1891)

> *President Benjamin Harrison offered these comments about the Wounded Knee massacre.*

That these Indians had some just complaints, especially in the matter of the reduction of the appropriation for rations and in the delays attending the enactment of laws to enable the Department to perform the engagements entered into with them, is probably true; but the Sioux tribes are naturally warlike and turbulent, and their warriors were excited by their medicine men and chiefs, who preached the coming of an Indian messiah who was to give them power to destroy their enemies. In view of the alarm that prevailed among the white settlers near the reservation and of the fatal consequences that would have resulted from an Indian incursion, I placed at the disposal of General Miles . . . all such forces as were thought by him to be required. He is entitled to the credit of having given thorough protection to the settlers and of bringing the hostiles into subjection with the least possible loss of life.

Source: James D. Richardson, ed., *Messages and Papers of the Presidents* (Washington, 1898), IX, 201–3.

PART V

THE STRUGGLE FOR SELF-DETERMINATION

INTRODUCTION: Ben Nighthorse Campbell

His grandfather fought against George Armstrong Custer at the battle of the Little Big Horn. In 1992 he became the first Indian elected to the U.S. Senate in over sixty years—and the only Senator to wear a ponytail.

His name is Ben Nighthorse Campbell, and his life story is a veritable Horatio Alger success story. It is a success story, however, with a critical difference: Campbell is a member of the Northern Cheyenne, and as a three-term member of the House of Representatives and as a Senator from Colorado, he has been an active proponent of self-determination for Native Americans.

He had a trying childhood. His father died of alcohol abuse; his mother suffered from tuberculosis. He spent years in an orphanage, and dropped out of high school to join the Air Force during the Korean War. He subsequently worked his way through San Jose State University, graduating in 1957. He worked as a jewelry maker and as a rancher, and served three terms in the House before being elected to the Senate in 1992.

As the only Indian member of Congress, he said he had "inherited a national constituency." He brought national attention to Native American issues when he introduced a bill to prevent Washington, D.C. from building a new football stadium unless the Washington Redskins changed the team's name.

A staunch defender of cultural diversity, he summed up his philosophy with these words: "I've never believed that to be a part of America, we all have to look alike, dress alike, talk alike."

161

His years in Congress witnessed many victories for Native Americans. These included grants to individual tribes to establish and run schools; and a law that required museums and the federal government to return all human remains and sacred objects that were taken from tribes without their consent. In 1993, the passage of the Religious Freedom Restoration Act guaranteed the right of Native Americans to practice traditional religions without state interference. Yet if much had been achieved, much more remained to be accomplished before Native Americans attained Campbell's goal of true self-determination.

22.
REFORMING INDIAN POLICY

"Colorado is as greedy and unjust in 1880 as was Georgia in 1830, and Ohio in 1795"
Helen Hunt Jackson (1881)

> *Like* Uncle Tom's Cabin, The Jungle, *and* Silent Spring, *Helen Hunt Jackson's* Century of Dishonor *aroused the nation's conscience and stimulated political action against injustice, in this case the nation's unjust treatment of Indians. Jackson's goals—education and individual land ownership—were embraced by many late nineteenth-century Indian reformers.*

There is not among these three hundred bands of Indians one which has not suffered cruelly at the hands either of the Government or of white settlers. The poorer, the more insignificant, the more helpless the band, the more certain the cruelty and outrage to which they have been subjected. . . .

It makes little difference . . . where one opens the record of the history of the Indians; every page and every year has its dark stain. The story of one tribe is the story of all, varied only by differences of time and place. . . . Colorado is as greedy and unjust in 1880 as was Georgia in 1830, and Ohio in 1795; and the United States Government breaks promises now as deftly as then, and with an added ingenuity from long practice. . . .

To assume that it would be easy . . . to undo the mischief and hurt of the long past . . . is the blunder of a hasty and uninformed judgment. The notion which seems to be growing more prevalent, that simply to make all Indians at once citizens of the United States would be a . . . panacea for all their ills . . . is a very inconsiderate one. . . . Nevertheless, it is true, as was well stated by one of the superintendents of Indian Affairs in 1857, that, "so long as they are not citizens of the United States, their rights of property must remain insecure against invasion. The doors of the federal tribunals being barred against them. . . . The utter absence of individual title to particular lands deprives every one among them of the chief incentive to labor and exertion. . . ."

Cheating, robbing, breaking promises—these three are clearly things which must cease to be done. One more thing, also, and that is the refusal of the protection of the law to the Indian's right of property. . . .

When these four things have ceased to be done, time, statesmanship, philanthropy, and Christianity can slowly and surely do the rest.

Source: Helen Hunt Jackson, *A Century of Dishonor* (New York, 1881), 337–38, 340–42.

"How lonesome I felt for my father and mother!"
Chief Luther Standing Bear (1879)

> *Luther Standing Bear was in the first class at the Carlisle Indian
> School, in Carlisle, Pennsylvania. Built in a former military barracks
> by Lieutenant Richard Henry Pratt, Carlisle served as an important
> model for Indian education during the late nineteenth and early twen-
> tieth centuries. As Standing Bear, a Sioux, explains, Carlisle's goal was
> to strip Indians of their cultural heritage and educate them in the ways
> of whites. During the summer, Carlisle's students lived with white
> farm families.*

It did not occur to me at that time that I was going away to learn the
ways of the white man. My idea was that I was leaving the reservation and
going to stay away long enough to do some brave deed, and then come
home again alive. If I could just do that, then I knew my father would be so
proud of me. . . .

One day when we came to school there was a lot of writing on one of
the blackboards. We did not know what it meant, but our interpreter came
into the room and said, "Do you see all these marks on the blackboard?

Students at the Carlisle Indian School in 1879. *(Courtesy, U.S. Department of the
Interior)*

Well, each word is a white man's name. They are going to give each one of you one of these names by which you will hereafter be known." . . .

Then the teacher took a piece of white tape and wrote the name on it. Then she cut off a length of the tape and sewed it on the back of the boy's shirt. Then that name was erased from the board. There was no duplication of names in the first class at Carlisle School! . . .

Next we had to learn to write our names. . . .

Next the teacher wrote out the alphabet on my slate and indicated to me that I was to take the slate to my room and study. . . .

How lonesome I felt for my father and mother! . . .

Next, we heard that we were soon to have white men's clothes. . . .

The clothes were some sort of dark heavy gray goods, consisting of coat, pants, and vest. We were also given a dark woolen shirt, a cap, a pair of suspenders, socks, and heavy farmer's boots.

Source: Chief Luther Standing Bear, *My People, the Sioux* (Boston: Houghton, Mifflin, 1928), 128–49.

"The importance of taking Indian youth from the reservations to be trained in industrial schools placed among communities of white citizens"
Friends of the Indian (1884)

> *Between 1883 and 1916, Indian reformers met annually at Lake Mohonk, New York, to formulate recommendations. One of the humanitarian reformers' major goals was abolition of the reservation system and distribution of land to individual families.*

1st. *Resolved,* That the organization of the Indians in tribes is, and has been, one of the most serious hindrances to the advancement of the Indian toward civilization, and that every effort should be made to secure the disintegration of all tribal organizations; that to accomplish this result the Government should . . . cease to recognize the Indians as political bodies or organized tribes. . . .

4th. *Resolved,* That all adult male Indians should be admitted to the full privileges of citizenship by a process analogous to naturalization, upon evidence presented before the proper court of record of adequate intellectual and moral qualifications. . . .

6th. *Resolved,* That . . . our conviction has been strengthened as to the importance of taking Indian youth from the reservations to be trained in industrial schools placed among communities of white citizens. . . .

14th. *Resolved,* That immediate efforts should be made to place the

Indian in the same position before the law as that held by the rest of the population. . . .

_____

Source: Second Annual Address to the Public of the Lake Mohonk Conference (Philadelphia, 1884), 3–7, 13–22.

"To allot the lands in the said reservation"
Dawes Act (1887)

> *The Dawes Act embodied one of the reformers' most cherished goals, the allotment of tribal lands to individual Indian families. "Excess" lands were then to be sold to whites, with the proceeds used to pay for Indian education.*

Be it enacted &c. That in all cases where any tribe or band of Indians has been, or shall hereafter be, located upon any reservation created for their use . . . the President . . . is authorized, whenever in his opinion any reservation or any part thereof of such Indians is advantageous for agriculture and grazing purposes, to cause said reservation . . . to be surveyed . . . and to allot the lands in said reservation in severalty to any Indian located thereon in quantities as follows:

To each head of a family, one-quarter of a section;

To each single person over eighteen years of age, one-eighth of a section; and

To each other single person under eighteen years now living . . . one-sixteenth of a section. . . .

SEC. 5. That upon the approval of the allotments . . . by the Secretary of the Interior, he shall cause patents to issue therefore in the name of the allotees . . . and declare that the United States does and will hold the land thus allotted, for the period of twenty-five years, in trust for the sole use and benefit of the Indian to whom the allotment shall have been made. . . .

And provided further, That at any time after lands have been allotted to all the Indians of any tribe . . . it shall be lawful for the Secretary of the Interior to negotiate with such Indian tribe for the purchase . . . of such portions of its reservation not allotted as such tribe shall . . . consent to sell. . . .

And the sums agreed to be paid by the United States as purchase money . . . shall be held in the Treasury of the United States for the sole use of the tribe . . . to whom such reservations belonged; and the same . . . shall be at all times subject to appropriation by Congress for the education and civilization of such tribe or tribes. . . .

_____

Source: U.S. Statutes at Large, 24:388–91.

"Away went my crop"
D. W. C. Duncan (1906)

A Cherokee tells a Senate committee how the Dawes Act had made it impossible to support his family through farming.

Under the old régime, when we were enjoying our vast estate in common here, we all had enough and more than enough to fill up the cup of our enjoyment. . . . While that was the case I had developed a farm of 300 acres up north of town. . . . But when the Dawes Commission sent its survey party around and cut me off up there all but 60 acres, I went to work on that, and to-day the allotment process . . . has written destruction of property and capital more terrible than that which was visited upon the isle of Galveston [Texas] years ago by the anger of the ocean. . . .

[U]nder the inexorable law of allotment enforced upon us Cherokees, I had to relinquish every inch of my premises outside of that little 60 acres. What is the result? There is a great scramble of persons to find land . . . to file upon. Some of the friends in here, especially a white intermarried citizen, goes up and files upon a part of my farm. . . . Away went my crop. . . . Now, that is what has been done to these Cherokees. . . .

The government of the United States knows that these allotments of the Indians are not sufficient. . . . Why, one American citizen goes out on the

A family of Navajo agricultural laborers in New Mexico in the 1950s made only about $1,000 a year. *(Courtesy, U.S. Department of the Interior)*

western plain in North Dakota to make a home. What is the amount of land allotted to him? Isn't it 160 acres?

_____

Source: Senate Report No. 5013, 59th Congress, 2d Sess., Pt. I, 180–90.

"A mighty pulverizing engine to break up the tribal mass"
President Theodore Roosevelt (1901)

The President defends the Dawes Act.

In my judgement the time has arrived when we should definitely make up our minds to recognize the Indian as an individual and not as a member of a tribe. The General Allotment Act is a mighty pulverizing engine to break up the tribal mass. . . . Under its provisions some sixty thousand Indians have already become citizens of the United States. We should now break up the tribal funds, doing for them what allotment does for the tribal lands; that is, they should be divided into individual holdings. . . . A stop should be put upon the indiscriminate permission to Indians to lease their allotments. The effort should be steadily to make the Indian work like any other man on his own ground. . . .

In the schools the education should be elementary and largely indus-

Life on the Fort Apache Reservation during the Great Depression. *(Courtesy, U.S. Department of the Interior)*

trial. The need of higher education among the Indians is very, very limited. . . . The ration system, which is merely the corral and the reservation
system, is highly detrimental to the Indians. It promotes beggary, perpetu-
ates pauperism, and stifles industry. It is an effectual barrier to progress. . . .
The Indian should be treated as an individual—like the white man.

Source: First Annual Message, December 3, 1901.

23.
A NEW DEAL FOR NATIVE AMERICANS

"Natural resources, such as timber and oil, were sold"
Meriam Report (1928)

> *The Meriam Report, which articulated strong criticisms of the Dawes
> Act, marked a critical turning point in the formulation of government
> policy. The report showed that the act had failed to transform Indians
> into family farmers, while depriving Native Americans of land and
> natural resources.*

When the government adopted the policy of individual ownership of
land on the reservations, the expectation was that the Indians would become farmers. Part of the plan was to instruct and aid them in agriculture,
but this vital part was not pressed with vigor and intelligence. It almost
seems as if the government assumed that some magic in individual ownership of property would in itself prove an educational civilizing factor, but
unfortunately this policy has for the most part operated in the opposite
direction. Individual ownership has in many instances permitted Indians to
sell their allotments and to live for a time on the unearned income resulting
from the sale. . . . Many Indians were not ready to make effective use of their
individual allotments. Some of the allotments were of such a character that
they could not be effectively used by anyone in small units. The solution was
to permit the Indians through the government to lease their lands to the
whites. In some instances government officers encouraged leasing, as the
whites were anxious for the use of the land and it was far easier to adminis-
ter property leased to whites than to educate and stimulate Indians to use
their own property. The lease money, though generally small in amount,
gave the Indians further unearned income to permit the continuance of a life
of idleness.

Surplus land remaining after allotments were made was often sold and the proceeds placed in a tribal fund. Natural resources, such as timber and oil, were sold and the money paid either into tribal funds or to individual Indians if the land had been allotted. From time to time per capita payments were made to the individual Indians from tribal funds. These policies all added to the unearned income of the Indian and postponed the day when it would be necessary for him to go to work to support himself.

Source: Lewis Meriam, *The Problem of Indian Administration* (Baltimore: Johns Hopkins University Press, 1928), 7–8.

"Any Indian tribe ... shall have the right to organize for its common welfare"
The Wheeler-Howard (Indian Reorganization) Act (1934)

This landmark act ended the policy of allotting tribal lands to individual Indians and selling the remaining lands to whites. It also restored limited tribal self-government and established funds for education.

AN ACT to conserve and develop Indian lands and resources; to extend to Indians the right to form business and other organizations; to establish a credit system for Indians; to grant certain rights of home rule to Indians; to provide for vocational education for Indians; and for other purposes. . . .
. . . That hereafter no land of any Indian reservation, created or set apart by treaty or agreement with the Indians . . . shall be allotted in severalty to any Indian. . . .
SEC. 3. The Secretary of the Interior, if he shall find it to be in the public interest, is hereby authorized to restore to tribal ownership the remaining surplus lands of any Indian reservation heretofore opened, or authorized to be opened. . . .
SEC. 5. The Secretary of the Interior is hereby authorized . . . to acquire . . . any interest in lands, water rights, or surface rights to lands, within or without existing reservations . . . for the purpose of providing land for Indians. . . .
SEC. 16. Any Indian tribe, or tribes, residing on the same reservation, shall have the right to organize for its common welfare, and may adopt an appropriate constitution and bylaws, which shall become effective when ratified by a majority vote of the adult members of the tribe, or of the Indians residing on such reservation. . . .

Source: U.S. Statutes at Large, 48:984–88.

"Ends the long, painful, futile effort to speed up the normal rate of Indian assimilation by individualizing tribal land"
John Collier (1934)

> *Indian Commissioner John Collier defends the Wheeler-Howard (Indian Reorganization) Act.*

The Wheeler-Howard Act, the most important piece of Indian legislation since the eighties, not only ends the long, painful, futile effort to speed up the normal rate of Indian assimilation by individualizing tribal land and other capital assets, but it also endeavors to provide the means, statutory and financial, to repair as far as possible, the incalculable damage done by the allotment policy and its corollaries. . . .

The repair work authorized by Congress . . . aims at both the economic and the spiritual rehabilitation of the Indian race. Congress and the President recognized that the cumulative loss of land brought about by the allotment system, a loss reaching 90,000,000 acres—two-thirds of the land heritage of the Indian race in 1887—had robbed the Indians in large part of the necessary basis for self-support. They clearly saw that this loss and the companion effort to break up all Indian tribal relations had condemned large numbers of Indians to become chronic recipients of charity; that the system of leasing individualized holdings had created many thousands of petty landlords unfitted to support themselves when their rental income vanished; that a major proportion of the red race was, therefore, ruined economically and pauperized spiritually. . . .

Through 50 years of "individualization", coupled with an ever-increasing amount of arbitrary supervision over the affairs of individuals and tribes so long as these individuals and tribes had any assets left, the Indians have been robbed of initiative, their spirit has been broken, their health undermined, and their native pride ground into the dust. The efforts at economic rehabilitation cannot and will not be more than partially successful unless they are accompanied by a determined simultaneous effort to rebuild the shattered morale of a subjugated people that has been taught to believe in its racial inferiority.

The Wheeler-Howard Act provides the means of destroying this inferiority complex, through those features which authorize and legalize tribal organization and incorporation, which give these tribal organizations and corporations limited but real power, and authority over their own affairs, which broaden the educational opportunities for Indians, and which give Indians a better chance to enter the Indian Service.

Source: Annual Report of the Secretary of the Interior, 1934, 78–83.

24.

FROM TERMINATION TO SELF-DETERMINATION

"To end their status as wards of the United States"
House Concurrent Resolution 108 (1953)

> *With this resolution, the House of Representatives and the Senate announced their support for a new Indian policy: "termination." Under this policy, Indians' status as government wards would be ended as soon as possible and Native Americans would assume all the responsibilities of full citizenship.*

Whereas it is the policy of Congress, as rapidly as possible, to make the Indians within the territorial limits of the United States subject to the same laws and entitled to the same privileges and responsibilities as are applicable to other citizens of the United States, to end their status as wards of the United States, and to grant them all of the rights and prerogatives pertaining to American citizenship. . . .

Resolved by the House of Representatives (the Senate concurring),

That it is declared to be the sense of Congress that, at the earliest possible time, all of the Indian tribes . . . located within the States of California, Florida, New York, and Texas . . . should be freed from Federal supervision and control and from all disabilities and limitations specifically applicable to Indians. . . .

———————

Source: U.S. Statutes at Large, 67:B132.

"A shift in . . . emphasis away from termination"
Philleo Nash (1961)

> *Philleo Nash, the Commissioner of Indian Affairs under President John F. Kennedy, declares that Indian policy must follow a "new trail" emphasizing "maximum self-sufficiency and full participation in American life."*

A "New Trail" for Indians leading to equal citizenship rights and benefits, maximum self-sufficiency and full participation in American life became the keynote . . . of the Department of the Interior shortly after the close of the 1961 fiscal year. . . .

Probably the most important single recommendation [by a special task force] was for a shift in program emphasis away from termination of Federal trust relationships toward greater development of the human and natural resources on Indian reservations.

This was coupled, however, with a recommendation that eligibility for special Federal service be withdrawn from "Indians with substantial incomes and superior educational experience, who are as competent as most non-Indians to look after their own affairs." . . .

In addition, the report recommended (1) more vigorous efforts to attract industries to reservation areas, (2) an expanded program of vocational training and placement, (3) creation of a special Reservation Development Loan Fund and enlargement of the present Revolving Loan Fund, (4) establishment of a statutory Advisory Board on Indian Affairs, (5) negotiation with States and counties, and resort to the courts where necessary, to make certain that off-reservation Indians are accorded the same rights and privileges as other citizens of their areas, (6) collaboration with States and tribes to bring tribal law and order codes into conformity with those of the States and counties where reservations are located, (7) acceleration in the adjudication of cases pending before the Indian Claims Commission, and (8) more active and widespread efforts to inform the public about the status of the Indian people and the nature of their problems. . . .

As a step toward transferring the responsibility for Indian education to local school districts, the Task Force urged renovation of present Federal school buildings, construction of new plants, and road improvements so that more Indian children can be bussed to classes. It also called for greater efforts to involve Indian parents in school planning and parent-teacher activities.

Source: Resources for Tomorrow: 1961. Annual Report, The Secretary of the Interior (Washington: Government Printing Office, 1961), 277–79.

"What we ask of America is not charity"
Declaration of Indian Purpose (1961)

> *Beginning with the founding of the National Congress of American Indians in 1944, Native Americans established national organizations to demand a greater voice in determining their own destiny. In 1961, some 700 Indians from sixty-four tribes met in Chicago to attack termination and formulate an Indian political agenda and a shared declaration of principles.*

. . . We, the Indian People, must be governed by principles in a democratic manner with a right to choose our way of life. Since our Indian culture is threatened by presumption of being absorbed by the American society, we believe we have the responsibility of preserving our precious heritage. . . .

We believe in the inherent right of all people to retain spiritual and cultural values, and that the free exercise of these values is necessary to the normal development of any people. . . .

We believe that the history and development of America shows that the Indian has been subjected to duress, undue influence, unwarranted pressures, and policies which have produced uncertainty, frustration, and despair. . . .

What we ask of America is not charity, not paternalism, even when benevolent. We ask only that the nature of our situation be recognized and made the basis of policy and action.

Source: *American Indian Chicago Conference*, University of Chicago, June 13–20, 1961, 5–6.

"I propose a new goal for our Indian programs"
President Lyndon Johnson (1968)

> *In Washington, D.C., Native American demands for self-determination began to be heard. In a special message to Congress, President Lyndon Johnson called for a new direction for national policy.*

I propose a new goal for our Indian programs: A goal that ends the old debate about "termination" of Indian programs and stresses self-determination; a goal that erases old attitudes of paternalism and promotes partnership self-help.

Our goal must be:

— *A standard of living for the Indians equal to that of the country as a whole.*

— *Freedom of Choice: An opportunity to remain in their homelands, if they choose, without surrendering their dignity; an opportunity to move to the towns and cities of America, if they choose, equipped with the skills to live in equality and dignity.*

— *Full participation in the life of modern America, with a full share of economic opportunity and social justice.*

I propose, in short, a policy of maximum choice for the American Indian: a policy expressed in programs of self-help, self-development, self-determination.

Source: *Public Papers of the Presidents of the United States: Lyndon B. Johnson, 1968–69*, Vol. I, 336–37.

A baby being carried
in a cradleboard in the
1950s. *(Courtesy, U.S.
Department of the
Interior)*

SEIZURE OF ALCATRAZ ISLAND

"We wish to be fair and honorable in our dealings with the Caucasian inhabitants of this land"
American Indian Center (1969)

> *In 1969, the struggle for Indian self-determination came dramatically to public attention when fourteen Native American college students occupied Alcatraz Island, in San Francisco Bay. The students said that under a Sioux treaty of 1868, the island—site of a former maximum security prison—should revert to Indian ownership. The argument that the United States needed to live up to treaty agreements with Native Americans would be repeated throughout the coming decades.*

We, the native Americans, re-claim the land known as Alcatraz Island in the name of all American Indians by right of discovery.

We wish to be fair and honorable in our dealings with the Caucasian inhabitants of this land, and hereby offer the following treaty:

We will purchase said Alcatraz Island for twenty-four dollars (24) in glass beads and red cloth, a precedent set by the white man's purchase of a similar island about 300 years ago. We know that $24 in trade goods for these 16 acres is more than was paid when Manhattan Island was sold, but we know that land values have risen over the years. Our offer of $1.24 per acre is greater than the 47 cents per acre the white men are now paying the California Indians for their land.

We will give to the inhabitants of this island a portion of the land for their own to be held in trust by the American Indian Affairs and by the bureau of Caucasian Affairs to hold in perpetuity—for as long as the sun shall rise and the rivers go down to the sea. We will further guide the inhabitants in the proper way of living. We will offer them our religion, our education, our life-ways, in order to help them achieve our level of civilization and thus raise them and all their white brothers up from their savage and unhappy state. We offer this treaty in good faith and wish to be fair and honorable in our dealings with all white men.

We feel that this so-called Alcatraz Island is more than suitable for an Indian Reservation, as determined by the white man's own standards. By this we mean that this place resembles most Indian reservations in that:

1. It is isolated from modern facilities, and without adequate means of transportation.
2. It has no fresh running water.
3. It has inadequate sanitation facilities.
4. There are no oil or mineral rights.
5. There is no industry and so unemployment is very great.
6. There are no health care facilities.
7. The soil is rocky and non-productive; and the land does not support game.
8. There are no educational facilities.
9. The population has always exceeded the land base.
10. The population has always been held as prisoners and kept dependent upon others.

Further, it would be fitting and symbolic that ships from all over the world, entering the Golden Gate, would first see Indian land, and thus be reminded of the true history of this nation. This tiny island would be a symbol of the great lands once ruled by free and noble Indians.

Source: American Indian Center, 1969.

"There are 1,959,234 American Indians ... a 37.9 percent increase over the 1980 recorded total"
Bureau of Indian Affairs (1991)

> *Far from being a vanishing people, the number of Native Americans has risen sharply in recent years. As their numbers have grown, so too has Native American political influence and the desire to rescue Native American history from past distortions.*

Population

According to U.S. Census Bureau figures, there were 1,959,234 American Indians and Alaska Natives living in the United States in 1990 (1,878,285 American Indians, 57,152 Eskimos, and 23,797 Aleuts). This is a 37.9 percent increase over the 1980 recorded total of 1,420,400. The increase is attributed to improved census taking and more self-identification during the 1990 count. The BIA's 1990 estimate is that almost 950,000 individuals of this total population live on or adjacent to federal Indian reservations. . . .

Reservations

The number of Indian land areas in the U.S. administered as Federal Indian reservations (reservations, pueblos, racherias, communities, etc.) total 278. The largest is the Navajo Reservation of some 16 million acres of land in Arizona, New Mexico, and Utah. Many of the smaller reservations are less than 1,000 acres with the smallest less than 100 acres. On each reservation, the local governing authority is the tribal government. The states in which the reservations are located have limited powers over them, and only as provided by federal law. On some reservations, however, a high percentage of the land is owned and occupied by non-Indians. Some 140 reservations have entirely tribally-owned land.

Trust Lands

A total of 56.2 million acres of land are held in trust by the United States for various Indian tribes and individuals. Much of this is reservation land; however, not all reservation land is trust land. On behalf of the United States, the Secretary of the Interior serves as trustee for such lands with many routine trustee responsibilities delegated to BIA [Bureau of Indian Affairs] officials.

Indian Tribes

There are 510 federally recognized tribes in the United States, including about 200 village groups in Alaska. "Federally-recognized" means these tribes and groups have a special, legal relationship to the U.S. government and its agent, the BIA, depending on the particular situation of each tribe.

Birth Rate—Birth rates were 28.0 births per 1,000 in 1986–88. The U.S. all races rate was 15.7 births per 1,000 in 1987.

Infant Death Rate—The infant death rate was 9.7 per 1,000 live births in 1986–88, while the U.S. all races rate was 10.1 per 1,000 births in 1987.

Life Expectancy—In 1979–81, life expectancy was 71.1 years (males, 67.1 years and females 75.1 years). These figures are based on 1980 census information.

Source: Bureau of Indian Affairs, *American Indians Today* (3rd ed.; Washington, D.C.: U.S. Government Printing Office, 1991).

GLOSSARY

Historical Terminology

Beringia: During one of the earth's periodic ice ages, water froze into glaciers, reducing sea levels 200 to 300 feet, exposing a subcontinent known as Beringia. This subcontinent connected Asia and North America and formed a migration route for hunters and animals searching for food.

Clovis tradition: A sophisticated form of toolmaking that appeared about 12,000 years ago.

Mississippian cultural patterns: A form of social organization that appeared among the Indian peoples east of the Mississippi beginning in the seventh century, characterized by permanent villages and towns, political and economic stratification, specialized crafts, and extensive trade.

Mound Builders: Early Indian peoples, including the Adena, Hopewell, and Mississippian cultures, who built large earthen monuments to serve as burial sites and as sites for temples and religious ceremonies.

Kinship Terminology

Lineage: A group of persons tracing descent from a common ancestor.

Clan: Two or more lineages claiming descent from a common ancestor.

Moiety: One of two basic complementary tribal subdivisions. Among some people, the members of one moiety were responsible for burying the dead of the other moiety.

Association: An organization whose members were not related. Among the Plains Indians, associations were often organized according to age.

Patrilineal descent: Land use rights and membership in the political system flow through the father.

Matrilineal descent: Group membership is determined by the mother's family identity.

Political Organization

Band: The form of political organization customarily found among hunter-gatherers. Bands usually have no permanent leaders; decisions are based on building consensus. Leadership tends to be situational, arising for short periods of time.

Tribe: Larger than a band, tribal organization is customarily associated with agriculture and more permanent settlements. Kinship is generally the central organizing principle. Leaders are usually chosen by consensus and rule by consensus.

Chiefdom: Usually larger than a tribe, chiefdoms show the beginning of social stratification and the emergence of a distinct ruling class. Customarily, the chiefs must redistribute the resources they control. Chiefdoms are often engaged in some kinds of extensive trade.

Federation: A union of a number of distinct tribes or chiefdoms.

State: Unlike bands, tribes, and chiefdoms, states have a true class structure and a distinct ruling class. It is a more extensive system of political control, often involving rule over subjugated groups.

Religious Terminology

Agrarian tradition: A religious system associated with farming communities, which was characterized by rituals associated with changing seasons. Unlike the hunting tradition, which had individual shamans, the agrarian tradition had an organized priesthood and cult societies.

Ghost Dance: A messianic religious ritual originating among the Paiute, which later spread to the Plains, and was supposed to bring the return of the spirits of the dead.

Hunting tradition: A religious system of beliefs that emphasized the ties between hunters and the animal world.

Kiva: A Pueblo Indian ceremonial structure that is usually round and partly underground.

Potlatch: A ceremonial feast held by Indians of the Northwest Pacific Coast marked by the host's lavish distribution of gifts.

Shaman: An individual with a special relationship with the spirit world. Whites often called shamans "medicine men" because they were responsible for curing the sick.

Southern cult: A system of religious ritual that shared many customs and symbols with Mexican Indian religions.

Sun dance: A religious ceremony among the Plains Indians to mark the renewal of nature.

Totem: An object, such as an animal or plant, that serves as the emblem for a lineage or clan. The totem often serves as a symbolic representation of a guardian spirit or an ancestor.

Totem pole: A carved or painted pillar erected by Indians of the Northwest Pacific Coast to mark an important event, such as a religious ceremony or acquisition of a title or the death of a relative.

Vision quest: A rite in which a young person or young adult goes to an isolated place to seek, in a vision, a protective spirit.

Forms of Shelter

Hogan: An earth lodge found among the Navajo, consisting of a frame built of poles or logs covered with dirt.

Longhouse: Large, rectangular structure found among the Iroquois. Some longhouses were 100 feet long and housed ten or more families.

Pit house: An insulated structure built in a pit several feet deep and covered with sod, dirt, or other materials.

Plank house: Form of housing found in the Pacific Northwest.

Pueblo: Multistoried apartment building built out of adobe (sun-dried bricks) found in Arizona and New Mexico.

Tipi: Cone-shaped structure built on a pole framework. On the Plains, it was covered with buffalo skins. Elsewhere, it was covered with animal skins or tree bark.

Wickiup: Form of shelter found among the Apaches and Paiutes constructed of brush and matting.

Wigwam: A dome-shaped structure found in the eastern woodlands that was built on a pole framework and covered with leaves and bark.

A GUIDE TO RECENT BOOKS IN NATIVE AMERICAN HISTORY

REFERENCE WORKS

ATLASES

Michael Coe, Dean Snow, and Elizabeth Benson, eds., *Atlas of Ancient America* (New York: Facts on File, 1986)

Francis Paul Prucha, *Atlas of American Indian Affairs* (Lincoln: University of Nebraska, 1990)

Thomas E. Ross and Tyrel G. Moore, eds., *A Cultural Geography of North American Indians* (Boulder: Westview, 1987)

Carl Waldman, *Atlas of the North American Indian* (New York: Facts on File, 1985)

BIBLIOGRAPHIC AND RESEARCH GUIDES

The Newberry Library Center for the History of the American Indian Bibliographical Series (see individual topics)

Felix S. Cohen's *Handbook of Federal Indian Law* (rev. ed.; Charlottesville: University of Virginia, 1983)

Polly Grimshaw, *Images of the Other: A Guide to Microform Manuscripts on Indian-White Relations* (Urbana: University of Illinois, 1991)

Edward E. Hill, *Guide to the Records in the National Archives of the United States Relating to American Indians* (Washington: National Archives, 1981)

Steven L. Johnson, *Guide to American Indian Documents in the Congressional Serial Set: 1817–1899* (New York: Clearwater, 1977)

Charles J. Kapper, ed., *Indian Affairs: Laws and Treaties* (2 vols.; Washington:U. S. Govt. Printing Office, 1904)

Robert M. Kvasnicka and Herman J. Viola, eds., *The Commissioners of Indian Affairs, 1824–1977* (Lincoln: University of Nebraska, 1979)

Francis Paul Prucha, *A Bibliographical Guide to the History of Indian-White Relations in the United States* (Chicago: University of Chicago, 1977)

———, *Indian-White Relations: A Bibliography of Works Published 1975–1980* (Lincoln: University of Nebraska, 1982)

Charles C. Royce, comp., *Indian Land Cessions in the United States*. Eighteenth Annual Report of the Bureau of American Ethnology. (Washington: U.S. Govt. Printing Office, 1899)

BIOGRAPHICAL DIRECTORIES

Biographical Dictionary of Indians of the Americas (2nd ed.; Newport Beach: American Indian Pub., 1991)

CHRONOLOGIES

Barbara A. LePoer, *Chronology of the American Indian* (2nd ed.; Newport Beach: American Indian Pub., 1985)

ENCYCLOPEDIAS AND HANDBOOKS

Dictionary of Daily Life of Indians of the Americas (Newport Beach: American Indian Pub., 1981)

Dictionary of Indian Tribes of the Americas (Newport Beach: American Indian Pub., 1980)

J. Norman Heard, *Handbook of the American Frontier* (Metuchen: Scarecrow, 1987)

Arlene B. Hirschfelder and Paulette Molin, *The Encyclopedia of Native American Religions* (New York: Facts on File, 1992)

F. W. Hodge, ed., *Handbook of American Indians North of Mexico* (2 vols.; Washington: Government Printing Office, 1907–10)

Howard R. Lamar, ed., *The Reader's Encyclopedia of the American West* (New York: Thomas R. Crowell, 1977)

William C. Sturtevant, general editor, *Handbook of North American Indians*, 20 vols. (Washington: Smithsonian, 1978–)

Carl Waldman, *Encyclopedia of Native American Tribes* (New York: Facts on File, 1988)

Bill Yenne, *Encyclopedia of North American Indian Tribes* (New York: Arch Cape, 1986)

SCHOLARLY JOURNALS

Akwe:kon Journal (formerly *Northeast Indian Quarterly*)
American Indian Culture and Research
American Indian Quarterly
Ethnohistory
Wassaja, The Indian Historian

STATISTICS

Paul Stuart, *Nations Within a Nation: Historical Statistics of American Indians* (New York: Greenwood, 1987)

TREATIES

Charles J. Kappler, comp., *Indian Affairs: Laws and Treaties* (5 vols.; Washington D.C.: U.S. Government Printing Office, 1904–1941)

OVERVIEWS AND SURVEYS

Arrell Morgan Gibson, *The American Indian: Prehistory to the Present* (Lexington: D.C. Heath, 1980)

William T. Hagan, *American Indians* (3rd. ed.; Chicago: University of Chicago Press, 1993)

Karen D. Harvey and Lisa D. Harjo, *Indian Country: A History of Native People in America* (Golden, Col.: North American Press, 1994)

Tom Hill and Richard W. Hill, Sr., eds., *Creation's Journey: Native American Identity and Belief* (Washington: Smithsonian, 1994)

Francis Jennings, *The Founders of America: From the Earliest Migrations to the Present* (New York: W.W. Norton, 1993)

Alice Beck Kehoe, *North American Indians: A Comprehensive Account* (2nd ed.; Englewood Cliffs, N.J.: Prentice Hall, 1992)

Hans Koning, *The Conquest of America: How Indian Nations Lost Their Continent* (New York: Monthly Review, 1993)

C. Matthew Snipp, *American Indians: The First of This Land* (New York: Russell Sage, 1989)

Edward H. Spicer, *The American Indians* (Cambridge: Harvard, 1982)

Herman J. Viola, *After Columbus: The Smithsonian Chronicle of the North American Indians* (Washington: Smithsonian, 1990)

Wilcomb E. Washburn, *The Indian in America* (New York: Harper and Row, 1975)

HISTORIOGRAPHY

Colin G. Calloway, ed., *New Directions in American Indian History* (Norman: University of Oklahoma, 1988)

Annette Jaimes, ed., *The State of Native America: Genocide, Colonization, and Resistance* (Boston: South End, 1992)

Calvin Martin, ed., *The American Indian and the Problem of History* (New York: Oxford, 1987)

W. R. Swagerty, ed., *Scholars and the Indian Experience* (Bloomington: Indiana, 1984)

Terry P. Wilson, *Teaching American Indian History* (Washington: American Historical Association, 1993)

DOCUMENT COLLECTIONS

Virginia Irving Armstrong, comp., *I Have Spoken: American History Through the Voices of the Indians* (Chicago: Sage Books, 1971)

James Axtell, ed., *The Indian People of Eastern America: A Documentary History of the Sexes* (New York: Oxford, 1981)

———, *Native American People of the East* (West Haven: Pendulum, 1973)

Nancy B. Black and Bette S. Weidman, eds., *White on Red: Images of the American Indian* (Port Washington, N. Y.: Kennikat Press, 1976)

Colin G. Calloway, ed., *Dawnland Encounters: Indians and Europeans in Northern New England* (Hanover: Univesity Press of New England, 1991)

———, *The World Turned Upside Down: Indian Voices from Early America* (Boston: St. Martin's Press, 1994)

Joseph H. Cash and Herbert T. Hoover, *To Be an Indian: An Oral History* (New York: Holt, Rinehart, and Winston, 1971)

Vine Deloria, comp., *Of Utmost Good Faith* (San Francisco: Straight Arrow Books, 1971)

Ives Goddard and Kathleen J. Bragdon, *Native Writings in Massachusetts* (Philadelphia: American Philosophical Society, 1988)

Charles Hamilton, *Cry of the Thunderbird* (New York: Macmillan, 1950)

Alvin M. Josephy, Jr., *Red Power: The American Indians' Fight for Freedom* (New York: American Heritage Press, 1971)

Jane B. Katz, ed., *I Am the Fire of Time: The Voices of Native American Women* (New York: Dutton, 1977)

———, *Let Me Be a Free Man: A Documentary History of Indian Resistance* (Minneapolis: Lerner Publications Co., 1975)

Steven Mintz, *Native American Voices* (St. James, N.Y.: Brandywine Press, 1995)

P. Richard Metcalf, *The Native American People of the West* (West Haven: Pendulum Press, 1973)

Wayne Moquin, comp., *Great Documents in American Indian History* (New York: Praeger, 1973)

Peter Nabokov, *Native American Testimony: A Chronicle of Indian-White Relations from Prophecy to the Present* (New York: Viking, 1991)

Theda Perdue, ed., *Nations Remembered: An Oral History of the Five Civilized Tribes, 1865–1907* (Westport: Greenwood Press, 1980)

Penny Petrone, *First People, First Voices* (Toronto: University of Toronto Press, 1983)

Bernd Peyer, *The Elders Wrote: An Anthology of Early Prose by North American Indians, 1768–1931* (Berlin: Reimer, 1982)

Francis Paul Prucha, *Documents of United States Indian Policy* (2nd ed.; Lincoln: University of Nebraska, 1990)

Patricia Riley, ed., *Growing Up Native American* (New York: Morrow, 1993)

Annette Rosenstiel, *Red & White: Indian Views of the White Man, 1492–1982* (New York: Universe Books, 1983)

Carl Ortwin Sauer, *Sixteenth Century North America: The Land and the People as Seen by Europeans* (Berkeley: University of California, 1971)

William S. Simmons, *Spirit of the New England Tribes: Indian History and Folklore, 1620–1984* (Hanover: University Press of New England, 1986)

W. C. Vanderwerth, comp., *Indian Oratory* (Norman: University of Oklahoma, 1971)

Virgil J. Vogel, *This Country Was Ours: A Documentary History of the American Indian* (New York: Harper & Row, 1972)

Wilcomb E. Washburn, ed., *The American Indian and the United States: A Documentary History* (4 vols.; New York: Random House, 1973)

———, *The Indian and the White Man* (Garden City: Anchor Books, 1964)

Ronald Wright, *Stolen Continents: The Americas Through Indian Eyes Since 1492* (Boston: Houghton, Mifflin, 1992)

COLLECTIONS OF INTERPRETIVE ESSAYS

All Roads Are Good: Native Voices on Life and Culture (Washington: Smithsonian Institution, 1994)

William W. Fitzhugh, *Cultures in Contact: The Impact of European Contacts on Native American Cultural Institutions, A.D. 1000–1800* (Washington: Smithsonian, 1985)

Frederick E. Hoxie, ed., *Indians in American History* (Arlington Heights: Harlan Davidson, 1988)

Eleanor B. Leacock and N. O. Lurie, eds., *North American Indians in Historical Perspective* (New York: Random House, 1971)

John H. Moore, ed., *The Political Economy of North American Indians* (Norman: University of Oklahoma, 1993)

Roger L. Nichols, ed., *The American Indian: Past and Present* (3rd ed.; New York: Knopf, 1986)

William B. Taylor and Franklin Pease, eds., *Violence, Resistance, and Survival in the Americas: Native Americans and the Legacy of Conquest* (Washington: Smithsonian, 1994)

Philip Weeks, ed., *The American Indian Experience: A Profile, 1524 to the Present* (Arlington Heights: Forum Press, 1988)

PREHISTORY

David S. Brose, James A. Brown, and David W. Penney, *Ancient Art of the Woodland Indians* (New York: H.N. Abrams, 1985)

Linda S. Cordell, *Prehistory of the Southwest* (Orlando: Academic, 1984)

L. S. Cressman, *Prehistory of the Far West* (Salt Lake City: University of Utah, 1977)

Brian M. Fagan, *Ancient North America* (New York: Thames and Hudson, 1991)

———, *The Great Journey: The Peopling of Ancient America* (New York: Thames and Hudson, 1987)

Stuart J. Fiedel, *Prehistory of the Americas* (New York: Cambridge, 1987)

William Iseminger, Dick Norrish, and John W. Strong, *Best of Cahokian: 16 Articles Appearing in the Cahokian* (Collinsville: Cahokian Mounds Museum, n.d.)

Jesse D. Jennings, ed., *Ancient North Americans* (San Francisco: W.H. Freeman, 1983)

Philip Kopper, *The Smithsonian Book of North American Indians: Before the Coming of the Europeans* (Washington: Smithsonian, 1986)

William N. Morgan, *Prehistoric Architecture in the Eastern United States* (Cambridge: MIT, 1980)

David B. Quinn, *North America from Earliest Discovery to First Settlements: The Norse Voyages to 1612* (New York: Harper and Row, 1977)

Lynda Norene Shaffer, *Native Americans Before 1492: The Moundbuilding Centers of the Eastern Woodlands* (Armonk: M.E. Sharpe, 1992)

Robert Silverberg, *Mound Builders of Ancient America: The Archaeology of a Myth* (Greenwich: New York Graphic Society, 1968)

Dean R. Snow, *Native American Prehistory: A Critical Bibliography* (Bloomington: Indiana, 1979)

EVE OF CONTACT

Chester B. DePratter, *Late Prehistoric and Early Historic Chiefdoms in the Southeastern United States* (New York: Garland, 1991)

Alvin Josephy, Jr., and Frederick E. Hoxie, eds., *America in 1492* (New York: Knopf, 1992)

Howard S. Russell, *Indian New England Before the Mayflower* (Hanover: University Press of New England, 1980)

COLUMBIAN ENCOUNTER

Warwick Bray, ed., *The Meeting of Two Worlds: Europe and the Americas, 1492–1650* (Oxford: Oxford, 1993)

Alfred W. Crosby, Jr., *The Columbian Exchange: Biological and Cultural Consequences of 1492* (Westport: Greenwood, 1972)

———, *Ecological Imperialism: The Biological Expansion of Europe, 900–1900* (New York: Cambridge, 1986)

Louis De Vorsey, Jr., *Keys to the Encounter: A Library of Congress Resource Guide for the Age of Discovery* (Washington: Library of Congress, 1992)

Ann F. Ramenofsky, *Vectors of Death: The Archaeology of European Contact* (Albuquerque: University of New Mexico, 1987)

Kirkpatrick Sale, *The Conquest of Paradise: Christopher Columbus and the Columbian Legacy* (New York: Knopf, 1990)

David Stannard, *American Holocaust: Columbus and the Conquest of the New World* (New York: Oxford, 1992)

David Hurst Thomas, ed., *Columbian Consequences: Archaeological and Historical Perspectives on the Spanish Borderlands East* (Washington: Smithsonian, 1990)

———, *The Spanish Borderlands in Pan-American Perspective* (Washington: Smithsonian, 1991)

EUROPEAN IMAGES OF INDIANS

Robert F. Berkhofer, Jr., *The White Man's Indian: Images of the American Indian from Columbus to the Present* (New York: Knopf, 1979)

Robert E. Bieder, *Science Encounters the Indian, 1820–1880* (Norman: University of Oklahoma, 1986)

Robert Drinnon, *Facing West: The Metaphysics of Indian-Hating and Empire Building* (Minneapolis: University of Minnesota, 1980)

Lee E. Huddleston, *Origins of the American Indians: European Concepts, 1492–1729* (Austin: University of Texas, 1967)

Roy H. Pearce, *The Savages of America* (Baltimore: Johns Hopkins, 1965)

Richard Slotkin, *Regeneration Through Violence: The Mythology of the American Frontier, 1600–1860* (Middletown: Wesleyan, 1973)

Patricia Trenton and Patrick T. Houlihan, *Native Americans: Five Centuries of Changing Images* (New York: H.N. Abrams, 1989)

HISTORICAL DEMOGRAPHY

Sherborne F. Cook, *The Population of the California Indians, 1796–1970* (Berkeley: University of California, 1976)

W. M. Denevan, ed., *The Native Population of the Americas in 1492* (2nd ed.; Madison: University of Wisconsin, 1992)

Henry F. Dobyns, *Native American Historical Demography* (Bloomington: Indiana, 1976)

———, *Their Number Become Thinned: Native American Population Dynamics in Eastern North America* (Knoxville: Univeristy of Tennessee, 1983)

Abram J. Jaffe, *The First Immigrants from Asia: A Population History* (New York: Plenum, 1992)

Clark Spencer Larsen, ed., *Native American Demography in the Spanish Borderlands* (New York: Garland, 1991)

Russell Thornton, *American Indian Holocaust and Survival: A Population History Since 1492* (Norman: University of Oklahoma, 1987)

John W. Verano and Douglas H. Ubelaker, eds., *Disease and Demography in the Americas* (Washington: Smithsonian, 1992)

COLONIAL PERIOD

Interpretations and General Works

James Axtell, *After Columbus: Essays on the Ethnohistory of Colonial North America* (New York: Oxford, 1988)

———, *The European and the Indian: Essays in the Ethnohistory of Colonial America* (New York: Oxford, 1981)

———, *The Invasion Within: The Contest of Culture in Colonial North America* (New York: Oxford, 1985)

Jose Barreiro, ed., *Indian Roots of American Democracy* (Ithaca: Cornell, 1992)

Colin G. Calloway, *Crown and Calumet: British-Indian Relations, 1783–1815* (Norman: University of Oklahoma, 1987)

Jack D. Forbes, *A World Ruled by Cannibals: The Wetiko Disease of Aggression, Violence, and Imperialism* (Davis, Ca.: D-Q University Press, 1979)

Bruce A. Glasrud and Alan M. Smith, eds., *Race Relations in British North America, 1607–1783* (Chicago: Nelson-Hall, 1982)

Wilbur R. Jacobs, *Dispossessing the American Indian: Indians and Whites on the Colonial Frontier* (New York: Scribner, 1972)

Francis Jennings, *The Invasion of America: Indians, Colonialism, and the Cant of Conquest* (Chapel Hill: University of North Carolina, 1975)

Dorothy V. Jones, *License for Empire: Colonialism by Treaty in Early America* (Chicago: University of Chicago, 1982)

Karen Ordahl Kupperman, *Settling with the Indians: The Meeting of English and Indian Cultures, 1580–1640* (Totowa, N. J.: Rowan and Littlefield, 1980)

Calvin Martin, *Keepers of the Game: Indian-Animal Relationships and the Fur Trade* (Berkeley: University of California, 1978)

Gary Nash, *Red, White, and Black: The Peoples of Colonial America* (3rd. ed.; Englewood Cliffs: Prentice-Hall, 1992)

Ian Kenneth Steele, *Warpaths: Invasions of North America* (New York: Oxford, 1994)

David G. Sweet and Gary B. Nash, *Struggle & Survival in Colonial America* (Berkeley: University of California, 1981)

Stephen Saunders Webb, *1676: The End of American Independence* (Cambridge: Harvard, 1985)

SPANISH COLONIZATION

Warren L. Cook, *Flood Tide of Empire: Spain and the Pacific Northwest* (New Haven: Yale, 1973)

Ramon Gutierrez, *When Jesus Came, the Corn Mothers Went Away: Marriage, Sexuality, and Power in New Mexico, 1500–1846* (Stanford: Stanford, 1991)

Elizabeth A. H. John, *Storms Brewed in Other Men's Worlds: The Confrontation of Indians, Spanish, and French in the Southwest, 1540–1795* (College Station: Texas A&M, 1975)

Robert Allen Matter, *Pre-Seminole Florida: Spanish Soldiers, Friars, and Indian Missions, 1513–1763* (New York: Garland, 1990)

Jerald T. Milanich, *Earliest Hispanic/Native American Interactions in the American Southeast* (New York: Garland, 1991)

Abraham P. Nasatir, *Borderland in Retreat: From Spanish Louisiana to the Far Southwest* (Albuquerque: Univeristy of New Mexico, 1976)

Edward E. Spicer, *Cycles of Conquest: The Impact of Spain, Mexico, and the United States on the Indians of the Southwest, 1533–1960* (Tucson: University of Arizona, 1962)

David J. Weber, *The Spanish Frontier in North American* (New Haven: Yale, 1992)

NEW FRANCE

Alfred Goldsworthy Bailey, *The Conflict of European and Eastern Algonkian Cultures, 1504–1700* (2nd. ed.; Toronto: Univeristy of Toronto, 1969)

Olive Patricia Dickason, *The Myth of the Savage and the Beginnings of French Colonialism in the Americas* (Edmonton: University of Alberta, 1984)

William J. Eccles, *The Canadian Frontier, 1534–1760* (New York: Holt, Rinehart and Winston, 1969)

———, *France in America* (New York: Harper and Row, 1972)

Conrad Heidenreich, *Huronia: A History and Geography of the Huron Indians, 1600–1650* (Toronto: McClelland and Stewart, 1971)

Cornelius J. Jaenen, *Friend and Foe: Aspects of French-Amerindian Cultural Contact in the Sixteenth and Seventeenth Centuries* (1976)

James T. Moore, *Indian and Jesuit: A Seventeenth-Century Encounter* (Chicago: Loyola, 1982)

Bruce Trigger, *The Children of Aataentsic: A History of the Huron People to 1660* (2 vols.; Montreal: McGill-Queens, 1976)

———, *The Huron* (2nd ed.; Fort Worth: Holt, Rinehart and Winston, 1990)

NEW ENGLAND

Colin G. Calloway, *The Western Abenakis of Vermont, 1600–1800* (Norman: University of Oklahoma, 1990)

William Cronon, *Changes in the Land: Indians, Colonialists, and the Ecology of New England* (New York: Hill and Wang, 1983)

Yasuhide Kawashima, *Puritan Justice and the Indian: White Man's Law in Massachusetts, 1630–1763* (Middletown: Wesleyan, 1986)

Richard I. Melvoin, *New England Outpost: War and Soceity in Colonial Deerfield* (New York: Norton, 1989)

Kenneth M. Morrison, *The Embattled Northeast: The Elusive Ideal of Alliance in Abenaki-Euramerican Relations* (Berkeley: University of California, 1984)

Neal Salisbury, *Manitou and Providence: Indians, Europeans, and the Making of New England* (New York: Oxford, 1982)

Peter A. Thomas, *In the Maelstrom of Change: The Indian Trade and Cultural Process in the Middle Connecticut River Valley, 1635–1665* (New York: Garland, 1990)

Alden T. Vaughan, *The New England Frontier: Puritans and Indians, 1620–1675* (Boston: Little, Brown, 1965)

MIDDLE COLONIES

Richard Aquila, *The Iroquois Restoration: Iroquois Diplomacy on the Colonial Frontier* (Detroit: Wayne State, 1983)

Robert A. Goldstein, *French-Iroquois Diplomatic and Military Relations, 1609–1701* (The Hague: Mouton, 1969)

Francis Jennings, *The Ambiguous Iroquois Empire: The Covenant Chain Confederation of Indian Tribes with English Colonies from its Beginnings to the Lancaster Treaty of 1744* (New York: Norton, 1984)

Barry C. Kent, *Susquehanna's Indians* (Harrisburg: Pennsylvania Historical and Museum Commission, 1984)

Georgiana C. Nammack, *Fraud, Politics, and the Disposession of the Indians; The Iroquois Land Frontier in the Colonial Period* (Norman: University of Oklahoma, 1969)

Thomas Elliott Norton, *The Fur Trade in Colonial New York, 1686–1776* (Madison: University of Wisconsin, 1974)

Frank W. Porter III, *Indians in Maryland and Delaware* (Bloomington: Indiana, 1979)

Daniel K. Richter, *The Ordeal of the Longhouse: The Peoples of the Iroquois League in the Era of European Colonization* (Chapel Hill: University of North Carolina, 1992)

Daniel K. Richter and James H. Merrell, eds., *Beyond the Covenant Chain: The Iroquois and Their Neighbors in Indian North America, 1600–1800* (Syracuse: Syracuse, 1987)

Allen W. Trelease, *Indian Affairs in Colonial New York: The Seventeenth Century* (Ithaca: Cornell, 1960)

Sherman P. Uhler, *Pennsylvania's Indian Relations to 1754* (New York: AMS Press, 1984)

Anthony F. C. Wallace, *Death and Rebirth of the Seneca* (New York: Knopf, 1970)

C. A. Weslager, *The Delaware Indians: A History* (New Brunswick: Rutgers, 1972)

SOUTHEAST

Charles Hudson and Carmen Chaves Tesser, eds., *The Forgotten Centuries: Indians and Europeans in the American South, 1521–1704* (Athens: University of Georgia, 1994)

Karen Ordahl Kupperman, *Roanoke: The Abandoned Colony* (Totowa, N. J.: Rowman & Allanheld, 1984)

James H. Merrell, *The Indians' New World: Catawbas and Their Neighbors from European Contact Through the Era of Removal* (Chapel Hill: University of North Carolina, 1989)

David Beers Quinn, *Set Fair for Roanoke: Voyages and Colonies, 1584–1606* (Chapel Hill: University of North Carolina, 1985)

Helen C. Rountree, *Pocahontas's People: The Powhatan Indians of Virginia Through Four Centuries* (Norman: University of Oklahoma, 1990)

———, *The Powhatan Indians of Virginia* (Norman: University of Oklahoma, 1988)

Bernard Sheehan, *Savagism and Civility: Indians and Englishmen in Colonial Virginia* (Cambridge: Cambridge, 1980)

Daniel H. Usner, Jr., *Indians, Settlers, and Slaves in a Frontier Exchange Economy: The Lower Mississippi Valley Before 1783* (Chapel Hill: University of North Carolina, 1992)

Gene Waddell, *Indians of the South Carolina Low Country, 1562–1751* (Spartenburg: University of South Carolina, 1980)

J. Leitch Wright, Jr., *The Only Land They Knew: The Tragic Story of the American Indians in the Old South* (New York: Free Press, 1981)

GREAT LAKES REGION

George Irving Quimby, *Indian Culture and European Trade Goods: The Archaeology of the Historic Period in the Western Great Lakes Region* (Madison: University of Wisconsin, 1966)

Helen Hornbeck Tanner et al., eds., *Atlas of Great Lakes Indian History* (Norman: University of Oklahoma, 1987)

Richard White, *The Middle Ground: Indians, Empires, and Republics in the Great Lakes Region, 1650–1815* (Cambridge: Cambridge, 1991)

FRENCH AND INDIAN WAR

Francis Jennings, *Empire of Fortune: Crowns, Colonies, and Tribes in the Seven Years War in America* (New York: Norton, 1988)

AMERICAN REVOLUTION

Isabel Thompson Kelsay, *Joseph Brant, 1743–1807* (Syracuse: Syracuse, 1984)

Barbara Graymont, *The Iroquois in the American Revolution* (Syracuse: Syracuse, 1972)

Donald A. Grinde, Jr. and Bruce E. Johansen, *Exemplar of Liberty: Native America and the Evolution of Democracy* (Berkeley: University of California, 1991)

Bruce E. Johansen, *Forgotten Founders: Benjamin Franklin, the Iroquois, and the Rationale of the New Nation* (Ipswich: Gambit, 1982)

James H. O'Donnell III, *The Southern Indians in the American Revolution* (Knoxville: University of Tennessee, 1973)

EARLY NATIONAL AND ANTEBELLUM PERIODS

GENERAL WORKS

Gregory Evans Dowd, *A Spirited Resistance: The North American Indian Struggle for Unity, 1745–1815* (Baltimore: Johns Hopkins, 1992)

Philip Weeks, *Farewell, My Nation: The American Indian and the United States* (Arlington Heights: Harlan Davidson, 1990)

NORTHEAST AND OLD NORTHWEST

Robert S. Allen, *His Majesty's Indian Allies: British Indian Policy in the Defence of Canada, 1774–1815* (Toronto: Dundurn Press, 1992)

Allan W. Eckert, *Gateway to Empire* (Boston: Little, Brown, 1983)

R. David Edmunds, *The Shawnee Prophet* (Lincoln: University of Nebraska, 1983)

————, *Tecumseh and the Quest for Indian Leadership* (Boston: Little, Brown, 1984)

Wiley Sword, *President Washington's Indian War: The Struggle for the Old Northwest, 1790–1796* (Norman: University of Oklahoma, 1985)

Anthony F. C. Wallace, *The Death and Rebirth of the Seneca* (New York: Knopf, 1970)

Joyce G. Williams, *Diplomacy on the Indiana-Ohio Frontier, 1783–91* (Bloomington: Indiana, 1976)

SOUTHEAST AND OLD SOUTHWEST

Thomas D. Clark and John D. W. Guice, *Frontiers in Conflict: The Old Southwest, 1795–1830* (Albuquerque: University of New Mexico, 1989)

Florette Henry, *The Southern Indians and Benjamin Hawkins, 1796–1816* (Norman: University of Oklahoma, 1986)

Theda Perdue, *Slavery and the Evolution of Cherokee Society, 1540–1866* (Knoxville: University of Tennessee, 1979)

Daniel H. Usner Jr., *Indians, Settlers, and Slaves in a Frontier Exchange Economy: The Lower Mississippi Valley Before 1783* (Chapel Hill: University of North Carolina, 1992)

TRANS-MISSISSIPPI WEST

Sherburne E. Cook, *The Conflict Between the California Indians and White Civilization* (Berkeley: University of California, 1976)

Julie Roy Jeffrey, *Converting the West: A Biography of Narcissa Whitman* (Norman: University of Oklahoma, 1991)

Janet Lecompte, *Pueblo, Hardscrabble, Greenhorn: The Upper Arkansas, 1832–1856* (Norman: University of Oklahoma, 1978)

James Ronda, *Lewis and Clark Among the Indians* (Lincoln: University of Nebraska, 1984)

James D. Unruh, Jr., *The Plains Across: The Overland Emigrants and the Transmississippi West, 1840–1860* (Urbana: University of Illinois, 1979)

David J. Weber, *The Mexican Frontier, 1821–1846* (Albuquerque: University of New Mexico, 1982)

THE REMOVAL POLICY

Angie Debo, *And Still the Waters Run: The Betrayal of the Five Civilized Tribes* (Princeton: Princeton, 1940)

Arthur H. DeRosier, Jr., *The Removal of the Choctaw Indians* (Knoxville: University of Tennessee, 1970)

John Ehle, *Trail of Tears: The Rise and Fall of the Cherokee Nation* (New York: Doubleday, 1988)

John R. Finger, *The Eastern Band of Cherokees, 1819–1900* (Knoxville: University of Tennessee, 1984)

Grant Foreman, *The Five Civilized Tribes* (Norman: University of Oklahoma, 1934)

——, *Indian Removal* (Norman: University of Oklahoma, 1932)

Arrell M. Gibson, *The Chickasaws* (Norman: University of Oklahoma, 1971)

Michael D. Green, *The Politics of Indian Removal: Creek Government and Society in Crisis* (Lincoln: University of Nebraska, 1982)

Gloria Jahoda, *The Trail of Tears* (New York: Holt, Rinehart and Winston, 1975)

Jane F. Lancaster, *Removal Aftershock: The Seminoles' Struggles to Survive in the West, 1836–1866* (Knoxville: University of Tennessee, 1994)

William G. McLoughlin, *Cherokees and Missionaries, 1789–1839* (New Haven: Yale, 1984)

John K. Mahon, *History of the Second Seminole War, 1835–1842* (Gainesville: Univeristy of Florida, 1967)

Gary E. Moulton, *John Ross: Cherokee Chief* (Athens: University of Georgia, 1978)

Theda Perdue, *Nations Remembered: An Oral History of the Five Civilized Tribes, 1865–1907* (Westport: Greenwood, 1980)

Michael Paul Rogin, *Fathers and Children: Andrew Jackson and the Subjugation of the American Indian* (New York: Knopf, 1975)

Robert N. Satz, *American Indian Policy in the Jacksonian Era* (Lincoln: University of Nebraska, 1975)

Rennard Strickland, *Fire and the Spirits: Cherokee Law from Clan to Court* (Norman: University of Oklahoma, 1975)

Anthony F. C. Wallace, *The Long Bitter Trail: Andrew Jackson and the Indians* (New York: Hill and Wang, 1993)

Mary E. Young, *Redskins, Ruffleshirts, and Rednecks: Indian Allotments in Alabama and Mississippi, 1830–1860* (Norman: University of Oklahoma, 1961)

REFORM

Robert F. Berkhofer, Jr., *Salvation and the Savage: An Analysis of Protestant Missions and American Indian Response, 1787–1862* (Lexington: University Press of Kentucky, 1965)

Christopher Miller, *Prophetic Worlds: Indians and Whites on the Columbia Plateau* (New Brunswick: Rutgers, 1985)

Bernard W. Sheehan, *Seeds of Extinction: Jeffersonian Philanthropy and the American Indian* (Chapel Hill: University of North Carolina, 1973)

GOVERNMENT POLICIES

Reginald Horsman, *Expansion and American Indian Policy, 1783–1812* (East Lansing: Michigan State, 1967)

Francis Paul Prucha, *American Indian Policy in the Formative Years: The Indian Trade and Intercourse Acts, 1790–1834* (Lincoln: University of Nebraska, 1962)

Wiley Sword, *President Washington's Indian War: The Struggle for the Old Northwest* (Norman: University of Oklahoma, 1985)

Helen Horbeck Tanner, *The Greenville Treaty, 1795* (New York: Garland, 1974)

Robert A. Trennert, Jr., *Alternative to Extinction: Federal Indian Policy and the Reservation System, 1846–1851* (Philadelphia: Temple, 1975)

Robert M. Utley, *Frontiersmen in Blue: The United States Army and the Indian, 1848–1865* (New York: Macmillan, 1967)

Herman J. Viola, *Thomas L. McKenney: Architect of America's Early Indian Policy, 1816–1830* (Chicago: Sage, 1974)

CIVIL WAR AND RECONSTRUCTION

M. Thomas Bailey, *Reconstruction in Indian Territory: A Story of Avarice, Discrimination and Opportunism* (Port Washington: Kennikat, 1972)

Edmund J. Danziger, Jr., *Indians and Bureaucrats: Administering the Reservation Policy During the Civil War* (Urbana: University of Illinois, 1974)

W. Craig Gaines, *The Confederate Cherokee* (Baton Rouge: Louisiana State, 1989)

Robert Huhn Jones, *The Civil War in the Northwest: Nebraska, Wisconsin, Iowa, Minnesota, and the Dakotas* (Norman: University of Oklahoma, 1960)

POSTBELLUM PERIOD

GENERAL WORKS

Norman J. Bender, *New Hope For Indians: The Grant Peace Policy and the Navajos in the 1870s* (Albuquerque: University of New Mexico, 1989)

Robert Utley, *The Indian Frontier of the American West, 1846–1890* (Albuquerque: University of New Mexico, 1984)

Philip Weeks, *Farewell, My Nation: The American Indian and the United States* (Arlington Heights: Harlan Davidson, 1990)

THE PLAINS

Ralph K. Andrist, *The Long Death: The Last Days of the Plains Indians* (New York: Macmillan, 1964)

Donald J. Berthrong, *The Cheyenne and Arapaho Ordeal: Reservation and Agency Life in the Indian Territory, 1875–1907* (Norman: University of Oklahoma, 1976)

Richard N. Ellis, *General Pope and U.S. Indian Policy* (Albuquerque: University of New Mexico, 1970)

Robert S. McPherson, *The Northern Navajo Frontier, 1860–1900: Expansion Through Adversity* (Albuquerque: University of New Mexico, 1988)

H. Craig Miner, *The End of Indian Kansas: A Study of Cultural Revolution, 1854–1871* (Lawrence: Regents Press of Kansas, 1978)

William Haas Moore, *Chiefs, Agents and Soldiers: Conflict on the Navajo Frontier* (Albuquerque: University of New Mexico, 1994)

Glenda Riley, *Women and Indians on the Frontier, 1825–1915* (Albuquerque: University of New Mexico, 1984)

David Svaldi, *Sand Creek and the Rhetoric of Extermination* (Lanham: University Press of America, 1989)

Robert M. Utley, *Frontier Regulars: The United States Army and the Indian, 1866–1891* (New York: Macmillan, 1973)

Richard White, *The Roots of Dependency: Subsistence, Environment, and Social Change Among the Choctaws, Pawnees, and Navajos* (Lincoln: University of Nebraska, 1983)

REFORM

Brian W. Dippie, *The Vanishing American: White Attitudes and U.S. Indian Policy* (Middletown: Wesleyan, 1982)

Henry F. Fritz, *The Movement for Indian Assimilation, 1860–1890* (Philadelphia: University of Pennsylvania, 1963)

Everett Arthur Gilcreast, *Richard Henry Pratt and American Indian Policy, 1877–1906* (Ann Arbor: University Microfilms, 1967)

William Thomas Hagan, *The Indian Rights Association: The Herbert Welsh Years, 1882–1904* (Tucson: University of Arizona, 1985)

Frederick E. Hoxie, *A Final Promise: The Campaign to Assimilate the Indians, 1880–1920* (Lincoln: University of Nebraska, 1984)

Robert H. Keller, *American Protestantism and United States Indian Policy, 1869–1882* (Lincoln: University of Nebraska, 1983)

Robert Lewis Mardock, *The Reformers and the American Indian* (Columbia: University of Missouri, 1971)

Clyde A. Milner II, *With Good Intentions: Quaker Work Among the Pawnees, Otos, and Omahas in the 1870s* (Lincoln: University of Nebraska, 1982)

Loring Benson Priest, *Uncle Sam's Stepchildren: The Reformation of United States Policy, 1865–1887* (New Brunswick: Rutgers, 1942)

Francis Paul Prucha, *American Indian Policy in Crisis: Christian Reformers and the Indian, 1865–1900* (Norman: University of Oklahoma, 1976)

————, *The Churches and the Indian Schools, 1888–1912* (Lincoln: University of Nebraska, 1979)

Paul Stuart, *The Indian Office: Growth and Development of an American Institution* (Ann Arbor: UMI Research, 1979)

DAWES ACT

Leonard A. Carlson, *Indians, Bureaucrats and Land: The Dawes Act and the Decline of Indian Farming* (Westport: Greenwood, 1981)

Wilcomb E. Washburn, *The Assault on Indian Tribalism: The General Allotment Law (Dawes Act) of 1887* (Philadelphia: Lippincott, 1975)

TWENTIETH CENTURY

GENERAL HISTORIES AND INTERPRETATIONS

Stephen Cornell, *The Return of the Native: American Indian Political Resurgence* (New York: Oxford, 1988)

Mary B. Davis, ed., *Native America in the Twentieth Century* (New York: Garland, 1994)

Arrell Morgan Gibson, ed., *Between Two Worlds: The Survival of Twentieth Century Indians* (Oklahoma City: Oklahoma Historical Society, 1986)

Fremont J. Lyden and Lyman H. Legters, eds., *Native Americans and Public Policy* (Pittsburgh: University of Pittsburgh, 1992)

James S. Olson and Raymond Wilson, *Native Americans in the Twentieth Century* (Provo: Brigham Young, 1984)

Donald L. Parman, *The Indian in the American West During the Twentieth Century* (Norman: University of Oklahoma, 1994)

Kenneth R. Philp, ed., *Indian Self-Rule: First-Hand Accounts of Indian White Relations from Roosevelt to Reagan* (Salt Lake City: Howe, 1986)

Robert N. Wells, Jr., ed., *Native American Resurgence and Renewal* (Metuchen: Scarecrow, 1994)

JOHN COLLIER AND THE INDIAN NEW DEAL

John Collier, *From Every Zenith: A Memoir* (Denver: Sage, 1963)

Lawrence C. Kelly, *The Assault on Assimilation: John Collier and the Origins of Indian Policy Reform* (Albuquerque: University of New Mexico, 1983)

D'Arcy McNickle and Harold E. Fey, *Indians and Other Americans: Two Ways of Life Meet* (rev. ed.; New York: Harper and Row, 1970)

Donald L. Parman, *The Navajos and the New Deal* (New Haven: Yale, 1976)

Kenneth R. Philp, *John Collier's Crusade for Indian Reform, 1920–1954* (Tucson: University of Arizona, 1977)

Graham D. Taylor, *The New Deal and American Indian Tribalism: The Administration of the Indian Reorganization Act, 1934–1945* (Lincoln: Univeristy of Nebraska, 1980)

WORLD WAR II

Alison R. Bernstein, *American Indians and World War II* (Norman: University of Oklahoma, 1991)

POST–1945

David M. Brugge, *The Navajo-Hopi Land Dispute: An American Tragedy* (Albuquerque: University of New Mexico, 1994)

Larry W. Burt, *Tribalism in Crisis: Federal Indian Policy, 1953–1961* (Albuquerque: University of New Mexico, 1982)

Mary Crow Dog, *Lakota Woman* (New York: Harper, 1990)

Vine Deloria, *Custer Died for Your Sins* (New York: Avon, 1970)

——, *We Talk, You Listen* (New York: Dell, 1970)

Donald L. Fixico, *Termination and Relocation: Federal Indian Policy, 1945–1960* (Albuquerque: Univeristy of New Mexico, 1986)

Jack D. Forbes, *Native Americans and Nixon: Presidential Politics and Minority Self-Determination, 1969–1972* (Los Angeles: American Indian Studies Center, 1981)

Hazel Hertzberg, *The Search for an American Indian Identity: Modern Pan-Indian Movements* (Syracuse: Syracuse, 1971)

Jerry Kammer, *The Second Long Walk: The Navajo-Hopi Land Dispute* (Albuquerque: University of New Mexico, 1980)

Oren Lyons et al., *Exiled in the Land of the Free: Democracy, Indian Nations and the U.S. Constitution* (Santa Fe: Clear Light, 1992)

D'Arcy McNickle, *Native American Tribalism: Indian Survivals and Renewals* (New York: Oxford, 1973)

Elaine M. Neils, *Reservation to City: Indian Migration and Federal Relocation* (Chicago: University of Chicago, 1971)

Gary Orfield, *Ideology and the Indians: A Study of the Termination Policy* (Chicago: University of Chicago, 1965)

Alan L. Sorkin, *American Indians and Federal Aid* (Washington: Brookings Institution, 1973)

————, *The Urban American Indian* (Lexington: Lexington, 1978)

Kenneth S. Stern, *Loud Hawk: The United States Versus the American Indian Movement* (Norman: University of Oklahoma, 1994)

Margaret Connell Szasz, *Education and the American Indian* (Albuquerque: University of New Mexico, 1974)

Jack O. Waddell and O. Michael Watson, eds., *The American Indian in Urban Society* (Lanham: University Press of America, 1971)

REGIONAL STUDIES

ARCTIC AND SUB-ARCTIC

Asen Balikci, *The Netsilik Eskimo* (Prospect Heights: Waveland, 1970)

Charles A. Bishop, *The Northern Ojibwa and the Fur Trade* (Toronto: Holt, Rinehart and Winston, 1974)

Hugh Brody, *Maps and Dreams* (New York: Pantheon, 1981)

Norman A. Chance, *The Inupiat and Arctic Alaska* (Fort Worth: Holt, Rinehart and Winston, 1990)

Olive P. Dickason, *Canada's First Nations* (Norman: University of Oklahoma, 1992)

William W. Fitzhugh and Aron Crowell, eds., *Crossroads of Continents: Cultures of Siberia and Alaska* (Washington: Smithsonian, 1988)

June Helm, *Indians of the Subarctic: A Critical Bibliography* (Bloomington: Indiana, 1976)

Dorothy M. Jones, *Aleuts in Transition* (Seattle: University of Washington, 1976)

James Kari, ed., *Tatl'ahwt'aenn nenn' = the Headwaters People's Country: Narratives of the Upper Ahtna Athabaskans* (Fairbanks: Alaska Native Language Center, 1986)

William S. Laughlin, *Aleuts: Survivors of the Bering Land Bridge* (New York: Holt, Rinehart and Winston, 1980)

A. J. McClanahan, *Our Stories, Our Lives: A Collection of 23 Transcribed Interviews with Elders of the Cook Inlet Region* (Anchorage: CIRI Foundation, 1986)

Moreau S. Maxwell, *Prehistory of the Eastern Arctic* (Orlando: Academic Press, 1985)

Lael Morgan, *Art and Eskimo Power: The Life and Times of Alaska Howard Rock* (Fairbanks: Epicenter Press, 1988)

Richard K. Nelson, *Make Prayers to the Raven* (Chicago: University of Chicago, 1983)

Robin Ridington, *Trail to Heaven* (Iowa City: University of Iowa, 1988)

James W. Van Stone, *Point Hope: An Eskimo Village in Transition* (Seattle: University of Washington, 1962)

Jane Willis, *Geniesh: An Indian Girlhood* (Toronto: New Press, 1973)

CALIFORNIA

Lowell John Bean and Sylvia Brakke Vane, eds., *Ethnology of the Alta California Indians* (New York: Garland, 1991)

Edward D. Castillo, ed., *Native American Perspectives on the Hispanic Colonization of Alta California* (New York: Garland, 1991)

Sherburne F. Cook, *The Conflict Between the California Indian and White Civilization* (Berkeley: University of California, 1976)

———, *The Population of the California Indians, 1769–1970* (Berkeley: University of California, 1976)

Julia G. Costello, ed., *Documentary Evidence for the Spanish Missions of Alta California* (New York: Garland, 1991)

Rupert Coto and Jeannette Henry Costo, eds., *The Missions of California: A Legacy of Genocide* (San Francisco: Indian Historian Press, 1987)

James E. Downs, *The Two Worlds of the Washo* (New York: Holt, Rinehart and Winston, 1966)

William Henry Ellison, *Federal Indian Policy in California, 1846–1860* (San Francisco: R and E Research, 1974)

Jack D. Forbes, *Native Americans of California and Nevada* (Happy Land: Naturegraph, 1982)

Robert F. Heizer, ed., *The Destruction of the California Indians: A Collection of Documents from the Period 1847 to 1865* (Lincoln: University of Nebraska, 1993)

———, *Indians of California: A Critical Bibliography* (Bloomington: Indiana, 1976)

Robert F. Heizer and M. A. Whipple, *The California Indians* (Berkeley: University of California, 1971)

Albert L. Hurtado, *Indian Survival on the California Frontier* (New Haven: Yale, 1988)

Theodora Kroeber, *Ishi in Two Worlds* (Berkeley: University of California, 1961)

George Harwood Phillips, *Chiefs and Challengers: Indian Resistance and Cooperation in Southern California* (Berkeley: University of California, 1975)

———, *Indians and Intruders in Central California, 1769–1849* (Norman: University of Oklahoma, 1993)

James J. Rawls, *Indians of California: The Changing Image* (Norman: University of Oklahoma, 1984)

CANADA

Denys Delage, *Bitter Feast: Amerindians and Europeans in Northeastern North America, 1600–64* (trans. Jane Brierley; Vancouver: UBC, 1993)

Olive P. Dickason, *Canada's First Nations: A History of Founding Peoples* (Norman: University of Oklahoma, 1992)

Robert J. Surtees, *Canadian Indian Policy: A Critical Bibliography* (Bloomington: Indiana, 1982)

Bruce G. Trigger, *Natives and Newcomers: Canada's "Heroic Age" Reconsidered* (Kingston: McGill-Queens University, 1985)

GREAT BASIN

David Rich Lewis, *Neither Wolf Nor Dog: American Indians, Environment, and Agrarian Change* (New York: Oxford, 1994)

Omer C. Stewart, *Indians of the Great Basin: A Critical Bibliography* (Bloomington: Indiana, 1982)

GREAT LAKES

Charles E. Cleland, *Rites of Conquest: The History and Culture of Michigan's Native Americans* (Ann Arbor: University of Michigan, 1992)

Carol Devens, *Countering Colonization: Native American Women and Great Lakes Missions, 1630–1900* (Berkeley: University of California, 1992)

Harold Hickerson, *The Chippewa and their Neighbors* (Prospect Heights: Waveland, 1988)

Carol I. Mason, *Introduction to Wisconsin Indians: Prehistory to Statehood* (Salem: Sheffield, 1988)

Ronald J. Mason, *Great Lakes Archaeology* (New York: Academic, 1981)

Robert E. Ritzenthaler and Pat Ritzenthaler, *The Woodland Indians of the Western Great Lakes* (Milwaukee: Milwaukee Public Museum, 1983)

Helen Hornbeck Tanner, ed., *Atlas of Great Lakes Indian History* (Norman: University of Oklahoma, 1987)

Richard White, *The Middle Ground: Indians, Empires, and Republics in the Great Lakes Region, 1650–1815* (New York: Cambridge, 1991)

NEW ENGLAND AND THE NORTHEAST

Peter Benes, ed., *Algonkians of New England* (Boston: Boston University, 1993)

Russell Bourne, *The Red King's Rebellion: Racial Politics in New England, 1675–1678* (New York: Oxford, 1990)

Paul Brodeur, *Restitution: The Land Claims of the Mashpee, Passamaquoddy, and Penobscot Indians of New England* (Boston: Northeastern, 1985)

Lynn Ceci, *The Effect of European Contact and Trade on the Settlement Pattern of Indians in Coastal New York, 1524–1665* (New York: Garland, 1990)

Laurence M. Hauptman and Jack Campisi, eds., *Neighbors and Intruders: An Ethnohistorical Exploration of the Indians of Hudson's River* (Ottowa: National Museum of Canada, 1978)

William A. Haviland, *The Original Vermonters: Native Inhabitants Past and Present* (rev. ed.; Hanover: University Press of New England, 1994)

Warren Sears Nickerson, *Early Encounters—Native Americans and Europeans in New England*; edited by Delores Bird Carpenter (East Lansing: Michigan State, 1994)

Howard S. Russell, *Indian New England Before the Mayflower* (Hanover: University Press of New England, 1980)

Neal Salisbury, *Indians, Europeans, and the Making of New England, 1500–1643* (New York: Oxford, 1982)

Dean R. Snow, *The Archaeology of New England* (New York: Academic Press, 1980)

Peter A. Thomas, *In the Maelstrom of Change: The Indian Trade and Cultural Process in the Middle Connecticut River Valley, 1635–1665* (New York: Garland, 1990)

Elisabeth Tooker, *The Indians of the Northeast: A Critical Bibliography* (Bloomington: Indiana, 1978)

PACIFIC NORTHEAST

June McCormick Collins, *Valley of the Spirits* (Seattle: University of Washington, 1974)

John Fahey, *The Kalispel Indians* (Norman: University of Oklahoma, 1986)

Robert Steven Grumet, *Native Americans of the Northwest Coast: A Critical Bibliography* (Bloomington: Indiana, 1979)

Erna Gunther, *Indian Life on the Northwest Coast of America* (Chicago: University of Chicago, 1972)

Bill Holm, *Northwest Coast Indian Art* (Seattle: University of Washington, 1965)

Claudia Lewis, *Indian Families of the Northwest Coast* (Chicago: University of Chicago, 1970)

T. F. McIlwraith, *The Bella Coola Indians* (Toronto: University of Toronto, 1948)

Rosalind C. Morris, *New Worlds from Fragments: Film, Ethnography, and the Representation of Northwest Coast Cultures* (Boulder: Westview, 1994)

Jacqueline Peterson, *Sacred Encounters: Father De Smet and the Indians of the Rocky Mountain West* (Norman: University of Oklahoma, 1993)

Derek Pethick, *First Approaches to the Northwest Coast* (Vancouver: Douglas and McIntyre, 1976)

Jeffrey C. Reichwein, *Emergence of Native American Nationalism in the Columbia Plateau* (New York: Garland, 1990)

Robert H. Ruby, *Indians of the Pacific Northwest* (Norman: University of Oklahoma, 1981)

Robert H. Ruby and John A. Brown, *Indian Slavery in the Pacific Northwest* (Spokane: A.H. Clark, 1993)

Hilary Stewart, *Indian Fishing* (Seattle: University of Washington, 1977)

Clifford E. Trafzer, ed., *Northwestern Tribes in Exile: Modoc, Nez Percé, and Palouse Removal to the Indian Territory* (Sacramento: Sierra Oaks, 1987)

Clifford E. Trafzer and Richard D. Sheuerman, *Renegade Tribe: The Palouse Indians and the Invasion of the Inland Pacific Northwest* (Pullman: Washington State, 1986)

PLAINS

Gary Clayton Anderson, *Kinsmen of Another Kind: Dakota–White Relations in the Upper Mississippi Valley, 1650–1862* (Lincoln: University of Nebraska, 1984)

James Clifton, *The Prairie People: Continuity and Change in Potawatomi Indian Culture, 1665–1965* (Lawrence: Regents Press of Kansas, 1977)

Ella Cara Deloria, *Waterlily* (Lincoln: University of Nebraska, 1988)

Raymond J. DeMallie, ed., *The Sixth Grandfather: Black Elk's Teachings Given to John G. Neihardt* (Lincoln: University of Nebraska, 1984)

Eleanor Grobsmith, *Lakota of the Rosebud: A Contemporary Ethnography* (New York: Holt, Rinehart and Winston, 1981)

Philip S. Hall, *To Have This Land: The Nature of Indian/White Relations, South Dakota, 1888–1891* (Vermillion: University of South Dakota, 1991)

Joseph B. Herring, *The Enduring Indians of Kansas* (Lawrence: Regents Press of Kansas, 1990)

E. Adamson Hoebel, *The Plains Indians: A Critical Bibliography* (Bloomington: Indiana, 1977)

Stanley Hoig, *Tribal Wars of the Southern Plains* (Norman: University of Oklahoma, 1993)

Peter Iverson, ed., *The Plains Indians of the Twentieth Century* (Norman: University of Oklahoma, 1985)

David E. Jones, *Sanapia, Comanche Medicine Woman* (Prospect Heights: Waveland, 1972)

Charles L. Kenner, *The Comanchero Frontier: A History of New Mexican–Plains Indian Relations* (Norman: University of Oklahoma, 1994)

Roy W. Meyer, *The Village Indians of the Upper Missouri* (Lincoln: University of Nebraska, 1977)

Rennard Strickland, *The Indians in Oklahoma* (Norman: University of Oklahoma, 1980)

Waldo R. Wedel, *Prehistoric Man on the Great Plains* (Norman: University of Oklahoma, 1961)

W. Raymond Wood and Margot Liberty, eds., *Anthropology on the Great Plains* (Lincoln: University of Nebraska, 1980)

SOUTHEAST

Alex W. Barker and Timothy R. Pauketat, eds., *Lords of the Southeast: Social Inequality and Native Elites of Southeastern North America* (Washington: American Anthropological Association, 1992)

Robin C. Brown, *Florida's First People: 12,000 Years of Human History* (Sarasota: Pineapple, 1994)

John H. Hann, *Apalachee: The Land Between the Rivers* (Gainesville: University of Florida, 1988)

Charles Hudson, *The Southeastern Indians* (Knoxville: Univeristy of Tennessee, 1976)

James Howlett O'Donnell III, *Southeastern Frontiers: Europeans, Africans, and American Indians, 1513–1840* (Bloomington: Indiana, 1982)

John R. Swanton, *The Indians of the Southeastern United States* (Washington: Smithsonian, 1946)

Walter L. Williams, ed., *Southeastern Indians Since the Removal Era* (Athens: University of Georgia, 1979)

Peter Wood, Gregory A. Waselkov, and M. Thomas Hatley, eds., *Powhatan's Mantle: Indians in the Colonial Southeast* (Lincoln: University of Nebraska, 1989)

J. Leitch Wright, Jr., *Creeks and Seminoles: The Destruction and Regeneration of the Muscogulge People* (Lincoln: University of Nebraska, 1986)

SOUTHWEST

Carol J. Condie and Don D. Fowler, eds., *Anthropology of the Desert West* (Salt Lake City: University of Utah, 1986)

Linda S. Cordell, *Prehistory of the Southwest* (Orlando: Academic Press, 1984)

Henry F. Dobyns and Robert C. Euler, *Indians of the Southwest: A Critical Bibliography* (Bloomington: Indiana, 1980)

Jack D. Forbes, *Apache, Navaho and Spaniard* (Westport: Greenwood, 1980)

Richard I. Ford, ed., *The Prehistorical American Southwest: A Sourcebook* (New York: Garland, 1987)

Kendrick Frazier, *People of Chaco: A Canyon and Its Culture* (New York: W.W. Norton, 1986)

Geoge Gummerman, ed., *Themes in Southwest Prehistory* (Santa Fe: School of American Research, 1994)

Elizabeth A. H. John, *Storms Brewed in Other Men's Worlds: The Confrontation of Indians, Spanish, and French in the Southwest, 1540–1795* (College Station: Texas A&M, 1975)

Paul E. Minnis and Charles L. Redmond, eds., *Perspectives on Southwestern Prehistory* (Boulder: Westview, 1990)

Carroll L. Riley, *The Frontier People: The Greater Soutwest in the Protohistoric Period* (rev. ed.; Albuquerque: University of New Mexico, 1987)

Edward E. Spicer, *Cycles of Conquest: The Impact of Spain, Mexico, and the United States on the Indians of the Southwest, 1533–1960* (Tucson: University of Arizona, 1962)

———, *People of Pascua* (Tucson: University of Arizona, 1988)

Christine R. Szuter, *Hunting by Prehistoric Horticulturalists in the American Southwest* (New York: Garland, 1991)

David Weber, *The Spanish Frontier in North America* (New Haven: Yale, 1992)

Anne I. Woolsey and John C. Ravesloot, eds., *Culture and Contact: Charles C. Di Peso's Gran Chichimeca* (Albuquerque: University of New Mexico, 1993)

SPECIFIC PEOPLES

ABENAKIS

Colin G. Calloway, *The Western Abenakis of Vermont, 1600–1800: War, Migration, and the Survival of an Indian People* (Norman: University of Oklahoma, 1990)

Kenneth M. Morrison, *The Embattled Northeast: The Elusive Ideal of Alliance in Abenaki-Euramerican Relations* (Berkeley: University of California, 1984)

APACHES

Eve Ball, *Indeh, An Apache Odyssey* (Norman: University of Oklahoma, 1988)

Keith H. Basso, *The Cibecue Apache* (New York: Holt, Rinehart and Winston, 1970)

D. C. Cole, *The Chiricahua Apache, 1846–1876: From War to Reservation* (Albuquerque: University of New Mexico, 1988)

William B. Griffen, *Apaches at War and Peace: The Janos Presidio, 1750–1858* (Albuquerque: University of New Mexico, 1988)

———, *Utmost Good Faith: Patterns of Apache–Mexican Hostilities in Northern Chihuahua Border Warfare, 1821–1848* (Albuquerque: University of New Mexico, 1988)

James L. Haley, *Apaches: A History and Cultural Portrait* (Garden City: Doubleday, 1981)

Michael Edward Melody, *The Apache* (New York: Chelsea House, 1989)

Richard John Perry, *Apache Reservation: Indigenous Peoples and the American State* (Austin: University of Texas, 1993)

David Roberts, *Once They Moved Like the Winds: Cochise, Geronimo, and the Apache Wars* (New York: Simon and Schuster, 1993)

H. Henrietta Stockel, *Survival of the Spirit: Chiricahua Apaches in Captivity* (Reno: University of Nevada, 1993)

Edwin R. Sweeney, *Cochise: Chiricahua Apache Chief* (Norman: University of Oklahoma, 1991)

Donald E. Worcester, *The Apaches: Eagles of the Southwest* (Norman: University of Oklahoma, 1979)

ARAPAHOS

Loretta Fowler, *Arapahoe Politics, 1851–1978* (Lincoln: University of Nebraska, 1982)

BLACKFEET

William E. Farr, *The Reservation Blackfeet, 1882–1945* (Seattle: University of Washington, 1984)

Malcolm McFee, *Modern Blackfeet* (New York: Holt, Rinehart and Winston, 1972)

Hana Samek, *The Blackfoot Confederacy, 1880–1920* (Albuquerque: University of New Mexico, 1987)

CATAWBAS

Charles M. Hudson, *The Catawba Nation* (Athens: University of Georgia, 1970)

James E. Merrell, *The Indians' New World: Catawbas and Their Neighbors from European Contact through the Era of Removal* (Chapel Hill: University of North Carolina, 1989)

CHEROKEES

Mary Whatley Clarke, *Chief Bowles and the Texas Cherokees* (Norman: University of Oklahoma, 1971)

Roy S. Dickens, Jr., *Cherokee Prehistory: The Pisgah Phase in the Appalachian Summit Region* (Knoxville: University of Tennessee, 1976)

Dianna Everett, *The Texas Cherokees, 1819–1840* (Norman: University of Oklahoma, 1990)

John R. Finger, *Cherokee Americans: The Eastern Band of Cherokees in the Twentieth Century* (Lincoln: University of Nebraska, 1991)

———, *The Eastern Band of Cherokees, 1819–1900* (1984)

Raymond D. Fogelson, *The Cherokees: A Critical Bibliography* (Bloomington: Indiana, 1978)

W. Craig Gaines, *The Confederate Cherokees* (Baton Rouge: Louisiana State, 1989)

M. Thomas Hatley, *The Dividing Paths: Cherokees and South Carolinians Through the Era of Revolution* (New York: Oxford, 1992)

Duane H. King, ed., *The Cherokee Indian Nation: A Troubled History* (Knoxville: University of Tennessee, 1979)

William G. McLoughlin, *After the Trail of Tears: The Cherokees' Struggle for Sovereignty, 1839–1880* (Chapel Hill: University of North Carolina, 1993)

———, *Cherokee Renascence in the New Republic* (Princeton: Princeton, 1986)

Thomas E. Mails, *The Cherokee People* (Tulsa: Council Oak, 1992)
Gary E. Moulton, *John Ross, Cherokee Chief* (Athens: University of Georgia, 1978)
———, ed., *The Papers of John Ross* (Norman: Univeristy of Oklahoma, 1985)
Theda Perdue, *Slavery and the Evolution of Cherokee Society* (Knoxville: University of Tennessee, 1979)
Rennard Strickland, *Fire and the Spirits: Cherokee Law from Clan to Court* (Norman: University of Oklahoma, 1975)
Thurman Wilkins, *Cherokee Tragedy: The Ridge Family and the Decimation of a People* (Norman: University of Oklahoma, 1986)
David Williams, *The Georgia Gold Rush* (Columbia: University of South Carolina, 1992)

CHEYENNES

E. Adamson Hoebel, *The Cheyenne: Indians of the Great Plains* (2nd ed.; New York: Holt, Rinehart and Winston, 1978)
Stan Hoig, *The Peace Chiefs of the Cheyennes* (Norman: University of Oklahoma, 1980)
Margot Liberty, *Cheyenne Memories* (Lincoln: University of Nebraska, 1991)
John H. Moore, *The Cheyenne Nation* (Lincoln: University of Nebraska, 1987)
Peter J. Powell, *The Cheyennes: Maheoo's People: A Critical Bibliography* (Bloomington: Indiana, 1980)
———, *People of the Sacred Mountain* (San Francisco: Harper and Row, 1981)

CHOCTAWS

W. David Baird, *Peter Pitchlynn: Chief of the Choctaws* (Norman: University of Oklahoma, 1972)
Clara Sue Kidwell and Charles Roberts, *The Choctaws: A Critical Bibliography* (Bloomington: Indiana, 1980)
Jesse O. McKee and Jon A. Schlenker, *The Choctaws: Cultural Evolution of a Native American Tribe* (Jackson: University of Mississippi, 1980)
Carolyn Keller Reeves, ed., *The Choctaw Before Removal* (Jackson: University Press of Mississippi, 1985)
Samuel J. Wells and Roseanna Tubby, *After Removal: The Choctaw in Mississippi* (Jackson: University Press of Mississippi, 1986)

COMANCHES

T. R. Fehrenbach, *Comanches: The Destruction of a People* (New York: Knopf, 1974)
Morris W. Foster, *Being Comanche: A Social History of an Indian Community* (Tucson: University of Arizona, 1991)
William T. Hagan, *Quanah Parker, Comanche Chief* (Norman: University of Oklahoma, 1993)
———, *United States–Comanche Relations: The Reservation Years* (New Haven: Yale, 1976)
Stanley Noyes, *Los Comanches: The Horse People, 1751–1845* (Albuquerque: University of New Mexico, 1993)

CREES

Hugh Aylmer Dempsey, *Big Bear: The End of Freedom* (Vancouver: Douglas & McIntyre, 1984)
John Sheridan Milloy, *The Plains Cree: Trade, Diplomacy, and War, 1790 to 1870* (Winnipeg: University of Manitoba, 1990)
Dale R. Russell, *Eighteenth Century Western Cree and Their Neighbors* (Hull: Canadian Museum of Civilization, 1991)

CREEKS

W. David Baird, ed., *A Creek Warrior for the Confederacy: The Autobiography of Chief G. W. Grayson* (Norman: University of Oklahoma, 1988)

Kathryn E. Holland Braund, *Deerskins & Duffels: The Creek Indian Trade with Anglo-America, 1685–1815* (Lincoln: University of Nebraska, 1993)

David H. Corkran, *The Creek Frontier, 1540–1783* (Norman: University of Oklahoma, 1967)

James Fletcher Doster, *The Creek Indians and Their Florida Lands, 1740–1823* (New York: Garland, 1974)

Michael D. Green, *The Creeks: A Critical Bibliography* (Bloomington: Indiana, 1979)

———, *The Politics of Indian Removal: Creek Government and Society in Crisis* (Lincoln: University of Nebraska, 1982)

Benjamin W. Griffith, Jr., *McIntosh and Weatherford: Creek Indian Leaders* (Tuscaloosa: University of Alabama, 1988)

Joel W. Martin, *Sacred Revolt: The Muskogees' Struggle for a New World* (Boston: Beacon, 1991)

Henry deLeon Southernland, *The Federal Road Through Georgia, the Creek Nation, and Alabama, 1806–1836* (Tuscaloosa: University of Alabama, 1989)

J. Leitch Wright, Jr., *Creeks and Seminoles: The Destruction and Regeneration of the Muscogulge People* (Lincoln: University of Nebraska, 1986)

CROWS

Keith W. Algier, *The Crow and the Eagle* (Caldwell: Caxton, 1993)

Rodney Frey, *The World of the Crow Indians* (Norman: University of Oklahoma, 1987)

DELAWARES

Herbert C. Kraft, *The Lenape, Archaeology, History, and Ethnography* (Newark: New Jersey Historical Society, 1986)

Earl P. Olmstead, *Blackcoats Among the Delaware: David Zeisberger on the Ohio Frontier* (Kent: Kent State, 1991)

Regula Trenkwalder Schonenberger, *Lenape Women, Matriliny, and the Colonial Encounter* (Bern: P. Lang, 1991)

Anthony F. C. Wallace, *King of the Delawares: Teedyuscung, 1700–1763* (Syracuse: Syracuse, 1990)

C. A. Weslager, *The Delaware Indians* (New Brunswick: Rutgers, 1972)

FLATHEADS

John Fahey, *The Flathead Indians* (Norman: University of Oklahoma, 1974)

GROS VENTRES

Loretta Fowler, *Shared Symbols, Contested Meanings: Gros Ventre Culture and History, 1778–1984* (Ithaca: Cornell, 1987)

HOHOKAMS

Emil W. Haury, *The Hohokam, Desert Farmers and Craftsmen: Excavations at Snakestown, 1964–65* (Tucson: Univeristy of Arizona, 1976)

Randall H. McGuire, *Death, Society, and Ideology in a Hohokam Community* (Boulder: Westview, 1992)

HOPEWELL

David S. Brose and N'omi Greber, eds., *Hopewell Archaeology* (Kent: Kent State, 1979)

Hurons

Elisabeth Tooker, *An Ethnography of the Huron Indians, 1615–1649* (Syracuse: Syracuse, 1991)

Bruce G. Trigger, *The Children of Aataentsic: A History of the Huron People to 1660* (Montreal: McGill-Queens, 1976)

——, *The Huron* (2nd ed.; Fort Worth: Holt, Rinehart and Winston, 1990)

Ioways

Martha Royce Blaine, *The Ioway Indians* (Norman: University of Oklahoma, 1979)

Iroquois

Richard Aquila, *The Iroquois Restoration: Iroquois Diplomacy on the Colonial Frontier, 1701–1754* (Detroit: Wayne State, 1983)

James W. Bradley, *Evolution of the Onondaga Iroquois* (Syracuse: Syracuse, 1987)

——, *Onondaga Iroquois Prehistory* (Syracuse: Syracuse University, 1971)

Jack Campisi and Laurence Hauptman, eds., *The Oneida Indian Experience* (Syracuse: Syracuse, 1988)

Michael K. Foster, Jack Campisi, and Marianne Mithun, eds., *Extending the Rafters: Interdisciplinary Approaches to Iroquoian Studies* (Albany: State University of New York, 1984)

Joseph A. Francello, *The Seneca World of Ga-No-Say-Yeh* (New York: P. Lang, 1989)

Laurence M. Hauptman, *The Iroquois and the New Deal* (Syracuse: Syracuse, 1981)

——, *The Iroquois in the Civil War* (Syracuse: Syracuse, 1993)

——, *The Iroquois Struggle for Survival: World War II to Red Power* (Syracuse: Syracuse, 1986)

Barbara Graymont, *The Iroquois in the American Revolution* (Syracuse: Syracuse, 1972)

Francis Jennings, *The Ambiguous Iroquois Empire* (New York: W.W. Norton, 1984)

Francis Jennings, William N. Fenton, and Mary A. Druke, eds., *The History and Culture of Iroquois Diplomacy* (Syracuse: Syracuse, 1985)

Daniel H. Page, *Sacred Life: A North American Indian Ethnohistory Emphasizing the Iroquoians of the Eastern Woodlands* (Barrie, Ont.: Pine Tree, 1987)

Daniel K. Richter, *The Ordeal of the Longhouse: The Peoples of the Iroquois League in the Era of European Colonization* (Chapel Hill: University of North Carolina, 1990)

Daniel K. Richter and James H. Merrell, eds., *Beyond the Covenant Chain: The Iroquois and Their Neighbors in Indian North America, 1600–1800* (Syracuse: Syracuse, 1987)

Anthony F. C. Wallace, *The Death and Rebirth of the Seneca* (New York: Knopf, 1970)

Kansas

William E. Unrau, *The Emigrant Indians of Kansas: A Critical Bibliography* (Bloomington: Indiana, 1979)

——, *The Kansa Indians* (Norman: University of Oklahoma, 1971)

Kickapoos

Arrell Morgan Gibson, *The Kickapoos* (Norman: University of Oklahoma, 1963)

Joseph B. Herring, *Kenekuk, the Kickapoo Prophet* (Lawrence: University Press of Kansas, 1988)

Kiowas

Alice Marriott, *Greener Fields* (New York: Doubleday, 1962)

Mildred P. Mayhall, *The Kiowas* (2nd ed.; Norman: University of Oklahoma, 1971)

Jim Whitewolf, *Jim Whitewolf: The Life of a Kiowa Apache Indian* (New York: Dover, 1969)

KLAMATHS

Theodore Stern, *The Klamath Tribe* (Seattle: University of Washington, 1966)
Lucy Thompson, *To the American Indian: Reminiscences of a Yurok Woman* (Berkeley: Heyday Books, 1991)

KWAKIUTLS

Philip Drucker and Robert Heizer, *To Make My Name Good: A Reexamination of the Southern Kwakiutl Potlatch* (Berkeley: University of California, 1967)
Ruth Kirk, *Wisdom of the Elders* (Vancouver: Douglas & McIntyre, 1986)

LUMBEES

Karen I. Blu, *The Lumbee Problem: The Making of an American Indian People* (New York: Cambridge, 1980)
Adolph L. Dial, *The Only Land I Know: A History of the Lumbee Indians* (San Francisco: Indian Historian, 1975)
Gerald M. Sider, *Lumbee Indian Histories: Race, Ethnicity, and Indian Identity* (Cambridge: Cambridge, 1993)

MASHPEES

Jack Campisi, *The Mashpee Indians: Tribe on Trial* (Syracuse: Syracuse, 1991)
Russell M. Peters, *The Wampanoags of Mashpee: An Indian Perspective on American History* (Somerville: Media Action, 1987)

MENOMINEES

Patrick K. Ourada, *The Menominee Indians: A History* (Norman: University of Oklahoma, 1979)
Nicholas C. Peroff, *Menominee Drums: Tribal Termination and Restoration, 1954–1974* (Norman: University of Oklahoma, 1973)

METIS

Madeline Bird, *Living Kindness: The Memoirs of Metis Elder* (Yellowknife: Outcrop, 1991)
Julia D. Harrison, *Metis: People Between Two Worlds* (Vancouver: Douglas & McIntyre, 1985)
Diane Payment, *"The Free People"* (Ottawa: National Historic Parks, 1991)
Jacqueline Peterson and Jennifer S. H. Brown, eds., *The New Peoples: Being and Becoming Metis in North America* (1985)

MISSISSIPPIANS

David H. Dye and Cheryl Anne Cox, eds., *Towns and Temples Along the Mississippi* (Tuscaloosa: University of Alabama, 1990)
Thomas E. Emerson and R. Barry Lewis, *Cahokia and the Hinterlands* (Urbana: University of Illinois, 1991)
Claudia Gellman Mink, *Cahokia: City of the Sun* (Collinsville: Cahokia Mounds Museum, 1992)
Peter N. Peregrine, *Mississippian Evolution* (Madison: Prehistory, 1992)
Mary Lucas Powell, *Status and Health in Prehistory: A Case Study of the Moundville Chiefdom* (Washington: Smithsonian, 1988)

Bruce D. Smith, *The Mississippian Emergence* (Washington: Smithsonian, 1990)
J. B. Stoltman, ed., *New Perspectives on Cahokia* (Madison: Prehistory, 1991)

MODOCS

Odie B. Faulk, *The Modoc People* (Phoenix: Indian Tribal Series, 1976)

MOHAWKS

Richard Dean Campbell, *The People of the Land of Flint* (Lanham: University Press of America, 1985)

NANTICOKES

C. A. Weslager, *The Nanticoke Indians—Past and Present* (Newark: Univeristy of Delaware, 1983)

NAVAJOS

Garrick Bailey and Roberta Glenn Bailey, *A History of the Navajos: The Reservation Years* (Santa Fe: School of American Research, 1986)
Henry F. Dobyns, *The Navajo Indians* (Phoenix: Indian Tribal Series, 1977)
James F. Downs, *The Navajo* (New York: Holt, Rinehart and Winston, 1972)
Cheryl Howard, *Navajo Tribal Demography, 1983–1986* (New York: Garland, 1993)
Peter Iverson, *The Navajo Nation* (Westport: Greenwood, 1981)
———, *The Navajos* (New York: Chelsea House, 1990)
Clyde Kluckhohn and Dorothea Leighton, *The Navaho* (Garden City: Doubleday, 1962)
Karl W. Luckert, *The Navajo Hunter Tradition* (Tucson: University of Arizona, 1975)
Robert S. McPherson, *The Northern Navajo Frontier, 1860–1900: Expansion Through Adversity* (Albuquerque: University of New Mexico, 1988)
William Haas Moore, *Chiefs, Agents and Soldiers: Conflict on the Navajo Frontier, 1868–1882* (Albuquerque: Univeristy of New Mexico, 1994)

NEZ PERCÉS

Haruo Aoki and Deward E. Walker, Jr., *Nez Perće Oral Narratives* (Berkeley: University of California, 1989)
Clifford M. Drury, *Chief Lawyer of the Nez Percé Indians, 1796–1876* (Glendale: A.H. Clar, 1979)
Alvin M. Josephy, Jr., *The Nez Percé Indians and the Opening of the Northwest* (1965)

OJIBWAS

Charles A. Bishop, *The Northern Ojibwa and the Fur Trade* (Toronto: Holt, Rinehart and Winston, 1974)
Edmund Jefferson Danziger, Jr., *The Chippewas of Lake Superior* (Norman: University of Oklahoma, 1978)
A. Irving Hallowell, *The Ojibwa of Berens River, Manitoba: Ethnography into History* (Fort Worth: Harcourt Brace Jovanovich, 1991)
Harold Hickerson, *The Chippewa and Their Neighbors* (rev. ed.; Prospect Heights: Waveland, 1988)
Melissa L. Meyer, *The White Earth Tragedy: Ethnicity and Dispossession at the Minnesota Anishinaabe Reservation, 1889–1920* (Lincoln: University of Nebraska, 1994)
Peter S. Schmalz, *The Ojibwa of Southern Ontario* (Toronto: University of Toronto, 1991)
Helen Hornbeck Tanner, *The Ojibwas: A Critical Bibliography* (Bloomington: Indiana, 1976)

Gerald Vizenor, *The People Named Chippewa* (Minneapolis: University of Minnesota, 1984)

PAIUTES

Pamela Ann Bunte and Robert J. Franklin, *From the Sands to the Mountain: Change and Persistence in a Southern Paiute Community* (Lincoln: University of Nebraska, 1987)

Gae Whitney Canfield, *Sarah Winnemucca of the Northern Paiutes* (Norman: University of Oklahoma, 1983)

Robert C. Euler, *The Paiute People* (Phoenix: Indian Tribal Series, 1972)

Ronald L. Holt, *Beneath These Red Cliffs: An Ethnohistory of the Utah Paiutes* (Albuquerque: University of New Mexico, 1992)

PAPAGOS

Alice Joseph, Rosamond B. Spicer, and Jane Chesky, *The Desert People: A Study of the Papago Indians* (Chicago: Univeristy of Chicago, 1949)

Ruth M. Underhill, *Papago Woman* (New York: Holt, Rinehart and Winston, 1979)

PAWNEES

Martha Royce Blaine, *Pawnee Passage, 1870–1875* (Norman: University of Oklahoma, 1990)

———, *The Pawnees: A Critical Bibliography* (Bloomington: Indiana, 1980)

PISCATAWAYS

Paul Byron Cissna, *The Piscataway Indians of Southern Maryland: An Ethnohistory from Pre-European Contact to the Present* (n.p.: n.p., 1986)

POKAGONS

James A. Clifton, *The Pokagons, 1638–1983* (Lanham: University Press of America, 1984)

POTAWATOMIS

James Clifton, *The Prairie People: Continuity and Change in Potawatomi Indian Culture, 1665–1965* (Lawrence: Regents Press of Kansas, 1977)

R. David Edmunds, *Kinsmen Through Time: An Annotated Bibliography* (Metuchen: Scarecrow, 1987)

———, *The Potawatomis: Keepers of the Fire* (Norman: University of Oklahoma, 1978)

POWHATANS

J. Frederick Fausz, *The Powhatan Uprising of 1622* (Ann Arbor: University Microfilms, 1981)

Helen C. Rountree, *Pocahontas's People: The Powhatan Indians of Virginia Through Four Centuries* (Norman: University of Oklahoma Press, 1990)

———, *The Powhatan Indians of Virginia* (Norman: University of Oklahoma, 1988)

———, ed., *Powhatan Foreign Relations, 1500–1722* (Charlottesville: University Press of Virginia, 1993)

PUEBLOS

Richard O. Clemmer, *Continuities of Hopi Culture Change* (Ramona: Acoma, 1978)

Edward P. Dozier, *Hano: A Tewa Indian Community in Arizona* (New York: Holt, Rinehart and Winston, 1966)

————, *The Pueblo Indians of North America* (Prospect Heights: Waveland, 1970)
J. Manuel Espinosa, ed., *The Pueblo Indian Revolt of 1696 and the Franciscan Missions in New Mexico* (Norman: University of Oklahoma, 1988)
Ward Alan Minge, *Acoma: Pueblo in the Sky* (Albuquerque: University of New Mexico, 1976)
Peter Nabokov, *Indian Running* (Santa Barbara: Capra Press, 1981)
Alfonso Ortiz, *The Tewa World: Space, Time, Being and Becoming in a Pueblo Society* (Chicago: University of Chicago, 1969)
Joe S. Sando, *The Pueblo Indians* (San Francisco: Indian Historian, 1976)
Peter M. Whiteley, *Deliberate Acts: Changing Hopi Culture Through the Oraibi Split* (Tucson: University of Arizona, 1988)

ROGUES

Stephen Dow Beckham, *Requiem for a People: The Rogue Indians and the Frontiersmen* (Norman: University of Oklahoma, 1971)

SEMINOLES

James W. Covington, *The Seminoles of Florida* (Gainesville: University Press of Florida, 1993)
Merwyn S. Gabarino, *Big Cypress: A Changing Seminole Community* (New York: Holt and Winston, 1972)
James Henri Howard, *Oklahoma Seminoles* (Norman: University of Oklahoma, 1984)
Harry A. Kersey, Jr., *Pelts, Plumes, and Hides: White Traders Among the Seminole Indians, 1870–1930* (Gainesville: University Press of Florida, 1975)
Jane F. Lancaster, *Removal Aftershock: the Seminoles' Struggles to Survive in the West, 1836–1866* (Knoxville: University of Tennessee, 1994)
Kevin Mulroy, *Freedom on the Border: The Seminole Maroons in Florida, the Indian Territory, Coahuuila, and Texas* (Lubbock: Texas Tech, 1993)
Brent Richards Weisman, *Like Beads on a String: A Cultural History of the Seminole Indians in Northern Peninsular Florida* (Tuscaloosa: University of Alabama, 1989)
Patricia R. Wickman, *Osceola's Legacy* (Tuscaloosa: University of Alabama, 1991)
J. Leitch Wright, Jr., *Creeks and Seminoles: The Destruction and Regeneration of the Muscogulge People* (Lincoln: University of Nebraska, 1986)

SHAWNEES

Jerry E. Clark, *The Shawnee* (Lexington: University Press of Kentucky, 1977)
James H. Howard, *Shawnee!: the Ceremonialism of a Native Indian Tribe and Its Cultural Background* (Athens: Ohio University, 1981)

SHOSHONIS

Hank Corless, *The Weiser Indians: Shoshoni Peacemakers* (Salt Lake City: University of Utah, 1990)
Steven J. Crum, *The Road on Which We Came: A History of the Western Shoshone* (Salt Lake City: University of Utah, 1994)
Brigham D. Madsen, *Chief Pocatello: The "White Plume"* (Salt Lake City: University of Utah, 1986)
————, *The Lemhi: Sacajawea's People* (Caldwell: Caxton, 1979)
————, *The Shoshoni Frontier and the Bear River Massacre* (Salt Lake City: University of Utah, 1985)
Virginia Cole Trenholm, *The Shoshonis: Sentinels of the Rockies* (Norman: University of Oklahoma, 1964)

SIOUX

Eleanor Grobsmith, *Lakota of the Rosebud: A Contemporary Ethnography* (New York: Holt, Rinehart and Winston, 1981)

Herbert T. Hoover, *The Sioux: A Critical Bibliography* (Bloomington: Indiana, 1979)

Herbert T. Hoover and Karen P. Zimmerman, comp., *The Sioux and Other Native American Cultures of the Dakotas: An Annotated Bibliography* (Westport: Greenwood, 1993)

Edward Lazarus, *Black Hills/White Justice: The Sioux Nation Versus the United States, 1775 to the Present* (New York: HarperCollins, 1991)

Roy W. Meyer, *History of the Santee Sioux* (Lincoln: University of Nebraska, 1967)

Ethel Nurge, ed., *The Modern Sioux* (Lincoln: University of Nebraska, 1970)

Ernest L. Schusky, *The Forgotten Sioux* (Chicago: Nelson-Hall, 1975)

SPOKANES

Robert H. Ruby and John A. Brown, *The Spokane Indians* (Norman: University of Oklahoma, 1970)

UTES

Robert W. Delaney, *The Southern Ute People* (Phoenix: Indian Tribal Series, 1974)

Joel C. Janetski, *The Ute of Utah Lake* (Salt Lake City: University of Utah, 1991)

Charles S. Marsh, *People of the Shining Mountains: The Utes of Colorado* (Boulder: Pruett, 1982)

WASHOS

James E. Downs, *The Two Worlds of the Washo* (New York: Holt, Rinehart and Winston, 1966)

YAKIMAS

Richard D. Daugherty, *The Yakima People* (Phoenix: Indian Tribal Series, 1973)

Helen H. Schuster, *The Yakima* (New York: Chelsea House, 1990)

————, *The Yakimas: A Critical Bibliography* (Bloomington: Indiana, 1982)

YUMAS

Jack D. Forbes, *Warriors of the Colorado: The Yumas of the Quechan Nation and Their Neighbors* (Norman: University of Oklahoma, 1965)

SPECIAL TOPICS

AGRICULTURE

Cecil Harvey, comp., *Agriculture of the American Indian: A Select Bibliography* (Washington: Science and Education Adminsitration, 1979)

R. Douglas Hurt, *Indian Agriculture in America: Prehistory to the Present* (Lawrence: University Press of Kansas, 1987)

Richard S. MacNeish, *The Origins of Agriculture and Settled Life* (Norman: University of Oklahoma, 1992)

BIOGRAPHY AND AUTOBIOGRAPHY

Stephen E. Ambrose, *Crazy Horse and Custer: The Parallel Lives of Two American Warriors* (Garden City: Doubleday, 1975)

William H. Armstrong, *Warrior in Two Camps: Ely S. Parker: Union General and Seneca Chief* (Syracuse: Syracuse, 1978)

W. David Baird, *Peter Pitchlynn: Chief of the Choctaws* (Norman: University of Oklahoma, 1972)

Philip L. Barbour, *Pocahontas and Her World* (Boston: Houghton Mifflin, 1970)

Margaret B. Blackman, *During My Time: Florence Edenshaw Davidson, A Haida Woman* (Seattle: University of Washington, 1982)

H. David Brumble III, *American Indian Autobiography* (Berkeley: University of California, 1988)

Harvey Lewis Carter, *The Life and Times of Little Turtle* (Urbana: University of Illinois, 1987)

Edward J. Cashin, *Lachlan McGillivray, Indian Trader: The Shaping of the Southern Colonial Frontier* (Athens: Univeristy of Georgia, 1992)

George Chapman, *Chief William McIntosh: A Man of Two Worlds* (Atlanta: Cherokee Pub., 1988)

Ella Cara Deloria, *Waterlily* (Lincoln: Univeristy of Nebraska, 1988)

Raymond J. DeMallie, ed., *The Sixth Grandfather: Black Elk's Teachings Given to John G. Neihardt* (Lincoln: University of Nebraka, 1984)

Hugh Aylmer Dempsey, *Big Bear: The End of Freedom* (Vancouver: Douglas & McIntyre, 1984)

Allan W. Eckert, *A Sorrow in Our Heart: The Life of Tecumseh* (New York: Bantam, 1992)

R. David Edmunds, *The Shawnee Prophet* (Lincoln: University of Nebraska, 1983)

———, *Tecumseh and the Quest for Indian Leadership* (Boston: Little, Brown, 1984)

Bil Gilbert, *God Gave Us This Country: Tekamthi and the First American Civil War* (New York: Atheneum, 1989)

G. W. Grayson, *A Creek Warrior for the Confederacy*; edited by W. David Baird (Norman: University of Oklahoma, 1988)

Joseph B. Herring, *Kenekuk, the Kickapoo Prophet* (Lawrence: University Press of Kansas, 1988)

Peter Iverson, *Carlos Montezuma and the Changing World of American Indians* (Albuquerque: University of New Mexico, 1982)

David E. Jones, *Sanapia: Comanche Medicine Woman* (New York: Holt, Rinehart and Winston, 1972)

Isabel Thompson Kelsay, *Joseph Brant, 1743–1807* (Syracuse: Syracuse, 1984)

Theodora Kroeber, *Ishi in Two Worlds* (Berkeley: University of California, 1961)

Arnold Krupat, ed., *Native American Autobiography* (Madison: University of Wisconsin, 1994)

Daniel F. Littlefield, Jr., *The Life of Okah Tubbee* (Lincoln: University of Nebraska, 1988)

Thomas E. Mails, *Fools Crow* (Lincoln: University of Nebraska, 1990)

Jay Miller, ed., *Mourning Dove* (Lincoln: University of Nebraska, 1990)

D. Earl Newsom, *Kicking Bird and the Birth of Oklahoma: A Biography of Milton W. Reynolds* (Perkins, Okla.: Evans, 1983)

Leo Simmons, ed., *Sun Chief: the Autobiography of a Hopi Indian* (New Haven: Yale, 1971)

P. David Smith, *Ouray, Chief of the Utes* (Ouray: Wayfinder, 1986)

James P. Spradley, *Guests Never Leave Hungry: The Autobiography of James Sewid, a Kwakiutl Indian* (1969)

Robert Utley, *The Lance and the Shield: The Life and Times of Sitting Bull* (New York: Henry Holt, 1993)

Thurman Wilkins, *Cherokee Tragedy: The Story of the Ridge Family and the Decimation of a People* (2nd ed.; Norman: University of Oklahoma, 1986)

Hertha D. Wong, *Sending My Heart Back Across the Years: Tradition and Innovation in Native American Autobiography* (New York: Oxford University, 1992)

Grace Woodward, *Pocahontas* (Norman: University of Oklahoma, 1969)

BUREAU OF INDIAN AFFAIRS

Robert M. Kvasnicka and Herman J. Viola, eds., *The Commissioners of Indian Affairs, 1824–1977* (Lincoln: University of Nebraska, 1979)

Theodore W. Taylor, *The Bureau of Indian Affairs* (Boulder: Westview, 1984)

CAPTIVITY NARRATIVES

John Demos, *The Unredeemed Captive: A Family Story from Early America* (New York: Knopf, 1994)

June Namias, *White Captives: Gender and Ethnicity on the American Frontier* (Chapel Hill: University of North Carolina, 1993)

Richard Slotkin, *Regeneration Through Violence* (Middletown: Wesleyan, 1973)

ECOLOGY

William Cronon, *Changes in the Land: Indians, Colonists, and the Ecology of New England* (New York: Hill and Wang, 1983)

J. Donald Hughes, *American Indian Ecology* (El Paso: Texas Western, 1982)

David Rich Lewis, *Neither Wolf Nor Dog: American Indians, Environment, and Agrarian Change* (New York: Oxford, 1994)

EDUCATION

Indian Nations at Risk Task Force, Final Report to the Secretary of Education (Washington: U.S. Government Printing Office, 1991)

Michael C. Cleman, *American Indian Children at School, 1850–1930* (Jackson: University Press of Mississippi, 1993)

David H. DeJong, *Promises of the Past: A History of Indian Education in the United States* (Golden: North American Press, 1993)

Estelle Fuchs and Robert J. Havighurst, *To Live on this Earth: American Indian Education* (Garden City: Anchor Books, 1973)

Basil H. Johnston, *Indian School Days* (Norman: University of Oklahoma, 1989)

Margaret Szasz, *Education and the American Indian: The Road to Self-Determination Since 1928* (2nd. ed; Albuquerque: University of New Mexico, 1977)

———, *Indian Education in the American Colonies, 1607–1783* (Albuquerque: University of New Mexico, 1988)

FOLKLORE

Mark A. Lindquist and Martin Zanger, eds., *Buried Roots and Indestructible Seeds: The Survival of American Indian Life in Story, History and Spirit* (Madison: University of Wisconsin, 1995)

FUR TRADE

Jennifer S. H. Brown, *Strangers in Blood: Fur Trade Company Families in Indian Country* (Vancouver: University of British Columbia, 1980)

James R. Gibson, *Feeding the Russian Fur Trade: Provisionment of the Okbotsk Seaboard and the Kamchatka Peninsula, 1639–1856* (Madison: University of Wisconsin, 1969)

Carolyn Gilman, ed., *Where Two Worlds Meet: The Great Lakes Fur Trade* (St. Paul: Minnesota Historical Society, 1982)

Conrad Heidenreich and Arthur J. Ray, *The Early Fur Trade: A Study in Cultural Interaction* (Toronto: McClelland and Stewart, 1976)

Carol M. Judd and Arthur J. Ray, *Old Trails and New Directions: Papers of the Third North American Fur Trade Conference* (Toronto: University of Toronto, 1980)

Shepard Krech III, ed., *Indians, Animals, and the Fur Trade: A Critique of "Keepers of the Game"* (Athens: University of Georgia, 1981)

Calvin Martin, *Keepers of the Game: Indian-Animal Relationships and the Fur Trade* (Berkeley: University of California, 1978)

Arthur J. Ray, *Indians in the Fur Trade* (Toronto: University of Toronto, 1974)

E. E. Rich, *The Fur Trade and the Northwest to 1857* (Toronto: McClelland and Stewart, 1967)

Lewis O. Saum, *The Fur Trader and the Indian* (Seattle: University of Washington, 1965)

Sylvia Van Kirk, *Many Tender Ties: Women in Fur-Trade Society, 1670–1870* (Norman: University of Oklahoma, 1980)

GENDER

Margaret B. Blackman, *During My Time: Florence Edenshaw Davidson, A Haida Woman* (Seattle: University of Washington, 1982)

Carol Devens, *Countering Colonization: Native American Women and Great Lakes Missions, 1630–1900* (Berkeley: University of California, 1992)

David E. Jones, *Sanapia: Comanche Medicine Woman* (New York: Holt, Rinehart and Winston, 1972)

Marla N. Powers, *Ogalala Women: Myth, Ritual and Reality* (Chicago: University of Chicago, 1986)

Glenda Riley, *Women and Indians on the Frontier, 1825–1915* (Albuquerque: University of New Mexico, 1984)

Lillian Schlissel, Vicki L. Ruiz, and Janice Monk, eds., *Western Women: Their Land, Their Lives* (Albuquerque: University of New Mexico, 1988)

John Upton Terrell, *Indian Women of the Western Morning: Their Life in Early America* (New York: Dial, 1974)

Ruth M. Underhill, *Papago Woman* (New York: Holt, Rinehart and Winston, 1979)

Sylvia Van Kirk, *Many Tender Ties: Women in Fur-Trade Society, 1670–1870* (Norman: University of Oklahoma, 1980)

GHOST DANCE

Michael Hittman, *Wovoka and the Ghost Dance: A Source Book* (Carson City: Grace Dangberg Foundation, 1990)

Alice Beck Kehoe, *The Ghost Dance: Ethnohistory and Revitalization* (New York: Holt, Rinehart and Winston, 1989)

William G. McLoughlin, *The Cherokee Ghost Dance* (Macon: Mercer, 1984)

Shelley Anne Osterreich, comp., *The American Indian Ghost Dance, 1870 and 1890: An Annotated Bibliography* (New York: Greenwood, 1991)

GOVERNMENT POLICY

R. Pierce Beaver, *Church, State, and the American Indians: Two and a Half Centuries of Partnership in Missions Between Protestant Churches and Government* (St. Louis: Concordia, 1966)

Robert L. Bee, *The Politics of American Indian Policy* (Cambridge: Schenkman, 1982)

Christine Bolt, *American Indian Policy and American Reform: Case Studies of the Campaign to Assimilate the American Indians* (London: Allen & Unwin, 1987)

Larry W. Burt, *Tribalism in Crisis: Federal Indian Policy, 1953–1961* (Albuquerque: University of New Mexico, 1982)

Sandra L. Cadwalader and Vine Deloria, Jr., eds., *The Aggressions of Civilization: Federal Indian Policy Since the 1880s* (Philadelphia: Temple, 1984)

Stephen E. Cornell, *The Return of the Native: American Indian Political Resurgence* (New York: Oxford, 1988)

Edmund J. Danziger, Jr., *Indians and Bureaucrats: Administering the Reservation Policy During the Civil War* (Urbana: University of Illinois, 1974)

Vine Deloria, Jr., and Clifford M. Lytle, *American Indians, American Justice* (Austin: University of Texas, 1983)

——, *The Nations Within: The Past and Future of American Indian Sovereignty* (New York: Pantheon, 1984)

Brian W. Dippie, *The Vanishing American: White Attitudes and U.S. Indian Policy* (Middletown: Wesleyan University, 1982)

William T. Hagan, *Indian Police and Judges: Experiments in Acculturation and Control* (New Haven: Yale, 1966)

——, *The Indian Rights Association: The Herbert Welsh Years, 1882–1904* (Tucson: University of Arizona, 1985)

Frederick E. Hoxie, *A Final Promise: The Campaign to Assimilate the Indians, 1880–1920* (Lincoln: University of Nebraska, 1984)

Wilbur Jacobs, *Dispossessing the American Indian* (Norman: University of Oklahoma, 1985)

Robert H. Keller, *American Protestantism and United States Indian Policy, 1869–1882* (Lincoln: University of Nebraska, 1983)

Lawrence C. Kelly, *The Assault on Assimilation: John Collier and the Origins of Indian Policy Reform* (Albuquerque: University of New Mexico, 1983)

Peter Matthiessen, *In the Spirit of Crazy Horse* (New York: Viking, 1983)

Nicholas C. Peroff, *Menominee Drums: Tribal Termination and Restoration, 1954–1974* (Norman: University of Oklahoma, 1973)

Kenneth R. Philp, *John Collier's Crusade for Indian Reform, 1920–1954* (Tucson: University of Arizona, 1977)

Francis Paul Prucha, *The Great Father: The United States Government and the American Indians* (2 vols.; Lincoln: University of Nebraska, 1984)

——, *Indian Policy in the United States* (Lincoln: University of Nebraska, 1981)

Ronald N. Satz, *American Indian Policy in the Jacksonian Era* (Lincoln: University of Nebraska, 1975)

Kenneth S. Stern, *Loud Hawk: The United States Versus the American Indian Movement* (Norman: University of Oklahoma, 1994)

Paul Stuart, *The Indian Office: Growth and Development of an American Institution, 1865–1900* (Ann Arbor: UMI Research, 1979)

Graham D. Taylor, *The New Deal and American Indian Tribalism: The Administration of the Indian Reorganization Act, 1934–1945* (Lincoln: University of Nebraska, 1980)

Robert A. Trennert, Jr., *Alternative to Extinction: Federal Indian Policy and the Beginnings of the Reservation System, 1946–1951* (Philadelphia: Temple, 1975)

Herman J. Viola, *Thomas L. McKenney: Architect of America's Early Indian Policy* (Chicago: Sage, 1974)

INDIAN MISSIONS

James P. Ronda and James Axtell, *Indian Missions: A Critical Bibliography* (Bloomington: Indiana, 1978)

LANGUAGE

Lyle Campbell and Marianne Mithun, eds., *The Languages of Native America* (Austin: University of Texas, 1979)

David Murray, *Forked Tongues: Speech, Writing, and Representation in North American Indian Texts* (Bloomington: Indiana University, 1991)

Gary Witherspoon, *Language and Art in the Navajo Universe* (Ann Arbor: University of Michigan, 1986)

LAND CLAIMS

Paul Brodeur, *Restitution: The Land Claims of the Mashpee, Passamaquoddy, and Penobscot Indians of New England* (Boston: Northeastern, 1985)

Linda S. Parker, *Native American Estate: The Struggle Over Indian and Hawaiian Lands* (Honolulu: University of Hawaii, 1980)

Imre Sutton et al., eds., *Irredeemable America: The Indians' Estate and Land Claims* (Albuquerque: University of New Mexico, 1985)

Wilcomb E. Washburn, *Red Man's Land/White Man's Law* (New York: Charles Scribner's, 1984)

LAW

James E. Falkowski, *Indian Law/Race Law: A Five Hundred Year History* (New York: Prager, 1992)

Sidney L. Harring, *Crow Dog's Case: American Indian Sovereignty, Tribal Law, and United States Law in the Nineteenth Century* (Cambridge: Cambridge, 1994)

Monroe E. Price and Robert Clinton, *Law and the American Indian* (2nd ed.; Charlottesville: Michie, 1983)

Rennard Strickland, *Fire and the Spirits: Cherokee Law from Clan to Court* (Norman: University of Oklahoma, 1975)

Charles F. Wilkinson, *American Indians, Time and the Law: Native Societies in Modern Constitutional Democracy* (New Haven: Yale, 1987)

Robert A. Williams, Jr., *The American Indian in Western Legal Thought* (New York: Oxford, 1990)

John R. Wunder, *Retained by the People: A History of American Indians and the Bill of Rights* (New York: Oxford, 1994)

LEADERSHIP

R. David Edmunds, ed., *American Indian Leaders: Studies in Diversity* (Lincoln: University of Nebraska, 1980)

Benjamin W. Griffith, Jr., *McIntosh and Weatherford, Creek Indian Leaders* (Tuscaloosa: University of Alabama Press, 1988)

LITERATURE AND FILM

Gretchen M. Bataille and Charles L. P. Silet, eds., *The Pretend Indians: Images of Native Americans in the Movies* (Ames: Iowa State, 1980)

————, *Images of American Indians on Film: An Annotated Bibliography* (New York: Garland, 1985)

Ward Churchill, *Fantasies of the Master Race: Literature, Cinema, and the Colonization of American Indians* (Monroe, Me.: Common Courage, 1992)

Ralph E. Friar and Natasha A. Friar, *The Only Good Indian: The Hollywood Gospel* (New York: Drama Book Specialists, 1972)

Michael Hilger, *The American Indian in Film* (Metuchen: Scarecrow, 1986)

John E. O'Connor, *The Hollywood Indian: Stereotypes of Native Americans in Films* (Trenton: New Jersey State Museum, 1980)

David R. Peck, *American Ethnic Literatures . . . An Annotated Bibliography* (Pasadena: Salem Press, 1992)

Roger O. Rock, comp., *The Native American in American Literature: A Selectively Annotated Bibliography* (Westport: Greenwood, 1985)

Elizabeth Weatherford, ed., *Native Americans on Film and Video* (2 vols.; New York: Museum of the American Indian, 1981, 1988)

MEDICINE

Trends in Indian Health, 1991 (Rockville: U.S. Department of Health and Human Services, Indian Health Service, 1991)

Virgil J. Vogel, *American Indian Medicine* (Norman: University of Oklahoma, 1990)

MILITARY POLICY

Francis Paul Prucha, *The Sword of the Republic: The United Army on the Frontier,
1783–1846* (New York: Macmillan, 1969)

Sherry Lynn Smith, *The View from Offiers' Row: Army Perceptions of Western Indians*
(Tucson: University of Arizona, 1990)

Robert M. Utley, *Frontier Regulars: The United States Army and the Indian, 1866–1891*
(New York: Macmillan, 1973)

———, *Frontiersmen in Blue: The United States Army and the Indian, 1848–1865* (New
York: Macmillan, 1967)

Robert Wooster, *The Military and United States Indian Policy, 1865–1903* (New Haven:
Yale, 1988)

MONEY

Don Taxay, *Money of the American Indians and other Primitive Currencies of the Americas* (New York: Nummus, 1970)

POTLATCH

John W. Adams, *The Gitksan Potlatch* (Toronto: Holt, Rinehart and Winston, 1973)

Mary Giraudo Beck, *Potlatch: Native Ceremony and Myth on the Northwest Coast*
(Anchorage: Alaska Northwest, 1993)

Helen Codere, *Fighting With Property: A Study of Kwakiutl Potlatching and Warfare,
1792–1930* (Seattle: University of Washington, 1966)

Douglas Cole and Ira Chaikin, *An Iron Hand Upon the People: The Law Against Potlatch on the Northwest Coast* (Seattle: University of Washington, 1990)

Philip Drucker and Robert Heizer, *To Make My Name Good: A Reexamination of the
Southern Kwakiutl Potlatch* (Berkeley: University of California, 1967)

Aldona Jonaitis, ed., *Chiefly Feasts: The Enduring Kwakiutl Potlatch* (Seattle: University
of Washington, 1991)

Sergei Kan, *Symbolic Immortality: The Tlingit Potlatch of the Nineteenth Century*
(Washington: Smithsonian, 1989)

Abraham Rosman, *Feasting With Mine Enemy: Rank and Exchange Among Northwest
Coast Societies* (New York: Columbia, 1971)

Ulli Steltzer, *A Haida Potlatch* (Seattle: University of Washington, 1984)

RELIGION

Denise Lardner Carmody and John Tully Carmody, *Native American Religions: An
Introduction* (New York: Paulist Press, 1993)

Raymond J. DeMallie and Douglas R. Parks, eds., *Sioux Indian Religion* (Norman: University of Oklahoma, 1987)

Patricia Galloway, ed., *The Southeastern Ceremonial Complex: Artifacts and Analysis*
(Lincoln: University of Nebraska, 1989)

Arlene B. Hirschfelder and Paulette Molin, *The Encyclopedia of Native American Religions* (New York: Facts on File, 1992)

Ake Hultkrantz, *Belief and Worship in Native North America*; edited by Christopher
Vecsey (Syracuse: Syracuse, 1981)

———, *The Study of Native American Religions*; edited by Christopher Vecsey (New
York: Crossroad, 1983)

———, *Native Religions of North America* (San Francisco: Harper and Row, 1987)

———, *The Religions of North American Indians* (Berkeley: University of California,
1979)

Maarten Jansen, Peter van der Loo, and Roswitha Manning, *Continuity and Identity in
Native America* (New York: E.J. Brill, 1988)

Joseph G. Jorgensen, *The Sun Dance Religion* (Chicago: University of Chicago, 1972)

216   A GUIDE TO RECENT BOOKS IN NATIVE AMERICAN HISTORY

Elisabeth Tooker, ed., *Native American Spirituality of the Eastern Woodlands* (New York: Paulist, 1979)
Robert M. Torrance, *The Spiritual Quest: Transcendence in Myth, Religion and Science* (Berkeley: University of California, 1994)
Ruth M. Underhill, *Red Man's Religion: Beliefs and Practices of the Indians North of Mexico* (Chicago: University of Chicago, 1965)

SEXUALITY

Walter L. Williams, *The Spirit and the Flesh: Sexual Diversity in American Indian Culture* (Boston: Beacon, 1986)

SLAVERY AND RACE

L. R. Bailey, *Indian Slave Trade in the Southwest* (Los Angeles: Westernlore, 1966)
Jack D. Forbes, *Africans and Native Americans: The Language of Race and the Evolution of Red-Black Peoples* (2nd ed.; Urbana: University of Illinois, 1993)
R. Halliburton, Jr., *Red Over Black: Black Slavery Among the Cherokee Indians* (Westport: Greenwood, 1977)
Theda Perdue, *Slavery and the Evolution of Cherokee Society* (Knoxville: University of Tennessee, 1979)
Robert H. Ruby and John A. Brown, *Indian Slavery in the Pacific Northwest* (Spokane: A.H. Clark, 1993)

TRIBAL GOVERNMENT

Russel Lawrence Barsh and James Youngblood Henderson, *The Road: Indian Tribes and Political Liberty* (Berkeley: University of California, 1980)
Donald A. Grinde, Jr. and Bruce E. Johansen, *Exemplar of Liberty: Native America and the Evolution of Democracy* (Los Angeles: UCLA, 1991)
Sharon O'Brien, *American Indian Tribal Governments* (Norman: University of Oklahoma, 1989)

URBAN RESIDENCE

Elaine M. Neils, *Reservation to City: Indian Migration and Federal Relocation* (Chicago: University of Chicago, 1971)
Alan L. Sorkin, *The Urban American Indian* (Lexington: Lexington Books, 1978)
Russell Thornton, Gary D. Sandefur, and Harold G. Grasmick, *The Urbanization of American Indians: A Critical Bibliography* (Bloomington: Indiana, 1982)